A Novel

PLEASING WHITE BOYS

A Story of Aspiration and Malice in Corporate America

LINDA SAULSBY

Published by BookBaby.com

Purple Sky Literary

First published in the United States of America by BookBaby.com

ISBN 978-1-54397-991-6 eBook 978-1-54397-992-3

Printed in the United States of America

Contents

For all those women

and

For my boys

There is no greater agony than bearing an untold story inside you.

- Maya Angelou

ξ PROLOGUE ξ

I

Mid-November 1990

Lia walked into the gun store and was surprised at how open and bright it looked. She felt nervous. She chose this store because it sat detached from the other shops, a small cement block with one small window, at the corner of a low, nondescript strip mall. When she occasionally drove by, there always seemed to be little activity in front of it. She did not want to risk any attention. Someone from Conallied seeing her walk into a gun store would think it seemed strange. When she pulled into one of the six unusually wide parking spaces in front of the store and turned off the engine, she hesitated.

What am I doing here? This feels claustrophobic and I haven't even walked in there yet. But I'm going to do this; I'm going to do this.

The store was larger than she had imagined. It had several aisles, and guns were stacked on racks almost to the ceiling. The well-worn wood boards creaked under her feet as she walked down the aisle opposite the entrance.

Why do they have wood floors in a gun store? Why not? Like I know so much about guns stores. I should not have worn heels. I should have come in on Saturday, not on a weekday in a business suit and high heels. No, too many people would be in here and staring at me on a Saturday. I'm the only

Black person in here, I'm the only woman in here, this morning anyway. I look so out of place. I've always been out of place. Jesus, rifles almost to the ceiling.

Lia walked to the end of the aisle and turned left down the next. Finally, three aisles over, the last aisle, against the opposite wall from the entrance to the store, she saw cases full of handguns. *Look at these guns. Wow, some of them are beautiful and so ornate. There's obviously people out there who revere guns and devote a lot of time to them. Jesus, look at the prices. These must be collector guns, the kind people never shoot but put in fancy cases and show them off.*

Lia walked to the end of the aisle and back to the front of the store.

There they are. Of course, they are in the front of the store. Isn't it what most people come in here to buy? Isn't it what I'm here to buy?

The big case ran the length of the storefront over to the entrance door. There were dozens of handguns in it. Two guys were working behind the case. Two customers were there, one talking with a clerk and one inspecting a handgun very closely. Lia leaned on the glass top of the case and started looking at the guns.

"Hi there." A tall, burly clerk greeted Lia. He had thin blond hair, unusually rosy cheeks, and a nice smile. A white t-shirt stretched over his bulging stomach, and it inexplicably displayed the Harley-Davidson logo and a black Lab puppy side by side. Lia resisted the urge to ask him about it.

"You're looking for a handgun?"

"Yes."

"For protection?"

"Yes." Lia lied.

He automatically assumes that I need the gun for protection.

"I take it you've never owned a gun before?"

"No, I haven't."

"I'm Boney; let me tell you about the different handguns and the various calibers that you can choose from."

Well, I can read the name on his badge, but I'm glad he introduced himself. I'm not sure why it makes me feel more comfortable, but it does.

Boney spent more than a half-hour with Lia, and he let her take the time to just look. He talked about the various kinds of handguns, the difference in calibers, manufacturers, and customary purposes for choosing to buy each of the six handguns that he selected to show her.

This almost feels comfortable now.

"Pick them up, see how they feel in your hand. Does it feel more comfortable holding it in one hand, or do you feel the need to support it with both hands. Either way is okay, but it is important for you to choose what feels most comfortable for the moment you may have use it. Point them toward that blue wall straight ahead and pull the triggers. Don't worry, none of them are loaded. Just find what's comfortable."

"I like this one." Lia handed him one of the smaller guns that she felt more relaxed holding in her hand than the others.

"That's a nice choice; this manufacturer makes a good firearm. It's a 25-caliber, and that's small. You really should think about a 32 or 38 caliber; they pack more of a wallop. But, it's most important that it feels comfortable to you. One thing though, if an intruder confronts you, don't let him get within arm's length if you can help it, and empty the gun. With a 25-caliber, you need to empty the gun in the attacker just to be sure. Remember that."

A gun in your mouth takes only one bullet.

"I'll take the 25-caliber."

"I'll show you how to load the bullets into the clip, and you need a bullet in the barrel to prime the pump, as they say. You'll need a box of ammo. I really suggest you take a shooting class. We have classes scheduled all the time; here's a brochure. I'll put it in the bag. It's a good idea for you."

A bit condescending, but I think he means well.

"Thank you," Lia replied noncommittally.

Boney took down a small cardboard box from one of the shelves behind him, and he removed a black case from it. Lia watched him open the case and place the gun in a carved out black styrofoam nest cut to the shape and size of the gun. Boney laid three pieces of printed information on top of the gun. Lia noticed one of the small pamphlets had photos of other guns.

"I've shown you the basics, but read the instructions carefully. Don't forget to send in your warranty card. This company is a stickler about warranty information and keeping accurate ownerships records.

I won't need a warranty, and I'm not buying another gun.

Boney covered everything in the case with a black felt cloth and closed it. He placed the case back into the cardboard box, and put it in a bag. Lia paid for her purchases, thanked Boney for his help, holding eye contact with him for more than a moment, and walked quickly to her Jeep Cherokee, a company executive perk.

In the short walk to the car, Lia was surprised at the weight of the contents of the bag. When she got in, Lia kept the bag on her lap for a moment and then peeked into it. With some effort, she pulled out the flap on the cardboard box and to look at the black case. The case had a strip of brown across the top with the manufacturer's name embossed in gold on it. She stared at the embossed name for a moment, and then replaced the flap.

Lia placed the bag on the floor with the name of the store facing down. Anyone who happened to look in her car window in the office parking lot would only see a nondescript white plastic bag. The heat in the car wrapped itself around Lia. She did not open a window for air, but instead looked up through the sunroof at the vivid blue sky and bright sun on the unusually mild early winter day. She stared until she found relief in the sun's glare and the expanse of the sky, which she knew was glorious in comparison to the anguish in her own small universe. She suddenly became keenly aware of her breath, and the claustrophobic feeling she had since getting out of her car had passed.

So, I did it. I bought a gun. It scared me, but I did it anyway. I'm nothing if not an efficient, get-it-done little nigger bitch. I know that's what they call me behind closed doors. Not all of them, but too many of them. Isn't it funny the things in life that seem to be lopsided somehow get accomplished, and the things that should work out end up in a pool of rejection and desolation rising up around your ankles. At least Boney was nice; he made it easy. He just assumed that I was buying the gun for protection. I didn't really lie to him. I bought the gun to protect myself from life.

When I don't show up at the office and don't call after a day or two, someone will come to check on me. Maybe it will be Wanda since she's my emergency contact. Can I do this to Wanda? Wanda, and certainly Keith, are the only people who would know to call and advise Dawson. Maybe someone from the office, likely Sara, will come first. I almost wish it could be Dan who comes. He would have the joy of finding my body and feeling guilty about it. Ha, he may feel nothing and point to my pathetic ending with self-satisfied pity and justification for my failure. "It's obvious she was emotionally ill, you know," he would say. Anyway, it will probably be Wanda. Even with what's happened, she is still my friend. Should I do this to her? And, what about Jordan? He's grown up, but he's still my baby. Can a mother do this to her baby? He would be devastated; he'd have Rob, though. Stop it, and deal with the reality that your child would suffer with grief. There's also Mama and Daddy; would they always wonder if it was something they did wrong? Ruthie would be strong for them; she'd take over everything at home and try to make it easier for everyone. Look what she's suffered in her life, and it's made her stronger. Ruthie would be so disappointed in me. It's just an option, Ruthie, just an option. And Laura, she will feel like she utterly failed me.

Why am I doing this? What the hell am I going to do with a gun? I hate guns. Why am I sitting here in this car? Am I mentally ill? Or, at least, emotionally fragile? Why have I imagined this morbid scenario in my mind? Morbid and strangely detailed? Am I determined to do something whether it makes sense or not? Well, here I am. Sitting here outside a gun store is happening. What's happened to me? Is this control?

II

Late November 1990

Lia Granger sat in the purple upholstered, ergonomic chair and swung slowly from side to side. She tried to mentally push back a headache that was beginning to creep in around the edges. When she arrived, no one appeared to be around, but the door was wide open, so Lia walked right in to Wanda's office and sat down to wait for her.

Don't do this to me. Please, not now. I'm alone, but if it weren't for Wanda, I'd have been utterly alone here. No friends. I don't have my old friends to fall back on. I don't have that kind of life. Would I know anyone here without Wanda? Would I have anyone to give anything to?

The screen saver on the computer monitor flashed a series of nature photos; it was more soothing than the little explosions of color on her computer's screen saver.

I love the sky. Why don't I have scenes of the sky on my screen saver? What a silly thought to have right now.

Lia had always liked Wanda's office; in fact, she had to admit some feelings of envy about it.

She's doing her own thing, she's her own boss, and she has created this wonderful space for herself.

The office reflected Wanda's creativity and sense of style. A wall of windows looked out to the man-made lake Wanda laughingly referred to as "Lake Woe-Is-Me." Lia had walked in more than once and found Wanda's back to the office door, standing at the window in deep thought. The weak sunshine on this chilly day streamed into the room, creating alternate splashes of light and dark shadows in the room. The walls were bright white and covered with numerous art reproductions, reprints of ads and logos designed by Wanda and several plaques and framed certificates she had received. All the office furniture was light oak, and a variety of purple, wine and rose-colored chairs were scattered around the large, odd-shaped room. A connecting alcove contained the graphic design tools of her trade. It contained two drafting tables where Wanda and her assistant, Ben, who also didn't seem to be around, did their creative work. Pens, pencils, markers and crayons of every color and description, a collection of small metal tools that Lia had no idea about, but she liked how they looked lined up by size, and a photocopier and fax machine filled the space. Wanda's office seemed an easy place to work, and just to be. Lia wondered, as she had many times before, how her life would be different if she developed her own business.

I wonder where I'd be today if I had taken the road of entrepreneurship, like Wanda, rather than putting my faith in the corporate ethic. Wanda's professional and financial success rests solely on her own ability and aggressiveness. She does not have to rely directly on the whim of white men for success.

Lia understood that a successful businesswoman like Wanda had to satisfy her clients who were primarily business people, mostly white men. They had talked about it, and Wanda always insisted that she had the freedom to work the way she pleased and, as long as she delivered what was agreed to with the client, her business would prosper. She would regularly bend Lia's ear, though, particularly when she was worried or had that third glass of wine, about never getting the really important contracts that white-owned firms were routinely awarded.

Still, I envy her; I do wish I had followed my entrepreneurial urges a long time ago. Especially today I wish it.

The usual solace of Wanda's office did not lessen the tension Lia felt, and her headache was settling in to stay. Wanda's outburst the last time they talked on the telephone had surprised, and then saddened her. Damn those bastards at EPD for building this anxiety between them.

III

Lia was surprised, and couldn't quite decide how she felt when her therapist, Laura Brown-Cramer, sat with her on the sofa. As Laura entered the office, she quickly walked to the big, wicker rocking chair she usually sat in, grabbed the high back, and dragged it to the corner of the room. The temperature in the office was very warm, just the way they both liked it, and provided a cozy haven from the wearying winter chill in Fielding. The small room now appeared to be off-balance, and the empty space and deep grooves left in the light gray carpet seemed to jump out at Lia and were a little discomforting to her.

What is this about?"

Laura settled into the thick cushions in the opposite corner of the sofa, folded one leg under her body and turned to face Lia.

"Are you ready for Christmas?" Laura's high-pitched, almost girlish voice was initially distracting when Lia first started seeing her, but she somehow always seemed to pull Lia into a conversation of revelation in an oddly seductive way. Laura was very good at what she did.

"I am as ready as I'm going to be. Trying to simplify it a little more each year. Plus, I have a move to get done.

"How are you today, Lia?"

"Oh, I don't know," Lia answered, knowing this response would elicit another question from Laura and wondering why she just didn't tell her what was on her mind right off the bat. She always ended up telling her everything, anyway, including those things she thought not even a therapist could truly understand. Lia made a conscious effort to relax, to allow her body to sink against the sofa's thick cushions, to let the feeling that came from Laura's close physical proximity envelope her. They shared the sofa comfortably. Pretty much the same age and body type, short stature, attractive, pretty decent figures, but not quite petite. They even laughed together one day about having the same skin color.

"Why is mine described as dark and ruddy, and yours is soft and caramel. That sounds so much better!"

There was no disquieting power exchange between them.

"You seem very sad today." Laura leaned over and lightly patted Lia's crossed knee. A quick, comforting touch.

Lia wondered again why Laura had abandoned her usual place in the rocker. She liked the feel of Laura so close to her; she imagined she could feel body heat, or energy, or something from her. Even in the rocker, she always sat very close to Lia. It had been positioned so that sometimes their knees almost touched. Laura's legs were always bare; she never wore pantyhose, sometimes socks like today. Now, Laura placed an arm along the back of the sofa. Her fingers were only a few inches from Lia's shoulder. It was almost sensual. Lia's thoughts seemed to form in slow motion, as if Laura's words penetrated her mind one at a time and then crystallized into an understandable sentence.

Jesus, why am I feeling so damned needy? And, why does Laura seem to so easily know it. I'm reading way too much into the fact that she's sitting in a different place. Relax. She knows this is our last session, at least for a long time. She's just being Laura, warm and friendly. I should just be happy she's been so helpful to me.

"I guess I do feel a little sad, but I don't know why I should. What's my excuse? I'm on my way down to Levale with a promotion and big assignment, Jordan is doing great, and I finally feel like I'm okay about not being married anymore."

"You've been coming to see me almost nine months now. I'm concerned about this sadness you still seem to be feeling, where it's coming from, why it's not lifting."

Lia shrugged her shoulders. Contrary to her nature, she simply did not know what to say. Laura looked intently at her for a few moments.

"Tell me about the best day in your life".

"Huh?"

"Think about the day that brings to mind your most pleasant memory and tell me about it."

It flowed right out of Lia.

"The moment is frozen in time for me. Not really the exact moment of the catch, but the moment just after. I saw Dwight Clark, the 49ers tight end, go up for the ball, but I did not see him come down with it. It seemed the entire crowd in the sold-out stadium rose in unison when Clark leaped high into the air. I'm too short; I couldn't see over the jumping, screaming bodies. So I stood there very still thinking that, at this moment, there was no place else in the world I'd rather be. I remember thanking God for the luck of good timing. We saw this game not long before moving east. We were going to really miss our football team. I had always been the only female football fanatic among our friends, and I liked it that way just fine."

"Lia," Laura interrupted, "what I really wanted . . ."

"I'd really like to finish telling you about it."

"Well, sure, go on."

"When we entered the stadium earlier, I was immediately struck by the appearance of the field. The grounds crew had really outdone themselves. The grass had been cut beautifully and had obviously been dyed deep green. The 49er end zone was a blaze of red and gold with 49ers written out in Victorian lettering. I remember that the Cowboys' end zone was very cool, classic blue and silver, a real contrast between the two. It was the football game we all hoped for, so much action and emotion. Then in the fourth quarter, with 51 seconds left in the game, third down and three yards to go, from the six-yard line, Joe Montana rolled to the right, threw up a looping pass and Clark made the catch that gave the 49ers the lead. The phrase 'The Catch' is very special to us San Franciscans, and it's still referred to all the time in the sports world. That moment was like suspended animation. The people were there, the colors were vivid, the light from the overcast sky was strangely bright, the air was cold, and during that moment, there was total silence for me. Then the pandemonium returned. The noise was deafening. Everyone was crying and hugging one another. It was glorious. I felt all of us who were there were absolutely golden. Blessed and golden."

Lia opened her eyes, surprised that she had closed them at all. Laura studied Lia's face as if puzzled by something.

I didn't choose to talk about an experience with Rob, or the day Jordan was born. It was a great day, but it's so random. I wonder what Laura is thinking.

"Why did you ask me that question; what does it have to do with anything?'

"I'm trying to better understand how you do, or don't, emotionally connect. It seems curious that your happiest experience was centered on a football game and did not involve a direct, personal experience with someone."

"No, it involved an experience with sixty thousand someones."

"Lia, I'm not trying to minimize that day, clearly it was wonderful. I'm troubled by your lack of emotional bonds that are real, that are authentic."

"I love my family in California, and they love me. Jordan is the most precious thing in my life and, thank God, I believe he thinks his Mom is pretty great too."

"Of course you do, and of course they do. We need to get you back to you feeling, to use your own word, golden. I want you to know that feeling again, but I don't want it to be short-term or motivated only by a special event or situation. I don't want you heading off to a new challenge in a new city feeling so sad. Based on all of our conversations, and what I understand about the environment you're working in, you need to store up some happiness to draw upon when you need it."

"Is Macy's having a sale on it?" Lia laughed and leaned in toward Laura.

I like Laura sitting on the sofa with me. I need her energy and spirit. Here I am sitting here with this amazing Jewish woman who has pulled more out of me than anyone else ever has before, and I should be concentrating on the insight and wisdom she can offer to me. This is our last session before I leave. So, why am I feeling distracted, drifting off inside my head?

It seemed to Lia early on that the typical therapist-patient relationship had grown to something deeper between them, a real friendship. She sometimes wondered if her sessions with Laura were simply paying for friendship because of the lack of it in Fielding. But Lia didn't want to view her time in this room it in a negative way. She was paying for therapy and also was blessed with the extra gift of Laura's friendship. She was fortunate that Laura managed to balance the two. Laura never once let Lia get away with being evasive or dishonest. Laura grinned and patted Lia's shoulder; she always sensed when Lia drifted off and could usually interpret her thoughts.

"Seriously, I'm concerned that you're not going to have the time . . ."

"Or the inclination?" Lia interrupted her.

"The time and the inclination to establish relationships and alliances that will fill out your life and provide strength to you."

"Uh oh, sounds like you're trying to say that I need a man; been there, done that."

"No, I'm talking about both men friends and women friends. Your old girlfriends are all in California; you're long gone from them. There's nothing like friendship between women to give you strength, you know that. I want to see you establish relationships that will sustain you, that have nothing to do with Conallied. You need relationships that are about supporting you, and not about some corporate goal or company politics. Personal confidantes are such an important part of the foundation that supports each of us. I'm not telling you anything you don't already know; you understand this, Lia."

Lia shrugged and mustered a weak smile. "I don't think I've been very good at separating the two, not for many years. But, when you spend twelve to sixteen hours a day trying to succeed in that world, it doesn't leave a lot of time for anything else. But, Laura, I know you're right."

"Well, just for a moment anyway, back to the subject of men or, more specifically, a man."

"I knew we were going to head there." Lia could feel just a little exasperation creeping around the edges. "I know I need to work on relationships that sustain me emotionally, and a nice relationship with a nice guy would be nice."

Why am I being so cynical?

"If I'm working hard on this new assignment and working on relationships, I'm afraid I'll end up not doing either of them well."

"How about a better balance. How about not trying to be all things to all people and keeping each part of your life in proper perspective?"

"That would be a neat trick."

I now don't want to sound cynical.

"Lia, what I want you to understand is that the energy you devote to nurturing a personal relationship is not just a nice concept, but something you do for yourself. You deserve it. By the way, how does Dawson feel about you leaving Fielding?"

"I haven't talk to him yet. Oh, I'm sure he knows about my promotion to this new assignment, but I haven't talked directly with him lately."

"Lia, you're leaving town next week."

"So, you're saying that I need to talk to him to be sure that he's not sad or mad or whatever; take care of his feelings?"

"Did it ever occur to you that by talking to Dawson you might also take care of yourself, of your feelings, in the process? It seems to me that this is a man who cares deeply about you. Lia, this is a loose end you need to tie up."

"I know, I know."

I don't know if I can even have a conversation with Daw.

"Are you going to miss him?"

"Yes, I think I will." Lia thought her voice reflected uncertainty.

"Daw and I are very close friends, and it's been nice. But I'll be in Levale; he'll be here in Fielding. Anything more wouldn't be workable, anyway. Conallied wouldn't tolerate it. Even though he tries to downplay it, it is a real issue. And, why should Daw put himself through it after thirty successful years with the company? And, God, I'd never survive the crap; they'd be so pissed they promoted me. The man is white, remember? I know of, or at least heard of, a couple of secretaries around Conallied who are in interracial relationships, but no one in management, not openly anyway, and absolutely not two people in the executive group. They all would freak, or many of them would!"

It would be fun to mess with their minds. No, that's not a good enough reason to be with someone, especially Daw.

"So you don't really know who would, or would not, be supportive."

"My point exactly. I don't have the time or inclination to go through it. It would be a masochistic act."

"You've never been afraid of taking chances; as a gregarious little girl, moving across the country with Rob, succeeding in a challenging career, taking on big assignments."

"I was just as excited as Rob to move to the East Coast and strike out on a new adventure, maybe even more so. I feel as though you are advising me to latch on to a man, to Dawson. I don't understand."

"Lia, you have lived a good deal of your life as the engine making things run. Why don't you sit back and let Dawson, or somebody, supply the energy, be the machine, give you love."

"Hey, they'll love me in Levale. Why wouldn't they?" Lia tried to joke her way out of this joust with Laura.

"I've got all the Conallied character traits down pat now. I've got the whole package; aggressive, get things done, deliver on commitments, change agent, that's one of the new buzz phrases you know. I guess I'm good at it because I was changing all kinds of shit, excuse my language, before it was cool."

"You know, I'm still reflecting on your earlier demeanor. I've never seen your body so relaxed, your disposition so natural as when you were recounting that Sunday at the football game. Your corporate persona is always present, even in this office with me. When you were talking about the game, you were completely out of that box".

Am I in a box?

"Out of that box?"

"Your I-have-to-be-the-best box, your I'm-so-in-control box, your corporate box."

God, she's so right.

"Oh." Lia gave in to Laura's interpretation without a fight.

"It seems to me that you have two sides of yourself battling for all of yourself."

"Well, it looks like one side is a bully."

"Sooner or later, you're going to have to sort all this out. I don't want you to suffer any professional trauma that might result from your quest to succeed in Conallied. Please think about what I've said, Lia."

"Oh good, another thing to sort out. The Energy Products Division won't keep me nearly as busy as you do. Laura, before we finish today, can I ask a favor? Can I call you once in a while? I don't know when I'll have the time to find a new therapist and, oh God, I can't stand the thought of starting again and slogging through all the history and muck. Maybe I just won't bother at all. Maybe we're done, and I've reached a jumping off point. Maybe I'm rambling."

Laura smiled warmly, took both Lia's hands into hers and gave them a firm squeeze.

"Of course, Lia. I have no problem with that. Call me when you need a tune-up session."

Lia laughed. "Naturally, I'll pay you for your time."

"However you want to arrange it is okay."

Laura let go of Lia's hands; Lia smiled back at her.

"Good luck, Lia. I know you'll be wonderfully successful in your new position. It all sounds tailor made for you. I'm going to miss you."

"I'll miss you, too. Well, I'm going to give this job a hundred and fifty percent. I think I can make a difference. I hope I can. Sorry, but if I feel myself getting stressed out, I'll sit back and think about the Sunday at that great football game."

"Well, I'm sure you'll do it while staring at the sky."

"You do know me, don't you? It's a testament to your therapy skills that I've been able to handle no windows in this office!"

"Thanks. Just capture some joy, and solace, when you need it."

They stood and shared a long and silent hug. Then Lia quickly opened the door and walked quickly down the hall out into unexpected sunshine, having pulled up yet another anchor, again ignoring the starting point from which her sadness came.

ξ

"Lia, my little niece, the big-time corporate executive!"

"Ruthie! Still calling me your little niece? It's so good to hear your voice. How are you?"

Lia was headed out the door on her last day in the office in Levale as the telephone rang. She was so glad she decided to grab it before the ringing stopped.

"Well I'm fine now that I've heard your voice. Honey, catching up with you is a challenge! Your mother told me about your latest promotion and the big move that you're about to make. I thought I would give my favorite niece a call."

"Hey, I'm not big-time, but I do have a great challenge ahead of me. I'm looking forward to it. So, how are you?"

"I'm doing really good. You know Dalton's been sick, but he's doing better now, thank God. We caught it early. How's Jordan?"

"He's fantastic; graduating in May, believe it or not."

"Time does march on, doesn't it? Will I ever see you? When are you going to come to California for a visit?"

"It's probably going to be a while. I'm actually spending only Christmas Day with Jordan. The day after he's headed on a skiing trip with Rob, and I'm headed south to Levale."

"I'd love to travel a little, bring my old bones to you, but I really don't want to leave Dalton right now."

"C'mon, you are not old! It's so good to hear that Dalton is doing better". Ruthie's long-time partner, a doctor, had been battling prostate cancer.

Lia got occasional reports from her mother about his progress, but didn't know his current condition.

"He's doing real good right now. I'm holding my breath; his doctors think he might be in remission."

"God, that would be wonderful. He's such a good guy. Are the beach and the sunsets as beautiful as I remember?"

"Yes, they are, honey. You know I've always appreciated how beautiful it is here, but now that I'm getting older, it becomes even more precious to me."

"It's been so long since I've seen you; but I'll bet you're still as beautiful as ever."

Ruthie, the much younger sister of Lia's father, had always been her favorite aunt and, although they saw one another infrequently now, Lia often thought about her. She suddenly wished she could have spent some time with Ruthie before going to Levale. Her presence had always been comforting; there wasn't much age difference between them, and they related well to one another.

"I know this is going to be a busy time for you with your new job, but why don't you think about coming to Monterey later in the year, even if it's only for a long weekend. You know there's plenty of space in this big house. I bet you'll need a break at some point."

"Sounds good to me. I can't promise exactly when it will be, but I'll definitely work it in somewhere along the way. I can see all the family while I'm out there."

"Just as long as you promise you will come. I know you, missy; you've always been an aggressive little thing, always pushing. I know you'll do well in Levale, as you've always done, but spend some time taking care of yourself, too."

This is beginning to be a theme.

"That's the second and last promise I'll ask you to make."

"Yes ma'am, I promise. I think your calling is a good omen."

"I'll be sending good wishes your way."

I need to stay in closer contact with Ruthie.

Talking to Ruthie left Lia feeling better than she had felt in a long time.

ξ

The flight attendant at the top of the stairs had the bluest eyes Lia had ever seen. She wondered if the woman wore some of those tinted contact lenses. She was very attractive, tall and slender, sported flaming red hair cut stylishly short and had a deep, smooth tan. She extended a perfectly manicured hand to Lia.

"Hi, I'm Maryanne. Simon's putting your bags in the cargo hold. I'll take your coat. There's just the two of you this morning; sit wherever you like and make yourself comfortable."

Maryanne then greeted Pascal, and the two of them exchanged cordial greetings. Lia stepped through the doorway and entered the cloistered world of an Conallied corporate jet.

Jesus, I don't believe this.

On the day before her departure from Fielding, Lia received a telephone call from Conallied's travel office.

"Lia, this is Cyndie in the travel office. Just wanted to advise you that Pascal Framonte is flying down to EPD tomorrow morning, and you've been scheduled for a hitch. Just drop your original plane ticket in an inter-office envelope and send it back to me. You need to be in the main lobby at 7:30am tomorrow morning. A limo will take you and Pascal down to the airport. Your driver will be Simon."

"Who arranged this?" Lia was surprised and intrigued.

"I got a call from Dawson Manford's office," Cyndie explained. "He approved it. Have a good trip; you'll enjoy it. Oh, good luck in Levale!"

"Thanks." Lia responded, feeling even more guilty about not talking with Daw.

"Hitching," Conallied's slang for riding on a corporate jet, was considered something of a special perk among all those below the top tier of the company and politically a feather in one's cap. Pascal Framonte was Jud Jeffries's global strategic guru. Lia really didn't know him, except for one occasion in London when she attended a week-long training session and participated in a case-study team presentation made to Pascal and his staff.

I wonder why he's visiting the Energy Products Division. I won't ask.

Conallied's fleet consisted of five jets of varying sizes. The largest was used exclusively by Jud Jeffries, Conallied's CEO. All five continuously flew the company's executives around the world to meetings, conferences and recreational events. They were staffed with flight and cabin crews enticed away from the major commercial airlines; these coveted jobs came by virtue of contacts and personal referrals.

The plane's passenger cabin was decorated in navy blue and slate gray. Plush carpet covered not only the floor, but the walls and ceilings as well. The sixteen seats that filled the front half of the cabin were wide, deep and covered in soft leather. Each passenger seat up front was equipped with individual audio and video set-ups. The rear half was outfitted with big swivel chairs and tables of varying sizes. One wall in this area was lined with shelves that held a small library of books, magazines and video and cassette tapes. A small alcove was outfitted with two computers, printer and fax machine. A recessed side bar held two crystal carafes with little tags marked "orange juice" and "cranberry juice" hand printed on them and silver decanters of coffee and hot water for tea, along with all the fixings. There was a full-size, wood-grained door marked as a restroom at the rear of the plane.

"Lia, we've got eight to ten minutes before I need you to buckle up for taxi and takeoff. If you want to scoot into the restroom, now would be a good time."

As she headed to the rear of the plane, Lia wondered how Maryanne knew she needed to go.

Damn, she's good at her job.

Navy blue glazed tile and heavy brass fixtures dominated the surprisingly spacious restroom. There was a small shower enclosed by glass, and blue and gray towels of various sizes monogrammed with Conallied's logo were stacked on shelves above the sink.

"There's a good-sized water tank somewhere in the bowels of this baby," Lia said aloud to herself.

Out of curiosity, she opened all the drawers under the sinks; they held a wide assortment of sundries and toilet articles, including sanitary napkins and tampons.

Nice going; I'll bet it's only recently that the company has stocked feminine hygiene products on its corporate jets.

"Well Lia, looking forward to your new challenge?" Pascal talked on the telephone during their fifteen-minute limo ride to the airport, so when she returned to her seat, this was their first opportunity to chat.

"Yes, I am," Lia responded to Pascal. She tried to keep her voice even and professional.

Why am I making such an extra effort? Chill out, stop worrying about silly things.

"We need a lot of help down there at EPD; we know you'll step up to the challenge."

I wonder who's included in the "we."

"Well, I'm going to give it 150%."

"We know you will. Good luck."

These were the only words they exchanged during the three-hour flight. Pascal worked and made telephone calls throughout the flight, and

Lia read and reread summaries of EPD's operations. She didn't want to give Pascal the impression that she was lazy or had nothing to do.

I can't doze off. It won't look good.

They were interrupted only by Maryanne serving a perfectly prepared ham and cheese omelet, along with a small tray of fresh fruit and muffins. About halfway through the flight, the captain and first officer, both named Bob, alternately came back to the cabin, greeted Lia, and spent a few minutes chatting and laughing with Pascal, as the jet glided smoothly through the thick layers of clouds and intermittent sunshine that peeked through that morning.

The deployment of equipment, supplies and staff to transport just two people in this manner must be tremendous. This way of living is very seductive, though. I could handle traveling around the country like this all the time.

The flawless service, the quiet ambience gently hugged by soft music, the atmosphere of importance, the environment of privilege, the expectation of perfection, seemed a normal routine and not a consciously sculptured world existing in an elevated, doggedly separate state apart from ordinary communities and the people in them. Lia sank down into the soft leather, stretched out across the wide leg rest, stared out the window and wondered, inexplicably it seemed, if she was blessed or cursed.

Pascal later said goodbye and reached over to shake her hand when the limo that picked them up at Levale's airport dropped him off at EPD's main entrance before taking Lia on to the hotel that had been arranged for her.

ع

The Energy Products Division's heating, ventilation and air conditioning products had been labeled for many decades as "We Make America Comfortable." The "We Make America Comfortable" quotation was a stroke of mastery in marketing conceived in 1922. The theme not only endured, but also had become a permanent part of the country's corporate identity pop culture. The Conallied EPD logo was printed, embossed and engraved on millions of product units in every town and city across the nation. Conallied sponsored nationally televised arts and cultural programming, and EPD products were featured in its slick commercials. Its products, ranging from small portable generators to massive nuclear power plants, ventilate, warm and cool just about everything. EPD's customers include millions of consumers across the country, other major manufacturers, real estate developers, railroads, airlines, municipal utilities and countries around the world. EPD's expanded global business strategy, still in its early years, required significant capital investment by Conallied. Long-term projected expenditures needed to be offset by strong earnings from profitable operations at EPD, as well as Conallied's other domestic Divisions. Jud Jeffries handed that challenge to all the Division leaders. Dan Castle, the head of EPD and the man Lia would be reporting to, had stridently resolved to succeed in meeting that challenge.

ξ

Levale, a quintessential company town, experienced a major growth spurt in the post-World War II years coinciding with the decision to locate Conallied Industries' Energy Products Division on its outskirts. EPD became the town's largest employer and remains so, with over 6,500 on the payroll in Levale and another 1,500 in field offices around the country. The town fathers gave the company hundreds of acres of essentially free land, along with every conceivable concession, including a direct railroad connector, to woo EPD to their growing town. Low-cost land, property tax abatements, cheaper labor, state-paid employee job training, low-interest construction loans, seats on local boards and councils, are the hallmarks of this common phenomenon of corporate America's locations. Over the decades, other corporations followed Conallied's lead and secured sweetheart deals of their own in Levale. Contrary to the popular images reflected in movies and on television, money and power are not concentrated primarily in glitzy, brightly lit skyscrapers, but in quiet, suburban, low-lying corporate complexes that are located on the outskirts of large cities and, increasingly, in bucolic, rural locations.

Levale, now grown to a city of just over 100,000, is depicted in Chamber of Commerce materials as the "Business Center of the Mid-South." Its small airport is quite modern and, not coincidentally, handles more corporate jet traffic than commercial flights. The city council was pleased it had in the past year negotiated with two major airlines to schedule daily large jet service between Levale and the cities of Atlanta, Dallas, and Chicago. This improved service created a new level of competition among the commuter jet carriers, which resulted in substantial improvement of the airport's airline schedules. Situated in northeastern corner of Kentucky, Levale lay just west of a low mountain range on a high plain. Flat and brown, the city stretches out to low, rolling foothills. The greenscapes dotting the region are the result of the labor of early inhabitants who wanted to create woodlands on the featureless terrain. The region is susceptible to sudden storms that create erratic weather patterns and dramatic skies. Not surprisingly, the lower economic classes are concentrated in the flatlands of the city, and the majority of the affluent scattered throughout the foothills.

EPD's acreage, once on the outer edge of the town limits, was now right in the middle of the city. In the mid-sixties, when the city experienced another growth period, EPD nervously acknowledged the teeming neighborhoods surrounding its "campus" by erecting a high brick wall around the entire perimeter of its grounds. Unlike the beautifully manicured grounds at corporate headquarters in Fielding, the Energy Products Division headquarters in Levale resembled a nondescript, sprawling military base. Levale's downtown area expanded at the southern end of the city, but the financial and business power of the region was concentrated in the corporate giants like Conallied's EPD, and their executive offices historically remained at the manufacturing sites instead of moving downtown. The tallest office tower, a gleaming twenty-four story building, had been constructed in the late eighties. A collection of shops, galleries and restaurants, and a theater-in-the-round sprang up in the area after the tower opened, and many of the older office buildings were remodeled. The citizens of Levale did not regularly flock downtown for entertainment because of few offerings, but the merchants managed to survive on trade from close-by neighborhoods. The city's upper class entertained themselves primarily at restaurants and two country clubs located in the foothills; the oldest had just celebrated its fiftieth anniversary. The new Vista Hills Country Club was the gathering place for many of the affluent, baby boomer crowd who came to the region with their corporate benefactors. Those who wanted bright lights and big city action traveled south to Atlanta, west to Dallas, or north to Chicago for long weekends. Outdoor enthusiasts went east to the mountains. Levale's reputation in America's corporate community was counterbalanced by its almost total lack of popular visibility by the country at large.

ξ

Lia Granger's place in the universe, currently marked by her promotion and relocation, while significant in the lore of Conallied and its Energy Products Division, resonated only slightly among the citizens of Levale as another corporate "suit" coming to their town.

ξ PART I ξ

First Winter

ξ CHAPTER 1 ξ

Daniel Castle walked into the spacious, main conference room at EPD with long, confident strides. His step was heavy on the polished hardwood floors, and he could be heard approaching halfway down the hall before he entered the room. Delayed by a conference call, he sent word for his staff to eat lunch without him. By the time he arrived, the cold buffet lunch had been removed by the ladies from Food Service. His staff was all waiting, seated around the large, oval mahogany table. Everyone shifted slightly as he entered the room. He sat in the empty chair next to Lia instead of the empty seat at the head of the table. Chairs scraped on the floor, body language was adjusted, and all the energy in the room flowed to Dan's direction and settled around him.

Wow, the dynamic in this room changed.

Dan was a big, hulking man with somewhat of a baby face. He did not carry himself in a pompous manner, but one didn't have to be very intuitive to know that he was the boss. He wore khakis, an open collar shirt, and soft leather loafers. He set the standard for the casual manner of dress at EPD. The atmosphere and dress in Fielding was corporate conservative formal; it had been a battle to institute casual Fridays, and a number of the staff still felt uncomfortable coming to headquarters in "business casual" clothing, even on Fridays.

This is so different than Fielding. I feel a little overdressed in my starched tailored shirt and wool slacks.

The Levale staff knew big changes were coming; they figured it was why Dan, one of the Company's "golden boys," had been placed in the Division out of corporate headquarters. Well educated, brash, creative, Castle had followed without variance the Company's predetermined path up the ladder during his thirteen-year tenure. He made things happen, and he made money; potential Conallied CEO material. It was common knowledge that the company maintained a short list of so-called executive "high potentials", generally in their 30's or early 40's, aggressive, the anointed. They were routinely mentioned as having the backbone to eventually run one of Conallied's core divisions and even one day to succeed Judson "Jud" Jeffries, the company's renowned CEO. Dan's people skills were poor, he knew it, everyone knew it. But, apparently, it didn't matter. The Company seemed prepared to look the other way. Lia had heard in Fielding that at least some of the big boys at corporate headquarters fretted over his inability to develop good relationships with the people around him. Ultimately, they decided to closely monitor him to prevent his messing up so badly in this regard they would be forced to acknowledge it and then do something about it.

Lia thought for a moment about the senior African-American in Conallied Company.

I wonder why I've never heard Lance Tolliver mentioned among the golden boys. He has fulfilled every requirement they always talk about, run a business with profit and loss responsibility, jump through every hoop placed his path, serve as a disciple of the Company doctrine, and never create any ripples in the Company's waters. I wonder what Lance is feeling.

Lia studied the faces around the table. She was the newest member of Dan's staff, and this was her first meeting with the full team. The staff was a mixture of old-line guys in the Energy Products Division and a handful of younger, aggressive types assembled by Castle to help "put the energy back into the Energy Products Division." There were two females at the table, one who managed EPD's massive supply chain and logistics operation, and Lia, who headed the critical national Consumer Services operation. Lia, as usual, was the only African American in the room, in fact, the only minority.

At least I'm not the only woman.

Lia knew she had to get to know these people, put them at ease with her, and establish relationships that would allow her to do her job and not let any of the proprietary feelings she suspected were just below the surface bubble up. She had been warned that EPD was filled with good old boys and working within the Division could be a political nightmare. But, she was now one of them, and it felt good to be among some of the best in corporate America.

This is where I want to be.

ξ

"Levale is an incestuous little hell hole." Keith Monroe's cynical laugh was so typical of him. "No, I take that back; it's a big hell hole!"

Lia was packing up her office at corporate headquarters in Fielding the previous month for shipping to Levale. Keith was not helping her with the task, lounging comfortably in one of her side chairs with his feet propped up in the other.

"Oh, please!" Lia shot back. "I've been a headquarters hack long enough, and so have you, Keith. It really became clear to me at the London management class that the action is out in the Divisions; that's where you make your mark. I'm taking on a new challenge in the new year".

In the past, Lia had envied Keith's comfortable, low stress position as Community Relations Director for the company. He was adept at navigating the corporate rapids, no small feat for an African American male in a none-too-friendly environment. On the other hand, Lia realized that his progression was now limited. Moving up meant moving out to the

Divisions where risk was reality. Keith was not a threat to anyone; that was his security. Lia, setting out into the rough waters, very well could be.

"Well, Lia, Dan Castle was up here last week and told me he was thrilled you were going to be a player on his team. I hope you know the definition of team player changes often in this company to suit the situation."

Lia knew he was right. "I've seen more careers ruined by a person being branded as 'not a team player' than anything else." She made the quotation marks in the air to emphasize the point.

"Just be careful. This job is perfect for you; you can ace this one with one hand tied behind your back, be a big hit, and move on. You're smart, intuitive and a great communicator. You have the best command of the English language of anyone I know. My sister, you know how to make folks see things your way. But remember, there are some real snakes crawling in the grass down there, good-old-boy snakes."

"Thank you, brother Keith, but you know I've dealt with snakes my entire career".

"Yeah, but they know when Castle gets done shaking up that place it won't ever be the same, and those rednecks are threatened as hell. And here comes your black face to restructure the whole damned Consumer Services organization. And, a goddamn woman, too. Holy shit, and a goddamn colored woman. You go get 'em honey child!"

They looked at one another and laughed out loud.

ξ

Energy Products had always been the Company's largest Division, and was once its most profitable. Times had changed, and it was generally acknowledged that EPD was in trouble. It was even hinted by some that Conallied could collapse if EPD failed. That was panic talk; Conallied failing would be akin to America itself collapsing. On the other hand, Conallied would surely be in very serious trouble if the Division crashed. It was one of the most visible, high profile Divisions, having direct contact with millions of consumers across the country. The regional branch offices and the smaller service offices are home to the service technicians who are dispatched to the homes of America. Print and television advertising campaigns featuring EPS techs had been a staple for decades. Only recently had men, no women, from a variety of racial backgrounds been featured in the ads; it created a bit of a stir, even though that small improvement was long overdue. While Conallied had other high-profile Divisions under the Company's umbrella, EPD was Middle America, steady and reliable.

The Energy Products Division's "plant" in Levale is a study of contrasts. It is a rambling, aging collection of mostly factories and warehouses. The blue collar, "line" population, the overwhelming majority of the Division's employees, labored on the manufacturing floors. The main administration building looked like all the others from the outside; a shiny, chrome and glass building wouldn't do much to enhance employee morale or public relations in a plant environment. However, it had been gutted and filled with plenty of plush carpets, polished wood and custom furniture in its interior. An added benefit in the older buildings is oversized offices, which were the envy of executives from other Divisions. The line workers were seldom seen upstairs in the administration building; the human resources department was located on the first floor just beyond the reception area. Even so, the line workers avoided going there. The executives visited the factories for major customer and vendor tours, special events, and, of course, when Jud Jeffries or someone on his staff showed up. They might also be seen on the factory floor as contract negotiations with the union neared. Both groups were not particularly motivated to cross lines. Inside the rambling, brick wall that encircled it, the imposing-looking plant was a small town unto itself. Railroad ties criss-crossed the grounds between the manufacturing and shipping areas. The eighteen low buildings of various sizes were separated by expanses of parking lots and meticulously groomed green areas. These small parks had benches and picnic tables scattered about for employee use. The largest of the parks, for some reason called

The Hill, was located in the center of the plant grounds. A large tent was set up there during the warm months, and employee teams could reserve it for group lunches, barbecues and other events. Adjacent to The Hill was a baseball field with wooden stands, four basketball courts and two tennis courts. A jogging trail had been carved out around the perimeter of the plant just inside the brick wall. Management and line employees mixed regularly at the plant's after-hours recreational activities in a way they did not while working. The first building inside the guarded main gate is a small theater for larger group meetings, and several, small meeting rooms are located on its lower level. The circular mezzanine above the lobby of the theater displayed EPD's new product lines. A small medical center sat on the southwest corner of the plant, and it was staffed by a full-time physician and a nurse. Two cafeterias, on the north and south ends of the plant, serviced the three shifts of employees working around the clock. EPD had been a decades-long institution in Levale, and its constancy through good and bad times underline the sense of superiority that pervades this corporate town.

Amidst this environment and the repositioning of the Division as Conallied's top revenue producer, Lia was smart enough to know that she was being tested. The company had taken its unusual specimen, put it in a Division jar, and was watching it progress under the microscope. If it could adapt, they would decide what to do with it next. They chose her. That's what mattered. For Lia, the process sometimes seemed perfectly reasonable, and in other instances, completely callous.

ξ

Lia couldn't believe she was actually sitting in Levale. Prior to her promotion and move there, it seemed an unlikely place to mark professional success. She had taken a very circuitous career route from California to Levale. From a little girl growing up in California, whose ideas, dreams and tastes were never what society had defined for her, Lia was constantly breaking out of molds. She was viewed as a "non-traditional" success story in Conallied Company. She was not recruited directly from college; she had returned to college as a working adult to complete the final two years of her undergraduate degree. She waited until Jordan started school before taking on the extra load. She had been an excellent student, and periodically toyed with the idea of graduate school. It seemed to her that the MBA frenzy had waned with the swing in the economy, and the absence of a graduate degree had not curtailed her career. Most of Conallied's long-time, senior executives did not have graduate degrees, though a larger number of the younger crop did. She had not touched all the right formal and informal bases in the company, she was not a twenty-year company veteran, she had not worked in a Division factory setting before, she couldn't drink bottle after bottle of beer and remain standing, she was good for only one tasteless joke in an evening, and she did not play golf. Most of her eighteen years of management experience had been gained outside the world of Conallied. But, she had brought in new perspectives and successfully completed two very challenging assignments at corporate headquarters that involved managing major organizational changes. The promotion to Levale was a big move and an opportunity to demonstrate her strengths in a business operations environment. Lia was especially pleased that the assignment involved Consumer Services. Assignments related to customer service were now sexy and considered choice opportunities for career advancement. It seemed that most of corporate America had got religion and was now focused on the customer.

ξ

Lia settled back in the comfortable, leather chair in EPD's main conference room and decided to let her body relax.

Jesus, I've been in countless meetings like this. Relax.

The surroundings were usually very nice in senior staff meetings in Conallied's Divisions around the country, and the service rendered by support staff was invariably indulgent. Always present was an unspoken, but foregone, understanding that vital work was being done. The atmosphere of arrogance and supremacy necessary to nurture and sustain that understanding was firmly in place. The sense of belonging, the knowledge that one is part of something that keeps the engines of industry running and thriving, is the narcotic that controls any impulse to question if the lifestyle is in conflict with one's nature. The fabric of corporate America feels sturdy, and it is continuously woven by its gatekeepers, mantra-like, to maintain its strength and resiliency. President Calvin Coolidge once said, "the business of America is business" and, notwithstanding the other critical institutions that comprise American society, that ideal represents the underpinnings of the gospel of Conallied. The company was the center of the universe for all inside it.

Lia was normally very animated in these kinds of meetings, but knew from watching other eager newcomers overplay their hand, her first meeting with Dan's full staff called for restraint.

It's your first week here. Just listen and learn.

Dan began by reporting the year-end results for EPD, which under normal circumstances, would be of great interest to his staff. Today, though, everyone just wanted Castle to get on with detailing his plans to restructure the Division during the new year. Lia studied the people who Keith had told were the key players in the group. Keith had friends in every Conallied Division around the country, and he was an amazing source of solid information and juicy gossip. Don Harmon, tall with a scholarly demeanor, is Dan's point man, serving as both an operations analyst and a strategic planner; he had been in the Division for several years, but was still considered a creative change agent. Douglas Jansen is the finance guy; he looked like a nerd, but had a reputation for being very smart and very ruthless. Clay Simpson, dressed impeccably among his casually dressed peers, handled all the communications and public relations for EPD. Joe Mather, who looked disheveled and distracted, headed up human resources. Virginia

Jamison, who started out on the Division's manufacturing assembly line, now headed up the Division's supply chain logistics and was apparently the only person who really got along well with Castle. Lia had heard comments that Virginia liked the perception and aggressively perpetuated it. Castle had a terrible reputation for working relationships with women, and Virginia seemed smart and savvy enough to position herself as his female success story. She was a tall, gangly woman with stringy blond hair that hung loosely down her back; her clothes didn't fit quite right, and she sat slouched in her chair. Apparently, this demeanor was okay in Levale; it would have never been acceptable in Fielding. But, she seemed to be very knowledgeable and was a fast and effective talker. Lia got the feeling that you would be asking for trouble if you interrupted her. She had been the first woman to head an EPD function, which was indeed an accomplishment in a very male-dominated Division. Virginia seemed determined to be better at being one of the boys than even the boys were.

I get it. Whatever strategy works to get you through.

"Now," Castle paused, "let's talk about what this group, this team, is going to accomplish during the next twelve months."

Bodies shifted again, less noticeable this time, but real. Lia got the feeling Dan enjoyed these moments.

I'm probably the calmest person in the room; I don't know enough yet to be afraid.

"EPD has fallen behind, way behind, and it's not acceptable. We're now at the bottom, compared to the other Divisions, in earnings and, not coincidentally, productivity as well. The Health Industries, Insurance Services, Software Development, and Radio Divisions have all beat us out. Radio was in the dumpster last year and has pulled off a great turnaround. We're going to do the same thing, and do it damned fast. Our competitors in the marketplace are kicking our asses on the product sales side and the consumer service side, too.

Uh oh, that's me.

We have a shitload of trouble here. Jud has put the pressure on all of us. But, the shit rolls downhill, and I guess I don't have to tell you who's next in line to get buried in it."

He laughed, and everyone laughed because he did.

You're next in line, Dan.

"Let me say this. EPD is going to look very different, and we're going to use this year to make it happen. This staff may look very different as a reflection of those changes. We've had three retirements and some key, new additions. We'll be constantly looking at what's needed for EPD's long-term future and what activities and functions have outlived their usefulness. Commitments have been made to Corporate. Well, hell, commitments were wrung out of us, but we'll make them. We're expected to deliver an additional $65 million to Corporate at year-end. One week from today, I want on my desk from each of you an overview of your function, two pages at most, don't bore me with a lot of detail. Outline your current accomplishments as well as the critical issues you face, your plans to streamline operations, increase productivity and improve quality in your department. I've brought Lia Granger from Fielding in to revamp the entire Consumer Services operation and get it back up to speed." He waved his hand in Lia's direction.

"So, Lia, I'll want you to give me your thoughts based upon what you've seen during your first couple of weeks."

Everyone in the room eyed Lia momentarily; Consumer Services touched every operation in the Division, and they didn't yet know her.

I hope my facial expression is okay.

"I'll read all your reports and set up either a meeting or conference call with each of you individually to discuss them. I will then determine what your dollar deliverable to the Division will be."

Wow, based on what I've heard, they're probably all thinking that they have already cut to the bone and how the hell are they going to increase productivity and quality, and cut costs, all at the same time. They've already eliminated the fat, now they were going to have to cut into the muscle. I'm hearing that the workforce is increasingly suspicious, and morale is way down. How am I going to deal with this? How am I going to do what needs to get done and respond to Dan's demands, Jud's demands?

"At our next meeting," Dan was on a roll; "we'll put the whole picture together and make decisions as necessary. We'll be taking a hard look at this Division at every monthly staff meeting. I don't want to spend a lot of time warming up old hash. Projects and initiatives aimed at increasing product sales and enhancing service will be identified, completed, demonstrable results presented to the team, always with a view to how it impacts where we need to take this Division. I'm interested in new ideas, new processes. Let's challenge everything. And, by the way, Jud is expecting a formal presentation from this team at end of the first quarter. Let's make sure we have something solid to say to him. Any questions? Thoughts? I always want open feedback anytime around this table."

Castle had a reputation for being abrupt and a man of few words; this occasion was no different. Silence filled the room for what became an uncomfortable few moments. Finally, it seemed, Virginia asked a question.

"Dan, how are we going to communicate this situation and any organizational changes to all of the employees, here at the plant and in the field? They all know something is up, and they're expecting us to tell them something after this meeting."

Castle's voice was tense, but quick. "We're not going to communicate anything yet. I mean we don't need to make any big announcements just yet, because there's nothing substantive to announce. We'll communicate only what we absolutely have to, which, for now, is nothing."

The group was clearly stunned. Castle was talking about the people who were actually going to have to make any new changes work. Body language was speaking again; everyone shifted and took quick glances at one another, but no one said anything.

I can't understand why this issue of communication with employees is not important enough to warrant more discussion, to cause someone to feel strongly enough to voice their concerns. Not even Don or Doug are saying anything. I want to say something, but I can't. It's my first staff meeting, too soon to be putting in my two cents. Anyway, what do I know?

Dan went on. "We need to be careful not to communicate anything until we have fully formulated the message. I'm confident we have the potential here for some really big wins. We can be heroes, winners, in this Division."

Lia glanced over at Pete Malvern, who was sitting to her left; he headed marketing for EPD. Like Lia, he was not home grown in the company. He was doodling on a yellow writing pad, and had printed in large, flourished letters "A REALLY BIG WIN FOR CASTLE."

Unless my instincts are really off, Pete's sentiment seems to be shared by most of these people; I feel it hovering in the air above the table.

They continued general discussion for a while longer. A few questions skirted around restructuring, but Virginia's concern about communication was the last direct question asked on the subject. Dan adjourned the meeting after exactly one hour.

Dan Castle never formally introduced Lia to the team, or them to her.

ξ

As they all drifted out into the hall, Joe Mather sidled up to Lia. She talked with him during the interview process, and was not particularly impressed with him. He had looked worried and bedraggled, came across like the Levale good old boy Keith had warned her about, and did not at all fit the strong team dynamic Dan had just talked about. Lia felt that their hour together for the interview had not gone particularly well, but it apparently didn't influence Castle's decision to meet with Lia and choose her. Lia had learned from an ex-EPD manager who worked at corporate headquarters in Fielding that Joe knew all the EPD history and where the bodies were buried, so he was able to hold on with Castle.

"Hi!" Joe greeted Lia with a little too much cheeriness. "I heard you got a hitch down here; they must really like you in Fielding. Oh, by the way, you might not want to sit next to Dan again at staff meetings; sit with some of the others. You don't want it to look like you're sticking too close to Dan. Some of the team won't like that."

He didn't say if the "others" included all of them or just certain individuals.

"Joe, the only empty chair at the table when Dan came in was next to me. That's why I was next to him."

"Well, just take my advice and be aware of it." He seemed to disregard Lia's explanation, and wandered away.

Well, that was more than a little strange.

Virginia approached, and slapped a hand over Lia's shoulder.

"So what do you think? Are you ready for this crazy group?"

Lia smiled; but for absolutely no reason she could put her finger on, she felt very uncomfortable in this close proximity to Virginia.

"The next year is *really* going to be interesting. Hey, if I can help you in any way, just pick up the phone. This place can get weird. Stick close to Dan in these meetings for a while. There's some sharks in this group. Now that you've got Consumer Services, these guys are nervous about what you're going to do and what plans you and Dan may have already discussed."

"Joe just gave me the opposite advice about sticking close to Dan!"

"Human resources people don't know shit from shinola."

Virginia's tone suggested nothing else need to be said. It occurred to Lia for the first time that Joe, the supposed people expert on Dan's staff, never said a word during the meeting about the potential impact of Castle's restructuring mandate on EPD's employees, even after she raised the issue with her question and gave Joe an opening. Unexplored questions and hidden agendas seemed to abound. Don Harmon was approaching them, and Virginia wandered toward him.

Lia made a point of joining the three branch managers with the most seniority, who all reported to her. They were clustered together on one side of the hallway. She had not met them yet, but recognized their photos in the Consumer Services materials she had been given. They were considered part of Dan's "extended staff," along with a handful of key managers from the manufacturing teams, and were occasionally invited to Dan's staff meetings, this time purportedly to meet Lia. They were talking about Castle, and Lia could sense both resentment and resignation in their attitude. Gunther Madison ran the largest of the six branches in the country, and apparently was the leader among the branch managers.

"Well, here we go again. These goddamn fast trackers go through here like diarrhea, wreaking havoc, and it's always us who have to deal with it. Hell, I guess this shit, too, will pass."

"Gunther, I don't know. This guy is going to make some dramatic changes if it kills him. He wants to be CEO of the whole fucking company." This was Walter Weldon, another senior guy whose body language seemed to Lia to be pretty low key and less intense than Gunther, or at least he had seemed so during the staff meeting.

As they chatted a few minutes longer, Lia smiled and nodded acknowledgement of their comments. Lia, though, was listening with half her brain; the other half was wrestling with other thoughts.

Am I imagining what's happening as I'm standing right here with them?

She stood in a small circle with them, but not one of the branch managers welcomed or acknowledged her, or looked directly at her. She was there, within inches of them, but not one included her in their conversation. Their body language also shut her out, a turned shoulder, a slight shifting of the feet to take up the available space, a maneuver practiced in this moment that clearly had been perfected by years of use.

I know it when I see it. I know it when I feel it. They don't even want to get to know me, their boss. They don't want to learn that I just might be okay.

They checked watches, talked about flight times out of Levale, and said good-byes to one another. No welcoming comments to Lia, no inquiries about her immediate impressions, no curiosity about any early plans she may have, no offers of advice, no opportunity for her to chat with them about visits to their branches. No change in what she had often experienced, and handled, in the past.

ξ

Lia made her way out of the maze of the administration building and back to her office in the Consumer Services building on the other side of the plant grounds. She felt confused and edgy. She wanted to call someone, but did not.

Why didn't they want to pop in and chat with her in a more private setting? Or, say hello to some of the people in the building? I just got to EPD, for God's sake! I'm not even going to call Keith, and certainly not Dawson. Hell, the Radio Division was where I wanted to be anyway. It's all about communication; it has always been my strongest leadership skill. Conallied disregarded my request for an assignment in the Radio Division.

Lia reviewed her weekly schedule and penciled in an unplanned meeting the next day with her staff, which she had originally scheduled at the end of the week. She plowed into a pile of messages, mostly consumer complaints, including two important commercial customers, before reviewing Consumer Services financial reports. There was work to be done. Lia stopped to stare out the window for a few moments. The sky looked strong. Thick, gray storm clouds were gathering on this January afternoon; a pretty hefty storm was coming.

ξ

At this moment of contemplation gazing at the sky, Lia's instincts did not alert her that she would, by all accounts, successfully restructure EPD's Consumer Services processes and procedures, increase productivity, boost morale, maximize revenue, and at the end of the day, fail monumentally. By habit, Lia hummed the words to the nursery rhyme, *Itsy Bitsy Spider*, as she worked.

ξ

Four times during her career at Levale, Lia had survived the ritual of meeting her new administrative staff. It was always like a first, tentative dance during which neither partner wanted to step on the other's toes. The goal was to make a sufficiently good impression in the hope they give her the benefit of doubt and follow her lead. A group dinner had been arranged for the following evening after Lia's arrival in Levale. She would have preferred to meet them on her first day in the office the following Monday morning and then plan a dinner. Apparently, this pre-planned dinner was a long-held EPD tradition. Dan had told her very little in advance about her staff. Lia suspected it was because he knew very little. He had been in his position only a few months, and he had not paid much attention to his staff, let alone the staff level below his direct reports. All she knew was among her staff there were five men, no women, four of them had spent their entire working careers in Conallied, and the fifth had been hired from the outside, but had been with the company for seven years.

Lia didn't expect anything more than polite chitchat and maybe some sharing about their backgrounds. She decided to adopt the attitude that it couldn't hurt, and it might be a better way to break the ice. Her staff would be coming to the restaurant directly from the office, so Lia was comfortable that the slacks, blouse and leather jacket she wore would be in keeping with EPD's casual dress code. She walked the one block from her hotel to the restaurant, a steak house that specialized in huge cuts of meat. When she inquired about the restaurant, the hotel's desk clerk told her the food was great and that she would definitely enjoy herself. Lia correctly guessed who her staff group was as soon as she spotted a huddle of men standing just inside the restaurant entrance.

Here I go.

"Hello, I'm Lia Granger," she said as she approached them and extended her hand; five arms thrust simultaneously toward her.

"I'm Lucas Mayhew." He stepped forward and gripped her hand so hard she winced. He then took the lead to introduce her to the others. Gordon Schwartz, Carl Talbot, Jerome Barrett and Gerard Swopes all smiled and made cordial small talk. The group was shown to a large, round table at the rear of the restaurant, and they settled in. The place was large and noisy, so Lia presumed that this table had been arranged in advance.

"I am so glad to finally meet all of you." Lia smiled and made eye contact with each of them.

Their waiter appeared, handed out menus and took their drink orders. He turned to Lia first, and there was the briefest moment during which Lia knew the guys were waiting to follow her lead on ordering alcohol. She ordered a glass of the restaurant's special reserve Riesling, and felt a barely distinguishable sense of relief around the table. Nonetheless, she was a little taken aback when Lucas ordered a double scotch straight up.

"We're glad you're finally here. We have no shortage of challenges, and we need a good leader to help us," Gordon said with a flourish that Lia sensed was his usual way of talking.

"Oh boy, sucking up already", Carl laughed.

"You'd better watch him, Ms. Granger", Jerome said in a joking tone.

"Oh goodness, call me Lia; all of you please call me Lia."

Lucas whirled his water glass between his palms, his fingers outstretched. "I'm not so sure about of all these challenges Gordon is talking about. My buddy is prone to exaggeration; in the grand scheme of things, we're managing to do just fine in our little universe here."

Lucas' hard gaze directly into Lia's eyes, more than his words, raised a little red flag inside her head.

I'm going to have to keep an eye on this guy.

"Lucas is our resident philosopher, and a country philosopher at that," Gerard smiled, but it seemed to Lia that his voice conveyed both amusement and consternation toward Lucas.

"Hey, I'm a good old boy from the hills of West Virginia. I'm just lucky that the Lord has given me a lot of good gray matter and Conallied has provided opportunities for me to use it."

"See what I mean," again Gerard smiled, but now it was he who stared directly into Lia's eyes.

The waiter returned with the drinks and took their dinner orders.

"Let's have a toast," Carl lifted his glass of beer. "To Lia, our new leader, good luck to you and our entire team."

"Hear, hear," said Gordon.

"Yes indeed," said Lucas.

"Good luck Lia; you'll be real pleased with the group of employees we have. You'll really like your secretary, Sara. She's a real sweet gal and very efficient. I know she will have everything ready for you on Monday morning."

After their dinners were served and comments exchanged about the size and quality of the steaks, they settled into dinner conversation about Levale, its weather, neighborhoods and shopping, and shared information about children, spouses and significant others. Lia was stuffed after making a good effort with her huge T-bone steak and didn't have dessert, although she insisted that the others indulge themselves. Over dessert and coffee, Lia turned to Gerard to follow up on his earlier comments about the employees.

"I understand we have just over three hundred people? I know this is a very general question, but what do you think of them?"

"Yes, we're at three hundred eleven, somewhat understaffed, but okay. With a few exceptions, I think they're a great bunch of people. These people are hungry for real leadership, though. We have all done the best we can, but we never see Castle or anyone else on his staff. All we get is second-hand information and rumors about how EPD is really doing, and the employees have no sense of being a part of the whole of the Consumer Services organization, let alone the whole Division. It's amazing when you think about how important Consumer Services is."

"Well, we'll do something about that. Not only will Consumer Services become an even more visible part of EPD, but we're going to have an influence on the bottom line, too. I've got a number of ideas I want to discuss with you guys, and all three hundred and eleven employees will be involved at some point. We're going to have some fun!"

"That's a stupid thing to say." Lucas, who had remained silent through most of dinner, shook his head as if in disgust.

Forks stopped in mid-air, Carl put down the water glass that had only gotten halfway to his mouth, Jerome stared at Lucas in disbelief, Gordon and Gerard sat silently.

Hello? Did I hear him correctly?

"Excuse me?"

"That just sounded so silly for someone who hasn't even reported for duty yet and doesn't know anything about this Division or us."

Lia stared at him for a few moments, pushed her teacup back and clasped her hands in front of her on the table.

"Clearly, that scotch was not your only drink this evening."

"Yes indeed, it is." The tone of his voice was strong and challenging.

"I'm sorry to hear that. So, that doesn't account for your lack of respect and common courtesy."

"Now you're trying to put me in my place, aren't you? You don't sound like this great leader we've heard about. You sound naïve. And, you could never define for me what respect or courtesy or tradition means. You wouldn't know what tradition is."

This is unbelievable. Hold it together.

Lia sat there for a moment grasping for a way to comprehend what had just happened. Never in her seventeen years in the corporate world had she ever experienced anything this overt, this kind of verbal hostility openly directed toward her.

Lucas must be really boiling inside to control it so poorly. Did he want my job? Had it been promised to him? What the hell is his story? That he would behave like this on the first goddamned night he meets me is unbelievable. Would he have ever done this to a white man, any man, even one he did not like? Absolutely not.

Lia made two decisions very quickly. She was not going to let this angry redneck bastard unravel her tonight, and his days in her operation would soon be over.

There's not a snowball's chance in hell that I'm going to let this snake's venom poison my efforts right from the start or infect the camaraderie I intend to build with my staff.

Gerard spoke up. "Lia, I'll walk you back to your hotel. Hey guys, why don't you get the check and take care of it."

"I'm the finance man, I'll take care of it," Jerome tried to sound lighthearted. "Hey boss, you'll see it on my next expense statement. I hope the extra cheesecake I ordered didn't bust our budget."

"Thanks Jerome. I'd like to meet with all of you on Monday morning. Why don't we gather in my office at ten o'clock; that will give me a couple of hours to get settled in with Sara."

"We'll be there at ten o'clock sharp; Gordon will make sure of it. He's so punctual it'll drive you crazy."

"That's okay with me; I'm kind of a punctuality nut myself."

Gerard touched her elbow, and they all stood up. As they headed to the door, Lucas stepped ahead of them leading the way. Lia put her hand on his shoulder to stop him. While Gerard walked ahead, Lia spoke to Lucas.

"I'd like to see you in my office at nine-thirty on Monday morning." Without waiting for an answer, she walked ahead of him and out the door where Gerard was waiting.

As they walked down the street, Gerard spoke first. "That was fucking unbelievable, if you'll please excuse my language. It was way beyond improper. I heard it, but I can hardly believe it happened."

"Well, unfortunately it did, and I will deal with it on Monday. I feel a little uncomfortable discussing Lucas with you because he is your peer, but you're my human relations manager and helping me sort out people problems is part of your job. Lucky you, I'll bet you didn't think you would have to put on your HR hat tonight, huh?"

"When it comes to people, I'm never surprised. Actually, I'm not surprised at what Lucas said, just at what he did. Does that make sense?"

"It makes perfect sense".

They arrived at the entrance to her hotel.

"Gerard, Lucas is out. He clearly does not want to be on my team, so let's accommodate him. I'll do whatever is fair in terms of reassignment to another EPD department; he can't remain in Consumer Services, or a new Conallied Division, or if he wants to terminate, severance pay, benefits, whatever is right. We ought to offer the guy some counseling, too. I'll look to you to take care of whatever paperwork is necessary."

Lia knew if she had pulled the same stunt on Dan Castle that Lucas did this evening, there would be no option of reassignment or severance pay and benefits; just fired, publicly, right on the spot and considered a shocking failure by Conallied leaders. Although this was a case of gross insubordination, Lia knew she had to appear to not overreact and to be fair in how she handled his departure from her team.

"Okay, I'll speak with Joe Mather about how we want to handle this, after you talk with Lucas, of course. He should be involved if you're terminating someone at this level, especially with his years of service. It's too bad; Lucas is a very smart guy, but he's hopelessly stuck in place. I wanted to think that he'd make an effort not to be an impediment, but we need to move forward, and I don't think he can march in your army".

"I'll restructure the service associates into two groups between Gordon and Carl. I'm also planning to bring a quality and productivity manager on board. I have someone in mind, but I'd like you to talk with her and give me your impression. Her name is Marva Herman, and I think she'll be an excellent resource for the managers and associates and a good addition to our team."

"I'll be happy to talk with her. This is good; although they may not say so, Gordon and Carl will be pleased, too. Lucas has always dominated them, and now they can speak up and really show their management skills."

"I'll see you on Monday morning. Good night, Gerard."

"Good night, Lia"

This has been one hell of an evening and introduction to my new staff. I can't stress about what happened. I can't.

When she got to her room, Lia undressed and fell asleep as soon as she got into bed. The absence of any angst over what had happened on her very first evening in Levale and her quick decision about what to do was a healthy sign, and it would not prevent her from leaving the starting gate. She slept well.

ξ

Lucas Mayhew. Over the years, Lia had met and worked with dozens like him. He is the corporate mid-manager model, continuously reproduced in large numbers by companies like Conallied. While men like Dan Castle serve as the spark plugs of corporate America, the Lucas Mayhews are the engine. They chug along, mostly out of sight, keeping the troops in the trenches working hard to follow the plan handed down to them from above. Corporate policy is formulated in the Dan Castle circles in short bursts of energy, tension and creativity fueled by intellect and arrogance. Men and women like Lucas do almost all the heavy lifting -- they and the people they supervise in never-ending cycles. Academically unremarkable, some never attended any college, they range from white, short-sleeve polyester shirts with pocket protectors filled with pens, to long-sleeve, oxford cotton button-down shirts with designer ties. The vast majority will never be chosen by top management to join their ranks. Their payoff, the guarantee offered in exchange for loyalty to the company, comes to them in a number of highly effective enticements. Good salary and benefits, annual bonuses, and generous pension plans provide the foundation. The icing on the cake, a periodic taste of the good life extended to them, comes in the form of meetings at resorts, golf outings, training sessions that cater to pre-determined professional development needs, and dinners with customers or vendors at private clubs and expensive restaurants. Their good fortune to live in nice, usually suburban neighborhoods, drive late model cars, educate children in better school districts, take vacations, possess the ideal of the American good life, is tethered to the Conallieds of the world. The total effectiveness of the corporate structure and its processes is demonstrated by the illusion of their view of the world. There is no vista beyond the walls of corporate America. It, and they, is the center of the universe, and anything else they may perceive revolves around their position at the center. Lia had witnessed mid-level managers who, dazed and confused at being restructured or downsized, could not begin to conceive of any other environment in which to make a living or live life. Downsizing, or the threat of it, creates paranoia and the determination to hang on even tighter.

Into this lurch come the Lia Grangers of the world, few in number, but creating a ripple that is perceived as a wave. They assumed that Lia cut in line, knocked them back, and grabbed an upper rung on the ladder. She is perceived as a loss of something, not always quite definable. There is no appreciation that African-Americans aspire to the same good life and, as they work and strive for it, fight the never-ending racial and cultural battles, as well.

ξ

"It's unfortunate that our first official conversation has to be about an unpleasant matter, and even before my formal first day in the office. I'm sorry."

I don't know why I'm apologizing.

Although it was not absolutely necessary, Lia called Dan the following morning to advise him of the situation with Lucas.

"I'm shocked, Lia. I noticed that Lucas seemed to be an intense fellow, but it sure sounds like he may have stepped over the line."

May have? There's no question that if he had done this to you, he would be gone. But, he never would have dared do this to you.

"It has to be done. His behavior was insubordination of the worst kind, blatant and hostile. There is no shade of gray here. This is a black and white, open and shut situation."

Her choice of words was not deliberate, but the double meaning that could be read into them was inescapable.

"Well, it's done. Let's have Gerard work with human relations here in my office. Have him call Joe Mather on my staff. We want to be sure the disposition of this matter is handled without any problems."

"Sure, Gerard had already planned to call Joe."

Good, you guys handle this jerk; we've got a lot of work to do over here.

After Dan hung up, Lia felt he was not thrilled with this turn of events; neither was she.

A bit of a rocky start, but no regrets, no need for paranoia.

ξ

"Come in Lucas."

He appeared at Lia's office door at nine-thirty on the dot. He startled her because, rather than knocking on the open door or announcing his presence in some way, he stood silently and waited for Lia to notice him. Lia pointed him to one of the two chairs opposite her desk. She much preferred to sit close to visitors in her office, either at the conference table or in side chairs, but not this time.

"Lucas, I'm afraid that it's not going to work having you on our team. Your insubordination the other evening was an embarrassment to me and to your colleagues, and it was grossly inappropriate."

Lucas sat silently, and did not respond.

Okay, he's not going to say anything.

"I've talk with Dan Castle, and he is aware of what happened and my need to take some action.

I'm going to give this a shot, anyway.

But, Lucas, I thought a lot about this situation over the weekend, and I want to listen to whatever you have to say. I really do want to understand what's going on and what motivated your action. I also have to say that I feel I'm entitled to an apology."

Why am I being so gracious to this guy? He should be eager to explain himself to me.

No response from Lucas. Lia pushed on. "It is possible for you and me to start over, even though we haven't even started yet."

Maybe the slightest little bit of humor will break the tension.

"Lucas, we can talk this out and try to work through it."

Still no response. The silence in Lia's office was deafening.

I give up.

"I have asked Gerard to follow up with you, and we will do whatever is fair. This is effective immediately. I would appreciate your collecting your personal items and leaving as soon as possible. If you prefer to come back this evening to collect your belongings in private, you may do so. We can arrange that for you."

Lucas's face had turned deep red, almost purple, and sweat beads had popped out on his forehead. His deep blue eyes bore into Lia's for a long moment. He stood up and left her office without uttering a word.

ξ CHAPTER 2 ξ

At dusk, her favorite time of day, Lia stepped out on the deck behind her home in Fielding, and the warmth of the sun, its restorative powers, immediately made her feel better. Her sense of well being was greatly enhanced by sunlight. She also liked the quiet out back. Even when all the neighborhood children were home from school, the sounds of their play and laughter seemed somehow muted. It was a real luxury not to have people living too closely around you. She leaned against the railing of the long deck and thought how thick the spring growth was this year throughout the two acres of trees on their land. The struggle of the young trees to take root out front made the old trees in back seem more beautiful than ever. It will be wonderful back here in the fall, she thought. Fall was her favorite time of year. The shimmering colors, warm days and cool nights, along with the start of football season, all felt good to Lia. It crossed Lia's mind that her football knowledge and passion had served her well in business gatherings with men over the course of her career.

She watched the critters romp through the woods, a city girl who never thought she would co-exist with animals of any sort who were not on a leash. Everything seemed to be in its place, and she liked it that way. The house was clean and filled with nice things. On the deck, the furniture and potted plants looked especially nice. She had grown accustomed to the space and place. In fact, she had finally become comfortable in New England even though the social life was limited and the connection with the community had happened only through Rob's political activities. If you had told her when she was growing up on the West Coast that she would one day live on the opposite coast, it would have seemed very unlikely. Actually, the first stop before moving to Fielding had been Washington, DC. It had been a social and cultural quantum leap from California, especially when she realized she was really living in a southern city instead of the eastern city she thought Washington would be. But "The District," as it was called by natives of the area, was special its aura of power reflected in the oversized monuments, grand congressional and administrative buildings and world-changing events that routinely took place there. She grew to love its mix of high visibility excitement and local community dynamics. She had never experienced the "haves" and "have-nots" living so closely together, but came to appreciate it as a feature of the East Coast and enjoyed the colorful mix of people. At dusk, the setting sun was still warm on her legs and the privacy provided by the woods allowed her to wear only a long T-shirt.

I love it back here. I know I'm going to miss it someday.

She sat in a deck chair and tried to read while waiting for Rob. She had negotiated a promise from him to come home early so they could have dinner together. It always seemed a major effort for him, so it didn't happen very often. His professional reputation in Washington, DC served him well in Fielding, and the move had expanded his business consulting practice. His partner and friend, Eli, continued to work out of the office in Washington. When he came into the house, the greeting and kiss were overly enthusiastic, and she knew he expected a thank you for coming home for dinner. She didn't give it. He immediately made two business phone calls, figuring it was okay since she was occupied with setting out the food. Over dinner he talked about his upcoming presentation to a state legislative committee; Rob and Eli had expanded their business to include lucrative government contracts at the federal and state level. Afterward, he settled in the den with his laptop. Later, when the emails had been sent and it was too late to call anyone else, he asked what was happening with her.

She suggested they sit on the deck since it was still very pleasant outside. As he settled in and put his feet up, he remarked on the beauty of the trees and flowers, how great the air felt and that he should try to spend more time out back. Lia interrupted him, sighed deeply, and began the discussion of divorce.

Later, after the divorce, which happened as quickly and painlessly as she could have hoped, Lia's transfer from Fielding to Levale provided the reason to sell the house.

ξ

Lia and Rob married right after college graduation, and it lasted twenty-two years. Its major accomplishment was Jordan, now a college senior. When Lia reflected on their marriage, an exercise she indulged in a lot less often now, her thoughts were generally benign. It saddened her to think that, after spending twenty-two years with a man, her feelings were so muted. No lingering regret over lost love and no hate or bitterness, either. Their relationship had been a distant one for fully the last half of their marriage. Lia wanted to maintain an intact home for Jordan, and Rob needed home and hearth for his image. The house became nothing more than a symbol and was maintained even after Jordan had gone off to college. She rationalized that the marriage had been in a years-long process of ending; when it finally did, there was little emotional investment left for either of them. Lia's corporate career and Rob's entrepreneurial endeavors and calling to public service had set them on paths that too often diverged. Their early passion had given way to quiet co-habitation. Over the years, Lia and Jordan became a team of two, participating in his school activities, taking vacation trips, and visiting her family in California every few years. Repeated attempts to pull Rob into their circle usually ended in frustration and hurt.

What Lia didn't get at home, she found only intermittently elsewhere. She had a group of old, close friends that she grew up with in California, but she saw them increasingly less often in recent years. She had a few good friends at Conallied. Dawson Manford, the first colleague who was also a friend, first became an occasional and enjoyable lunch partner; Lia and Dawson edged toward a more serious relationship on more than one occasion, but would back away from their feelings when they sensed it might develop into something more serious. He tried to give her a sense of belonging among the executives in a way that another friend, Clara Houston, an executive secretary who reached out and helped her navigate the environment when she first joined Conallied, could not do in the company's hierarchical structure. Dawson's efforts to connect her inside Conallied helped, but never grew permanent deep roots. Some days she felt good in her skin at Conallied, and some days she didn't, and struggled emotionally because of it. Still, she managed to get visible, challenging assignments based on a simple formula she had used for years: nail the assignment and then ask for another. Lia resolved to be successful in Conallied, and hopefully, finally, to feel the comfort of belonging somewhere.

ع

Loneliness gradually and quietly settled in, like the dark clouds that silently appeared in the western sky above the plains that stretched outside Lia's kitchen window in Levale, and then rolled in carrying beautiful storms. A sky watcher since she was a little girl, Lia marveled at what she called the for-real storms in this part of the country that she had never before experienced. Lia's rendition of loneliness played out in soft, familiar tones. It was not the acute, crushing loneliness that comes with an emotional situation. No, it existed around the edges and was a part of her reality by living in places where she did not have deep roots. But, her new friendship with Wanda was a blessing, and Lia was grateful. Wanda spent a lot of time with her riding around Levale with the realtor EPD arranged to help Lia with house hunting. They had twice met for dinner, gone to the movies, and wandered around Levale taking advantage of what good shopping there was. Levale is Wal-Mart country; it didn't take the two of them very long to get around to discussing a weekend trip to Atlanta as soon as they could both clear their schedules. The majority of Lia's time was consumed with making the transition into her new position. It seemed she had spent her entire adult life managing career transitions. As a long-practiced routine, Lia worked long hours in the office and continued to do so into the late evening at home after spending an hour on her treadmill and having dinner, which was often the best take-out she could find. This habit had long worked well for she and Jordan; when she was married to Rob, he rarely made it home before eight o'clock in the evening, even when Jordan was young, so preparing dinner for him was not usually an issue. She always cooked a big dinner on Sunday for the three of them, which served as a good leftover dinner on Mondays. Monday night leftovers and watching Monday Night Football was a ritual Lia and Jordan enjoyed together. Lia was now determined to fill her personal void with professional achievement. The loneliness hovered around the edges, and Lia resolved, as she always had, to hold it at bay.

ξ

In summer of 1958, eleven-year-old Lia and her summertime friend, Lois, were in business. Lia declared they were going to start a business and, as usual, Lois went along with the program. They struggled to drag the old, metal desk from the basement around to the side of the house and placed it in their little alcove under the steps. It was an act of bravery for the two girls, both of whom were small for their age and often mistaken for being younger. They had always been afraid of the dusty, cluttered cavern of a basement with its low ceiling and dark, cobweb-filled corners. Lia wanted the desk, and she swallowed her fear and talked Lois into doing the same. Lia also found two old, wood chairs; they were cracked, and the layers of bright green, yellow and blue paint were peeling off, but they were much better than the crates they had first planned to use. They had both contributed part of their allowances and purchased two writing tablets, a small metal file box with 3x5 index cards, two giant, bright yellow and purple pencils, an eraser and a big, brown folder. Lois offered a big, white doily for the top of the desk. Lia had to point out that it wouldn't look businesslike. It did not surprise Lia that Lois wanted to use the doily; there were at least fifty of them around her grandparents' home. Lois's grandmother hand made them, and constantly made her wash and iron them to starched perfection. Lois was also responsible for all of the other household chores, to the exacting demands of her grandmother. It always made Lia angry, and queasy, when she watched Lois empty and clean the small trash cans her grandparents used to spit their chewing tobacco into. Lois never talked about her parents or what happened to them. Lia never asked, even though she wanted to; somehow asking the question frightened the usually brave Lia. As far as she knew, Lois had always lived with her grandparents, six houses down the street from Lia's own grandparents. Lia spent many weekends and every childhood summer with her maternal grandparents, even though they only lived across town from her parents and ever-expanding group of siblings. Lia was the first-born and always had a special relationship with her grandparents, who totally spoiled and catered to her. Her family would come over for Sunday dinner every couple of weeks, and sometimes Lia was glad when they went home, and she was the center of the universe again. Lia's spending so much time with her grandparents seemed to be okay with everyone. When she arrived on the first day of summer vacation, she would run down the street to announce her arrival to Lois. The two of them had repeated the annual ritual since they were both four years old.

Everything was set up in the girls' alcove office, but it was now close to dinnertime for both girls.

"I don't think we can start today, Lia, because by the time I eat and do the dinner dishes, it will be almost dark. Mother Bea won't let me come back outside."

"Okay, let's start tomorrow. I can be out at nine o'clock. Can you be out that early?"

"I'll get up early to finish my chores."

"Good, because we're going to be partners and split the money we make."

"I hope we make some money," Lois voice betrayed her doubt.

"I know people will think we're too young . . ."

"White people are gonna be surprised that we're colored, too, Lia."

"And, they will be surprised even more because we'll do a good job."

"Yeah. See you in the morning, Lia."

"Lois, let's wear our pink pants and tops. Will Mother Bea let you?"

"If it's clean, I'll just wear it. It was my birthday present, so I should be able to put it on whenever I want. We're gonna look so cute." Both girls giggled at the thought.

As Lois started down the street, she suddenly turned and asked, "Lia, what kind of business will we do?"

The question surprised Lia. She just wanted to be in business and had not thought about exactly what they would do. She hadn't been so smart, after all, she thought, but her mind was racing fast now.

"We're going to ask people passing by for their name, address, phone number and where they work and other stuff. We'll write it all down on our tablets and then copy the stuff neatly on the cards that we'll keep in the little box.

"We should put our names on the box," Lois was glad to offer an idea.

"Yes, we'll put just the main things on the cards and keep them in the box. We have those red cards with the alphabet on them to keep everything in order, and we've got the little key so nobody can steal the cards. Then, when someone needs to know who anybody really is, not just because they say so but to, you know, make it true and official, they can come see us. We'll charge everybody fifty cents, or maybe a dollar, to make a card for them."

"But how do we know people will talk to us?"

"Let's talk about that tomorrow".

This all sounded pretty good to Lia even though she had to think fast about it. Grown-ups just needed to give young girls a chance.

"Okay." Lois really didn't seem to understand completely, but Lia knew her friend would try it anyway.

"Will we have a real office, in a store or something, when we're grown up?"

"Definitely!"

ع

Lia's staff filed into her office while she was getting her morning tea. Sara always volunteered, but she didn't want her secretary getting it for her. She liked the idea that Sara was okay with handling the chore, but was uncomfortable with her actually doing it. Lia preferred having staff meetings in her office rather than in the adjoining conference room. She enjoyed the intimacy of sitting around her smaller conference table; she felt there was a more comfortable exchange of ideas and opinions, and the physical closeness made a real difference to her. She generally kept her office door open during meetings. Lia sensed that it made a couple of the guys a little nervous, but it encouraged trust from the employees.

No secrets in here.

Lia's corner office was long and narrow, floor to ceiling glass on two walls. An office designed after her own heart, the design seemed to allow the whole sky in, and Lia loved it. She did not change the furniture that was in the office when she arrived; oak wood, blue tweed upholstered chairs, navy blue leather desk chair and navy carpet with a band of tan around the edge. She personalized it with some of her own artwork, photographs of Jordan, and the plaques and awards he had earned at Conallied.

Marva, who Lia had just brought to Levale to join her staff to focus on productivity and quality, and Carl were engaged in good-natured verbal jousting about something or other, but quieted down when Lia came in.

"So what do we have to do, hand over our first-born kid to Castle?"

Lia could always count on Carl to be first with a crack. He seemed to be her most creative staff member, but he also had a lot of growing up to do.

"Lia's already had the pleasure of Dan Castle's staff meetings.

It didn't take long for bits and pieces to get out. Everybody knows everything around here. Even so, there's not much detail at this point.

Whew! I'm relieved I don't have a first born to donate, at least not one I know about!" Jerome, Lia's finance manager, joked. She was convinced the guy had missed his calling in life as a stand-up comic.

"He'll gladly take your wife, though, and your new puppy!"

Gordon, who usually displayed no sense of humor, provoked raucous laughter from the group with his quip.

I'm glad they're in a good mood this morning.

"Well folks, it ain't pretty."

It was not exactly a thrill to be the new boss in a position, so early in the game, to convey a message that was going to challenge and stress them out over the next year. On the whole, Lia felt pretty comfortable with her staff's acceptance of her. Gerard had commented to Lia his feeling that the dynamic among her staff was more positive now that Lucas Mayhew was no longer part of the group. He also shared with her that some managers across EPD felt she had gotten the position because she was an African-American female; EPD had been under a lot of pressure because of its woeful lack of diversity in its leadership ranks, particularly among minority women. But, Lia felt her staff respected her capabilities and leadership.

They realized that Castle wasn't going to give this responsibility to someone who couldn't hit a grand slam for him.

Marva had also clued her in to some of the discussions among her staff.

"They've been talking with the guys in the branches, and a lot of them think Castle hired you because it would look good to have an African-American on his staff, and a female at that. This move really enhances his image at corporate headquarters. But, you know, the guys here like you. They like your energy. They think you are the kind of person who can go toe to toe with Castle, if necessary, for the good of Consumer Services. They feel they can learn by watching you in action. You like that, don't you?"

"I suppose I do. I need all of you to help me make a lot of things happen, and we'll probably not have a lot of time to do it."

Lia had taken on a serious tone with Marva. She counted on her more than anyone to keep a beat on the mood around Service. Frankly, Lia needed Marva to watch her back but not separate herself from the rest of the staff while doing so. Lia had convinced Marva to come work for her before she even got to Levale. Lia had seen her in action around corporate headquarters and was impressed with her creative ideas and eagerness to do things differently. She was still too young to be jaded. Lia needed change agents on her team, and it sure wouldn't hurt her to add the diversity of an African-American female to her group, too. The white guys had hired folks who looked and thought just like themselves forever.

I'm continuing a long and fine tradition.

She laughed to herself and took a kind of perverse pleasure in the irony. Her paranoia ebbed and flowed, but was in check for the moment; she needed to let it go because she realized it sapped the energy she needed to navigate the political rapids and get the job done. She had seen the careers of too many African-Americans, and women, torpedoed over the years for reasons that had nothing to do with performance. Lia maintained no illusions that it couldn't happen to her.

But, somehow, she forgot.

ξ

"So, folks, we'll take on the challenges. I know it could be a long putt, but we can sink it."

Lia was wrapping up her thoughts on the message Castle delivered at his staff meeting. Her group had listened to her quietly, but intently. They all leaned in around the conference table, and Lia wanted to channel the tension among them into shared resolution. Lia took a deep breath, and they all looked at her expectantly.

"I have faith in this team that we'll get it done. We'll need to pull together every one of our three hundred people here and ask them to play a role. I don't have to tell any of you that we're the group that's on the front line with the consumers; we're highly visible. The changes Dan is planning will include us in a big way. He talked to his staff about being heroes; well, we, all of us around this table, can definitely be big heroes for EPD in Dan's eyes." Lia was excited; this is what she was good at, what she liked doing, and she wanted to transfer the energy to her staff.

ξ

Her small size and stature had always belied Lia's strong presence. From the time she was a little girl, her intensity had taken others by surprise, and she quickly earned respect from others in school and later at work. Lia was accustomed to getting comments about her drive and leadership. The comments ranged from genuinely complimentary to awkwardly guarded to thinly veiled hostility. She was well into her career and had joined Conallied in the corporate office in Fielding just six months earlier when a manager in another department displayed what seemed to Lia to be incredible ignorance, although he was totally sincere.

"Wow, you are great on your feet. You know, Lia, you don't come across like most other Black women."

Lia had taken a seat next to him in the front row of an auditorium after making a presentation on the newest trends in organizational development, a topic she loved to discuss, and she had to squash her immediate instinct to reach out and slap him. Instead, she stared daggers in his direction.

"Don't get me wrong," he stuttered, "it's just that you act differently, and you really communicate well."

So, you're displaying the "we-picked-a-good-one" mentality.

Lia was determined to maintain her calm. "When you say, 'most Black women,' who are you talking about?"

"Oh you know, the ones you see on television and sometimes out in public. It's just that they always seem to be so big, and so loud, and angry about everything. You know what I mean."

"No, I don't. Lia said the words very slowly.

"Oh, but some of the time they seem to be nice, and very religious, too. They're not always loud or bad people, that's not what I'm really saying. You're small, and you look young, but you have a lot of poise."

Oh, now you want to try to smooth it over.

These words of wisdom came from a supposedly smart man, a young, up-and-coming manager.

Lia put her hand up. "Let me stop you before you make a complete ass of yourself."

"Excuse me?" He looked genuinely startled and confused.

Suddenly, Lia was close to tears.

What the hell is wrong with me? He's the ignorant one. Why do I feel like crying?

She got up, walked to the back of the auditorium, and stood against the wall not listening to the other presentations, preoccupied with thoughts about what he had said and why she felt so badly. Lia had experienced too many similar conversations over the years; not all of them were as frustrating, but the theme was the same. Although they crossed paths from time to time, the two of them never spoke to one another again.

ξ

"Lia, what do you think Castle is going to want from us on the budget?"

Jerome sounded worried because, along with Lia, he had responsibility to justify the monthly financials submitted to the Division.

"I'm going to have that conversation with him in the next week or so. I really don't know at this point, but my guess is a pretty significant reduction in our costs and a definite bump up for our revenue projections. We can count on that."

"There's no way we can readjust our projections down again. We've already done it once at the end of last year, and we're barely into the friggin' new year!"

Gordon sounded genuinely worried, too, and looked a little fatigued; he sighed and made his case.

"Sorry, but it pisses me off. Lia, the only way we can get another three, five, or ten percent, or whatever the hell it's going to be, is to cut people. If we try to get more productivity than we're already getting, which is pretty damned high, we're going to lose them anyway. They are working at a pretty relentless pace already. This is a no-win. We need to constantly improve service to our customers to stay competitive, we know that, but there's no way we can meet their expectations with fewer bodies doing the work here and out in the branches. What's the guy thinking about? Looking good for now and to hell with the long term?"

Carl, who could always be counted on to provide enough nervous energy for the whole group, got up, paced around Lia's office once, and then leaned against one of the windows.

"The guys out in the branches have a totally bad attitude about all of this. The technicians don't know what Castle is going to do or what you're planning for Consumer Services. They're pretty freaked. The branch managers are not helping matters much either."

"How do you know all this?" Gerard asked.

In Lia's opinion, Gerard was the ideal human resources manager. Quiet, thoughtful, his questions and comments were infrequent, often subtle, and always right on target.

"They talk to me. I've known a lot of these guys for a long time. Just like the people here, they feel like their backs are against the wall and they're sure that a restructuring is going to result in lost jobs."

I'm not sure yet, either, but you may be right, Carl.

Consumer Services was a big part of the Energy Products Division, with over six hundred total employees. Lia had three hundred in Levale, most working as consumer service associates. They were housed in one of the newer buildings that sat on the edge of EPD's plant. Lia's staff and the associates occupied all four floors of the building. The associates were situated in clusters of cubicles that were custom designed for the operation. Because their fundamental work activity involved one-on-one communication with consumers, they all had the benefit of state-of-art computer and telecommunications equipment. She was going to have to give priority to spending more time with them. As a group, they lacked self-esteem and had been given absolutely no decision-making authority related to managing their jobs or handling difficult customer problems. Lia planned to change that.

Almost three hundred service technicians, based in the branch offices scattered around the country, serviced the array of products manufactured and sold by EPD. Functionally, the branch managers supervised the agents by geographical region, but structurally they were all part of Lia's Consumer Services operation. The structure created an almost inevitable tension between the branch managers and the leader of the Consumer Services operation.

Is this a test that companies like Conallied love to structure by design into assignments to test the mettle of its executives? Or, was it just stupid and too hard to undo after all these years? Who the hell knows at this point?

Hopefully, Dan's plans would provide the opportunity to make some organizational changes during the restructure. Lia knew she would be buying trouble if she tried to make it happen on just her own energy. The discussion after the staff meeting confirmed that for her.

Her staff continued to discuss what might be coming, knowing their coping skills would be stretched thin.

Jerome spoke up. "The truth of the matter, what all of us have to deal with is that we are expected to generate revenue, big-time revenue. Consumer Services should really be a key element of the Division's new marketing and public relations strategy in an updated and fresh way with the emphasis on taking great care of our customers. We should be a key component of how the Division sells the goddamn products. We shouldn't have to be salesmen, just service the customer well."

Lia wondered how Jerome had lasted this long in the jungle. He was a very smart guy who often displayed his sensitivity without discomfort and didn't exhibit the usual aggressive behavior that Conallied's culture ingrained in its managers. Lia admired his style, and it slightly irritated her at the same time. She was going to need him to be aggressive during the next year; aggressive while hopefully remaining true to his nature.

I think I might be envious of his ability to display his sensitivity and be a strong leader. Why am I afraid to be both?

"At the product service conference I went to in Chicago last month, our major competitor stole the spotlight with their presentation on the millions of dollars they're investing in the delivery of service, emphasis on how the actual delivery of service is carried out, because their marketing group convinced the business leadership that the best overall strategy to boost revenue is for service to support the sales operation. Their theory is that top-notch service sells more product, so service is viewed as an investment, not a direct revenue generator."

"It seems to me," Marva cut in, "that we are compelled to play both roles. I mean, consumers spend a finite amount of money on our products in a lifetime because they are so durable, so they've got to be wooed at the original point of sale with the promise of great service. People don't buy a new furnace or air conditioning system every day. We've got to capture their loyalty for the long-term very early in the game."

"There you go being logical again, Marva. It's very annoying." Carl slapped his knee as he laughed.

Jerome pressed on, refusing to drop his serious tone.

"They're actually trying to use Consumer Services to subsidize the whole damned Division. The attitude of our competitors is if they make a few bucks from their service operation that's great, but it's not their primary goal. I just sat in that conference hall and stayed quiet. There I was from big, bad Conallied, and I didn't have a thing to say."

"Jerome, we've had this discussion before. It's just not going to happen. Get used to it." Gordon sounded irritated, but he and Jerome had worked together for years; they were good friends.

"EPD is too far down this road now. They have determined that over the long term almost as much money can be made in Consumer Services rather than from actual product sales. I know that some are not comfortable with the strategy but, right or wrong, it's where we are."

Lia pressed ahead with her thoughts. "Well, I intend to be a supporter and friend of the service technicians; they just don't know it yet. Gordon's right; revenue pressures are never going to change. I'm absolutely convinced, though, if we are a team, and I mean really a team in the strongest terms, we can make these new dollar goals, whatever they are. Hell, we can even exceed them, through reviewing and streamlining the process of how we deliver service. The productivity gains can minimize, maybe even eliminate, the job losses everybody is worried about. I'm telling you guys, if we crunch the productivity, all this noise about downsizing will mostly go away. I'm going to start by going on the road to all six regional branches with my sermonette on teaming. Then, we're going to organize a series of roundtable sessions with our associates here and then joint sessions with the service techs in the regions. It blows my mind that the two groups don't know one another. We will figure out a process to do some joint sessions with the associates and techs. I can already see that they too often don't understand the pressures each group has to cope with. It took me about twenty minutes to figure out that reality. This working at cross-purposes, intended or not, has to stop. The Division can no longer afford it."

Lia waved her arms around from an open to a closed circle to emphasize their inclusion in her plans.

"Through the sessions, we'll do the practical work of improving the processes of service delivery; quantum improvements, not baby steps, I should stress. These teams can't be a fad or the flavor the month. I want them to be the primary vehicle we utilize to improve the entire Consumer Services operation. We have to institutionalize the teams to give them credibility."

"Sounds great. I'm ready. This sounds like a hell of a lot of work, but a lot of fun."

Thanks for the cheerleading, Marva.

"Lia, I'm with you all the way; let's go for it." Gordon uncharacteristically pounded the table.

As the staff wandered out of her office, Lia felt a sense of relief. She was learning a lot from her staff that would be helpful to her. She needed her team to genuinely embrace this initiative with enthusiasm. Right or wrong, it mattered to her that their support was real and not just lip service given to the new boss. She was now thankful that her staff had jelled nicely, and they all had seemed to embrace her plans for their operation. She felt they were up to the challenge.

Jesus, I've got a multitude of work to do here in Levale and on the road. Let's see how hostile it is out there. No, too soon to make that judgment; I have little to nothing to support that assumption at this point; I can't be the one with the bad attitude.

Lia flipped on the tape player in her office, dropped in the *Hideaway* cassette, and hummed along with the music. David Sanborn, at his absolute best, to steady and comfort her.

ξ

She drove back to the hotel that evening in the rental car, thinking how glad she was her own car and furniture were arriving within the week. Lia had been booked into the new, all-suite hotel near the plant during her relocation period; it would be home until she moved into her new house. Her suite on the top floor was not lavish, but nice enough, and had a living room, dining area, fully outfitted kitchenette and a loft bedroom. Over the years, Lia had spent many nights in hotel rooms in just about every state and several countries. She had stayed in luxury suites of five-star hotels on well-known boulevards and small rooms in economy motels right off interstate highways while visiting branch offices, manufacturing facilities, distribution plants and customer service centers in Conallied, as well as in other companies. On more than one occasion, she had awakened in the middle of the night and couldn't remember where she was, a professional hazard of corporate life.

She had decided to purchase a newly built townhouse and was approved for a fast closing date. A small, two-bedroom unit, but plenty of space for her, and Lia loved the surprisingly spacious deck that surrounded her corner property.

I hope this good luck with the house is a good omen.

The townhouse was in a small, picturesque development in an area of the foothills that was almost rural, a new experience she hoped would be pleasant. She was going to enjoy the calming effect of driving by the working farms going to and from the plant. She had not seen any other African-Americans in the area, but her next-door neighbors, a young professional couple with no children, seemed nice enough. Her new friend, Wanda, who lived in the middle of the city close to her graphic design office, lived in a big, Southern Victorian home in an old, well-maintained neighborhood that was a mix of original owners and younger, diverse professionals. Wanda's house, left to her by her mother, suited her vibrant style perfectly.

For someone who had moved a lot, Lia was not good at transient living. She had done so much moving over the years that her family and friends in California assumed she took it in stride. In reality, it had not gotten any easier. Her mother called almost every night since she arrived in Levale.

"Lia, are you going to be okay? I can't understand why you're going to live way up in the hills instead of in the city around people. There are plenty of rednecks down there, you know, and some of them would think nothing about bothering you. You're not scared at all? Don't you want to be downtown in the city where things are going on all the time? What does Rob think of it"?

"Mama, how is where I live any of Rob's concern? He's not my husband any longer, just to remind you.

"I just wish you'd settle down again; it seems you're just never going to really settle down".

"Mama, just because I haven't lived at the same address for years doesn't mean I'm not a settled person. I'll have a nice, cozy townhouse here and it's not way up in the hills. Jordan graduates from Michigan in a little over four months. Everything is very settled. We've talked about this before. You have to move if you want to prove yourself and get ahead in Conallied. They want devotion."

"You don't have to prove devotion to those people! You've always taken care of things for them. You were a strong child, and you're a strong woman. I'm going to worry about you sometimes, that's all there is to it. But, I suppose you'll be okay, Lia. You always have been."

ع

The following week Lia admired the darkening sky as she drove past the flatlands and started to wind into the foothills, and it calmed her. She had always been a sky watcher, never quite understood why she always sought out and saw something fascinating in the sky. Clear blue skies of varying hues seemed to inspire feelings of affirmation; stormy skies somehow generated strength in her; the transitions in the sky as a storm passed through was somehow hopeful. She decided some dramatic and hopeful music was in order and popped *The Phantom of the Opera* tape into the player.

ع

Lia needed to call Dawson; they hadn't talked since her promotion and move to EPD was announced. Daw was among the first people Lia met at Conallied, and she particularly enjoyed talking with him. On her first visit to Conallied's corporate headquarters, he had been one of a cadre of corporate leaders Trisha Lyman arranged to interview Lia. She assumed the ritual was arranged to ensure consensus that Lia had what it took to fit in. Trisha was one of the few female senior executives in Conallied. Even though she liked Lia a lot, she knew enough to cover her backside by having others give Lia the seal of approval. Lia met Trisha when they both served on a panel at a women's forum in Washington, D.C. They sat together during the luncheon that followed, and for some reason both felt an immediate kinship with each other. They stayed in contact after that. Lia was comfortable and doing well as an operations director at a nationally known public relations firm. It took Trisha over a year to persuade Lia to visit Conallied to discuss potential career opportunities. Arrangements were made for Lia to fly to Fielding, Conallied's corporate headquarters, and accommodations were reserved for her at Latimer House, Conallied's on-site residence for its traveling executives. Latimer House, a three-story wood structure, was connected to the headquarters building by a covered bridge filled with flowering plants of every color and description. The structure, almost one hundred years old, had been beautifully maintained. A large, bronze plaque affixed to a wall in the lobby described the building's origin and heralded its historical designation. The two upper floors contained eighteen small suites. The main floor consisted of an informal check-in desk, a large, well-appointed meeting room, a small lounge with a huge fireplace in the corner and a fully stocked, self-service bar running alongside one wall, a business library, and a small, elegant dining room. The highly polished, original wood throughout the facility was spectacular. Lia picked up a message to meet Trisha for dinner in the dining room at 6:30. As they sat in the half-filled dining room talking for more than two hours, Lia took in the atmosphere of corporate privilege; beautifully prepared gourmet meals, quiet and attentive service, complete comfort and safety always taken for granted. It was unspoken, but obvious, that a certain manner of living, working and interacting was maintained, but could potentially be adopted by a promising outsider. It was alluring and intoxicating. As Lia and Trisha were walking to the lobby and saying good night, she heard a burst of laughter coming from the lounge. A group of three men, holding brandy snifters in one hand and cigars in the other, were enjoying the pleasures of the institution they had been empowered, for generations, to sustain.

ξ

Dawson Manford was among a small cadre of Conallied finance executives who reported directly to Jud Jeffries, and he sat at his side at every important meeting around the globe. Trisha remarked to Lia that Dawson was very well liked. He was easygoing, almost irreverent in his manner and attitude toward the company; his demeanor was relaxed and open. It was especially refreshing to Lia, because everyone else had been stiff and awkward and asked her some really ignorant questions.

"I assume you took the SATs in high school; what were your scores?" A senior human resources manager she talked with earlier in the day asked this question.

He must be kidding. I'm sitting here with years of professional experience and achievement, and this idiot, a human resources manager no less, asks me about a test I took over twenty years ago in high school. Unbelievable.

"Since that was probably twenty-five years ago, I have no recollection whatsoever. I think I may remember my son's SAT scores from a few years ago if you're interested."

If I have to answer absurd questions like this, Conallied is not the place for me.

He held Lia's gaze for a long moment, but didn't respond. Lia tried to forget about it and not let it ruin the day.

"So, have we all bored you to death trying to impress you with how great we are? We know everything, but don't know a damn thing really, so that makes us a pretty wacky and dangerous crowd." Laughter twinkled in Daw's eyes and the lines at his temples did not age him. He laughed at his own comment, and it was genuine in its merriment. The sound of it dissolved Lia's edginess. He was not at all overweight, but his height and bulk seemed to fill the room. He appeared to be in his mid to late fifties, had a full head of thick black hair, the gray just starting to creep in at his temples. His mustache, however, was more gray than black. The fact that he had mustache was unusual; Lia had not seen very many men in corporate America sporting one, especially white men. Most African-American men grew mustaches, a cultural thing and one, small choice on which most refused to compromise for the sake of the corporate ethic. There were some, though, who didn't want to take a chance and maintained a clean-shaven look. Lia spent almost an hour and a half talking and laughing with Daw about life in general, families, raising teenagers, the hassles of relocating and the fun of hiking and camping. He laughed a lot.

I like this guy.

"Well, we've covered the waterfront, haven't we, and shit, we didn't even get to what a joy it is to work for Conallied. You know, we really do think our little place here is pretty special."

He waved his arm at the floor to ceiling window that looked out toward the manicured grounds on which the corporate headquarters sat. Lia spotted two groundskeepers outside, and wondered how many people were employed to maintain the unblemished facility and its surrounding acreage. It had to be a small army.

"You're talking to all of us headquarters hacks so we can decide if you have the stuff to be included. You may kiss my ring now."

Dawson spoke with exaggerated cynicism, but Lia knew there was a lot of truth in his humor. She had conducted and been through enough interviews to know.

"Is this a good place to be?"

"It can be, Lia," Dawson replied after pausing and then looking directly into her eyes.

His eyes are telling me there's much more to know, many more conversations we could have.

"Hey, your background looks great. Trisha's going to ensure that a nice challenge is identified for you. I liked talking to you a lot. Don't hesitate to call me if have any dumb questions you don't want to ask anyone else or if you need anything. Navigating this place can be death defying! Let's have lunch after you come aboard. I really mean it."

He flipped on his compact stereo as he walked around his desk to show Lia to the door. Barbra Streisand's voice quietly filled the office.

"Oh, I love her; she's absolutely my favorite singer. Actually, she's one of my heroines," Lia said.

"Really, I've got to learn how that came about when we have lunch. Call me after you're settled in."

"I don't know about that, if I'm in yet." Lia was chuckling now.

"You're in," he replied with a smile.

Dawson escorted her out to his secretary, a grandmotherly African-American woman, who was going to call Trisha to let her know the interviews were done. He smiled at Lia, shook her hand, and headed down the hall.

"Have a seat Ms. Granger." The secretary motioned to a small seating area near her desk. "Trisha will be down in just a moment. I hope everything went well today."

Her voice suggested more than cordial small talk; it was a real question. She spoke again before Lia could respond.

"You don't know how good it is to see a Black woman being interviewed for something important, and getting the red carpet treatment, too. I've been here eighteen years, most of it by myself, the only one. This is so wonderful. My name is Clara Houston. I know all the ins and outs of this place. Call me; I'll help you whenever I can."

"Thank you; I appreciate that."

Trisha greeted Lia, and they headed back up to her office, where she made Lia a formal offer to work for Conallied Company at corporate headquarters as a senior business operations vice president in the executive group.

ξ

"Hi Daw, how ya doing?" Lia tried to keep her voice light and upbeat.

"I'm okay. Are you all right? They haven't tried to roll over you yet, have they?"

"I just dare them!" Lia laughed. "No Daw, so far, so good."

She didn't mention Lucas Mayhew or the silent treatment from the branch managers at her first staff meeting.

"I've got about a million things to get done down here, and now Castle is about to put the big-time budget squeeze on everybody. They'll be there's no shortage of crapola to deal with."

She shared with him some of the initiatives she was planning to start on her own.

I feel like I'm seeking his approval; maybe I am.

Dawson brought the conversation back to the personal without commenting on the merit of her plans.

"Lia, I thought you would stop by my office on your last day here. I suppose I understand why you didn't, but I'm not certain. I was disappointed. I really miss you. Did you get my gift?" She heard him take a deep breath.

Oh Jesus.

"The charm is lovely, and I thank you for the thought. Forgive me for not acknowledging your gift before now. I was raised better than that. I needed to depart in my own way, you know that. But, now I'm down here alone, and there's no one to listen to me whine!" Lia tried to keep her voice light and playful.

"I still don't quite get it, Lia," Daw said, doggedly serious. "But, hell, I'd pay to see you whine. That's your trouble, you won't lean on anyone."

"People say they want you to lean on them, count on them, but when it gets right down to it, they really don't".

"That's what you say, Lia".

This conversation is heading down the road of conversations we've had before. I don't think I can take too many serious things happening all at the same time.

"Listen, I'm probably going to be coming down to EPD at the end of the first quarter to review the financials. Corporate is definitely turning the screws on EPD."

"Tell me about it," Lia remarked dryly.

"We can at least have dinner, can't we? I'll get away from the traveling posse that's going to make the trip."

"Sure we can. I'd love it. My social life here is limited."

God, dinner with Daw sounds good. It will be nice to see him. Face it, it'll be really nice to see him.

"Yeah, I know; I spent two miserable years there a long time ago."

ξ

Lia dialed the number at Rob's apartment in Shelburg, twenty miles north of Fielding. She expected to get his answer machine, and was surprised when he picked up the telephone. It was unusual for him to be home from the office this early in the evening. She was tempted to ask him about it, then controlled the urge. What he did was none of her business anymore.

"Hi Rob, how're you doing?"

"I'm doing good. Is everything okay?"

I'm calling to give you my new numbers. You may need them if there's something concerning Jordan, or whatever."

"Jordan told me that you'd transferred to Levale and are buying a new house. Sounds like you've been real busy."

"A townhouse, it's very nice. This is going to be a hell of an assignment, but I'm excited."

"Well, I'm sure it's what you wanted. I know you'll do a good job. I've been busy, too; I've been approached about running for the open county council seat."

"Wow, do you have time for that?"

"I'll make time if it looks like I can win."

Time was something Rob had never, really, given Lia. What leftovers he had were given to Jordan, but not until he had grown older. He couldn't be bothered with the demands of a small child. Lia wasted a lot of emotional energy early on trying to cope with his limitations, eventually gave up, and basically raised Jordan alone. Their lives had been separate for a long time, so she had taken the steps to make it official.

"I assume you got the final settlement papers from the court. I just got my copies last week; it took them forever."

"Yeah, I got mine, too. Everything was in order."

This conversation is a lot like the second half of our marriage; neat, courteous, distant.

"Oh Rob, my Mama says hi."

"Next time you two talk, tell her I said hello, too."

ξ

Gerard Stewart peered hesitantly into Lia's open office door. He was the only one on her staff who didn't just barge right in. Lia waved him in impatiently.

I wish he felt the freedom to just come on in like the others. I've told him it's okay. He has such good manners; it sometimes gets in his way of saying what's on his mind without a lot of deliberation. I guess it's not such a bad approach, now that I think about it.

"Let's talk about the associates roundtables," Lia started as she came around her desk to the meeting table. She situated herself so that the sun warmed her back. The sky was that particular, startling blue that sometimes happens in the dead of winter, and the sun was unusually bright.

"Lia, they are really looking forward to these meetings with you. They can't quite believe it's actually going to happen, but since it came directly from you, they're feeling optimistic."

"Is everybody feeling this way? I sure hope so."

"Well, you know there's always a small number who will be negative, but I think a lot of that is because they've never been listened to before. They've always been told how important they are to the Division, but have never been treated like they're important. Lia, these people are utterly unempowered. They don't have any say-so, and I think some will probably struggle with even a positive change. No, I take that back; there are some good thinkers in this group, and they'll lead the way."

"Gerard, what I want to do is meet with them in groups of twenty or so. I'd prefer smaller groups, but that would take forever. I want to have them here in my office to take the mystique away; they're actually afraid to come in this office. It'll be a little crowded, but I want them to be comfortable being in here. I want them to feel free to pop in later. You know the group better than I; how formal should this be?"

"You probably need to kick-start them with some kind of upbeat opening statement, not too formal, and then ask them very direct questions to generate discussion. Some will speak right up, but I think most will be a little intimidated."

"Okay, work with Sara to make up the lists and schedules. Make sure there's a good mix, females and males, ethnic backgrounds, young and old, some old-timers and recent hires. I think it's important we have diversity in these groups so we can get varied ideas and opinions."

"Yes, I agree. The associates are pretty tight with one another. There is some them-versus-us mentality in their interaction with the regional branches, that's a reality. I think you can deal with it, though, especially if they begin to feel some sense of empowerment, feel that you're really listening to them."

"I don't want any of my staff to sit in. Will they be okay with that? I want the associates to feel they can talk directly to me." Lia was a little anxious about this.

"The staff will be fine with it. They're up to their eyeballs anyway. In fact, they're intrigued to know what you'll hear when they're not around," Gerard answered.

"Gerard, I'm also going to use these sessions to identify associates who we'll involve in the teaming with the branch technicians. We'll tap some of the stronger ones. Then, I will want feedback from the staff on the folks I identify before we cast anything in concrete."

"Okay, Ms. boss lady, I'll get to work.

It was nice to hear Gerard lighten up a little.

They're going to love it!"

These sessions are going to consume a hell of a lot of time, but I've got to do it.

She'd have Sara schedule them around her road trip to the regional branch offices and use the next full month to kill both birds.

ξ

Lia and Wanda had been introduced by telephone exactly a year earlier by telephone before Lia left Conallied's corporate headquarters in Fielding for her new assignment in Levale. Clara Houston, an executive secretary in the office, had set up a three-way call to introduce Lia to the daughter of her old friend who lived in Levale. Clara was Wanda's godmother. She had embraced Lia and become her lifeline to the small African-American community in Fielding. She set up Lia with her hairdresser, thereby allowing her to avoid one of a number of worrisome problems common to corporate African-Americans when they are transferred to certain locations. Lia

57

went to church with Clara occasionally, and Lia had dinner with Clara and her family from time to time, including one Thanksgiving when both Lia and her son, Jordan, were included.

Clara was excited. "Lia, this is Wanda Coleman. I'm so glad you two are going to be in Levale together. I want y'all to know one another, become friends."

"Yes, Mama." Wanda laughed.

Wanda, whose mother Lia learned had passed away, called Clara "Mama" with both humor and affection in her voice.

"I am so proud of both of you. One of you is running her own business and the other is going to run a big part of our largest division. I never thought I'd see something like this. Lord have mercy!"

Lia was struck by the tone of pride and ownership in Clara's voice when she referred to Conallied as "our."

"It will be great to have another professional sister in Levale; there's only a handful of us here, you know." Wanda's voice was deep, rich and reassuring.

Maple syrup smooth, a touch of southern girl.

"Well, then, you two need to be friends, help out one another. Maybe you ladies can even find some interesting men, go out on a date sometimes."

"Mama Clara, Mama Clara, there's very few eligible African-American men in Levale, let alone good ones, and even fewer professional men. Lia, the situation here is pretty sad."

It's okay; the last thing I'm looking for right now is a man, professional or otherwise. I've just recently come out of a divorce, and I need a rest; I'm in down time right now."

"Girl, I can relate to that."

"You two Ms. Independents. Y'all just go on and continue to do your thing."

"Lia, let me know what day you're arriving. You're staying in a hotel until you get settled?"

"Yes. I'd really appreciate your recommendations about the areas where I should look for a house, or maybe a townhouse."

"Be happy to; I'll show you the highlights and the lowlights, and there's plenty of those."

"Yeah, I've heard that. I'm really looking forward to meeting you."

"Me, too, and we have our marching orders from Mama."

ξ

Wanda was waiting at the gate in the airport with a huge bunch of multi-colored, balloons when Lia arrived in Levale. One balloon, larger than the others, had the word "welcome" printed across it in large script.

"Welcome to Levale! I'm so glad you're here! You look just like Mama Clara described you. How was your trip?" Wanda gave Lia a quick hug. She was half a foot taller than Lia and much heavier, but not overweight. She had a shapely figure, and her shoulder-length hair was pulled back on one side held by a large African-motif hair clip that highlighted her dark brown skin. She was quite beautiful. Wanda was, as described by the boys in Lia's old neighborhood, a "brick house."

"Uneventful, the best kind. I'm really glad to meet you, too. It's a relief to finally be here. It's also nice to put a face with a voice. The balloons are great, thank you!"

"These should cheer up your hotel room. I know you'll probably get sick of it real fast."

I feel real good vibes from her.

"I know that's true. I'm going to start looking for a house right away. I'm one of those people who likes to nest."

"Well, I'm ready to show you around town and, if you like, I know a good realtor. She's an old friend from high school and the sister really knows how to work a deal."

"Thanks. I've been through this ritual a few times, and a good realtor can save the day. The whole, damned house-buying process is designed to drive a person crazy, and I think I'm going to need all my wits to transition into this new job."

"Well, I'll have her call you at the hotel. Let's get your luggage; do you have a lot of stuff"?

"Tons," Lia laughed as she took hold of the balloons and they headed down the short concourse toward the baggage claim area.

They clicked immediately and, for Lia, it was a wonderful gift. During the early weeks, Wanda showed her around Levale, often went along with Lia on house viewing excursions, and took her to the most interesting shops and the few good restaurants in town. Lia really enjoyed visiting Wanda's office and learning about the graphic design business. Lia always felt she had pretty good taste, with an eye for what looks good, and she found Wanda's work really interesting. She also envied her independence and freedom to largely determine her own professional fate. To Lia's surprise, it turned out Wanda was actually married, but she and her husband, Kanzi, had not lived together for two years. Clara had never said anything to Lia about him; she supposed Clara felt it was not her place and Wanda would tell her about him if she wanted to. He was a native of Nigeria and a career foreign service officer. They met in Washington, DC when he was on assignment there and Wanda worked for a large design firm. He was now posted in France.

"Damn! I missed out on Paris." Wanda bowed her head and slowly shook it from side to side in obviously mock sorrow. "I always wanted to live in Paris, but Kanzi and I couldn't go on. Under his highly educated, very charming exterior is an unloving and sexist jerk."

Lia smiled at Wanda. "You think highly of him, huh?"

"I was withering on the vine, and that's just what he wanted. My working was a big problem, and my dream to start a business of my own was out of the question. So, when he left for France, I came home to Levale. Mama was here, and a few old friends I grew up with. She's gone now, but I'm still here and my business keeps me anchored."

"Will you and Kanzi divorce," Lia asked quietly, hoping that she wasn't prying too much.

"At some point, I suppose. Neither of us has gotten around to it. It helps his career to remain married, and I'm sure it also helps him avoid getting too bogged down in any other relationship."

Well, this Kanzi thing is a little strange, but it's not my business. I have my own emotional baggage to worry about.

Lia, too, had dreamed of one day living in Paris, and she traveled there three times, one on her own for vacation and twice for Conallied meetings. She felt entirely comfortable there. Even her elementary understanding of the French language didn't seem to be a problem; French people seemed to appreciate her effort to speak their language, no matter how much she mangled it. She and Wanda shared many of the same philosophies and ideas about life, love, and the pursuit of happiness. It had been a long time since Lia had enjoyed a real friendship with another woman. It was going to be so nice to have her as a friend.

Thank you, Lord, thank you.

ξ

Wanda had left Lia a message about dinner this week. She called her back, and they made plans. Wanda promised to take her to the only decent Japanese restaurant in Levale, and Lia insisted it would be her treat to thank Wanda for hanging in there with her throughout the house hunting process. She turned to the credenza behind her chair and flipped on the tape deck. Barbra Streisand's incomparable voice wafted across the single, wide sunbeam shining through the window coming to rest at the edge of her desk.

ξ CHAPTER 3 ξ

Lia picked up the telephone to call Gunther Madison. He managed the largest region, and his branch office was located just outside Boston.

Why do I feel so uncomfortable simply picking up the phone? I must do this right; strike the right balance between building a cordial and professional relationship with him and soliciting his support to build cross-functional teams in EPD, without kowtowing to him, as everyone else seems to have done.

She hoped there was no real reason to be anxious, that she was making something out of nothing. The attitude of the branch managers after both the January and February staff meetings was troubling, although some of the others in Levale seemed to be warming up to her. Lia had endured this kind of treatment from white males her entire career, being shut out or allowed onto the edges of their informal circles, just enough to avoid being accused of doing otherwise. She was too old and experienced now to let it bother her any more. Castle would expect Lia to achieve certain goals. She would also develop her own goals beyond those. She wanted to throw a touchdown pass in EPD.

"Gunther, hi! How are you doing?"

"What's up?"

Okay, he wants to skip the small talk. That suits me, but I'll make an effort anyway.

"Let me ask you first, what do you think of all of the restructuring that Dan wants to do? I'm really interested in your take on this. I'll sure be glad when he's more definitive about exactly what he wants."

"Well, you know how it goes. It's always one damned thing or another. What can I do for you, Lia"?

Lia gave up and got to the point.

"I'm planning a road trip to all six branches to familiarize myself with all the Consumer Services operations. I want to visit your folks in Boston first and then go on to Walter's location in St. Louis and on to LA. I want to hit the larger branches first. I'll make quick stops in Denver, Memphis and Jacksonville before heading back to Levale. I need to introduce myself to everyone and give them all an opportunity to get to know me, as well. I want to make a strong statement about all of EPD Consumer Service teaming up to work together. I'm convinced that if we plan initiatives together, we can forge a strong link between the associates and technicians. I know we can make the productivity gains to generate the additional revenue that Dan's going to demand from all of us. I'm excited, because if we meet and even exceed Dan's targets, I think the downsizing plans will mostly go away or at least be scaled down a lot. The other half of this equation I'd like to focus on is the issue of customer expectations. I'm having a series of meetings here in Levale with the associates, and we're going to emphasize exceeding rather than just meeting expectations that were developed so long ago. So, as you can see, there's a theme here."

I'm beginning to run on too long. Take a breath. Get a response. Okay, I'm getting silence.

"Gunther, do you have any suggestions on how I can best communicate this message to your guys?"

"Well, I'm trying to think of a good time for you to come. We've been really busy. Probably the best opportunity is week after next. Most of the more senior guys will be here for our regional meeting and new product training. I could give you some time on the agenda. I'll let you know."

No other comment. No response to my questions. Dealing with this guy is not going to be easy.

"Thanks Gunther, I'd appreciate that."

Lia had no trouble scheduling the rest of her trip. Walter Weldon in St. Louis was very accommodating; he was so laid back, Lia felt it would go against his grain to be anything else. The responses from the other four were benign, and they only had to hear that she was visiting Gunther first to confirm dates at their locations. She didn't tell them that the exact date had yet to be scheduled with Gunther in Boston.

ξ

Lia was curled up on the sofa wrapped in her red blanket giving herself a hug staring out into the dark beyond the small deck off her living room. A long time ago she heard someone say that, when you had your arms folded around yourself, it was a hug. She needed it tonight. It had been a cold, wet day; the sky had been gray and misty, not strong at all. She decided to allow herself a relaxing evening. But, television offered nothing worth watching, and she had tossed the *Newsweek* on the floor. The absolute last thing she needed this evening was to read the cover story about the rise of racist groups around the globe. The telephone calls to the branches weighed on her mind. The reactions of the Directors ranged from Gunther's barely lukewarm "I'll let you know" to "well, okay, I guess it will be all right." Walter was the only one who seemed genuinely cooperative. It was a bad stroke of timing that he was retiring soon, or so she had heard; Lia could really use his support. It seemed that the combination of Gunther's perceived cooperation and the mandates they assumed Castle must have given her is what compelled them all to cooperate. Lia wanted to figure out how their cooperation could be motivated simply by eagerness for new ideas. Her career was filled with making things happen. She had gotten plenty of positive strokes along the way; as a child from a variety of adults and, as an adult, it had been mostly from white men who held all the authority positions. She wanted to make it happen again.

Don't try to run the whole race today, just run it like a relay.

She needed to stop thinking and turn off her brain; she was tired. Jordan was safe and secure at school, she was settled into her new home, and her current career challenge lay very clearly before her. She wrapped the blanket tighter around herself and stared out into the darkness. She soon fell asleep and remained there on the sofa all night.

ξ

"Hey Laura."

"Hey Lia. I've been thinking about you."

Lia swiveled her desk chair around to give herself full exposure to the bright sun. She closed her eyes and visualized Laura's face and her cozy office in Fielding.

"I've been going at 100 miles an hour since I got here. The bad news is this challenge is really big, the good news is this challenge is really big!"

" You get to be a big hero."

"That's for sure, and I can do that," Lia laughed.

"How's your new boss? What's his name, Dan?"

"Too soon to tell, but I have to work with some guys who'd just as soon see me fall off the edge of the earth. But what else is new?"

"So, how are you doing?"

"I guess I'm okay. I'm having weird dreams, though."

"What do you mean? What are they about?"

"I really can't remember very much of the detail at all. It's more how I feel when I wake up in the morning; sad and kind of shaky."

"How's your energy level?"

"I'm surprised I don't feel more tired during the day. I'm working long days and getting a lot done, I think."

"What have you done to relax?"

"I met Wanda, the woman I think I mentioned to you before I left. My friend in Fielding introduced me to her by telephone before I left. She's a good person, and very talented; one of those creative, artsy-craftsy types that are so impressive to me. We get together fairly often. She's not a sports fan like me but, then again, Levale certainly is not a sports town. I really, really miss that. We've already talked about a shopping trip to Atlanta; maybe I can drag her to a baseball or football game when we're there."

"Do you want me to call in a prescription to a pharmacy down there to help you with sleeping"?

"No. It's not falling asleep that's the problem. I just want to wake up in the morning with a sense of well being. I have enough to deal with during the day. I need dreamland to be peaceful!

I don't think I'm making much sense.

"I've got to run. I should have called when I had more time."

"Lia, please call me next week. I don't want so much time to go by before we speak again. If this uneasiness intrudes on your days, we should explore it further and come up with a little strategy to deal with it."

"Okay, I'll do that, I promise. How much do I owe you for this phone call? Or, I guess we should really call it a session."

"The first session is free".

"This is hardly our first session."

"It's our first via the telephone. Don't argue with me."

"What a woman. Talk to you soon."

"Take good care. Bye Lia."

Lia's next telephone conversation was with Dan.

"Hi there, how's it going? I'm sorry I'm not meeting with you in person. I'm on the road, in Fielding for a couple of days and then to Mexico. We're growing there, at least. Once you get things where we need them to be in Levale, I'll put Mexico's consumer relations under your control. Right now, it's being handled locally, and the standards are low. We'll need to bring the operation up to U.S. standards." He sounded like he was in a pretty good mood.

"So far, so good. There's sure no shortage of challenges on my plate over here." Lia kept her voice in the same good humor tone as his.

He laughed. "Hey, why do you think I hired you; I know you can handle it. Lia, I need you to sink a long one for me this year. I'm going to need you guys to bring in an additional twenty percent in revenue. I know this is as stretched as it gets for a goal, but I'm going to count on you."

Lia stared out at the sun again.

Twenty percent? He must be on drugs.

Lia understood the strategy; she had used it herself in the past. Challenge your staff with more than they can possibly accomplish, and usually they will deliver what you actually need. Sometimes, they even meet and surpass the challenge. Up and down the line, it's a win for everybody involved. But, with a hole to dig out of and such a short timeframe to deliver, Dan had to appreciate that another twenty percent would be a very formidable task.

"Also, Lia, I've read your preliminary status report about Consumer Services and changes that should be made going forward. It's well written, and you've made some good observations. I agree with your assessment that Consumer Services needs to repackage the service agreements and then train the associates and technicians to aggressively sell them. I'll talk to Marketing about developing some new national promotions to help your efforts. I'm also going to need you to reduce the service operation's costs by a hundred thousand."

Oh, a twenty percent increase in revenue and a hundred thousand reduction in costs. Who's crazier, Dan for asking, or me for even trying to do it?

"I know that's a hammer, but I'm hammering everybody hard. I'm not going to tell you how to do it. You and your people know your staffing and productivity issues better than I do. You've got some good people there; I know you'll pull it off."

Lia had been told that Dan was outstanding at assessing a problem situation and giving direction to his people to get it resolved quickly. It got him to where he is today. He also had a reputation, though, for leaving a trail of dead bodies along the road to the solution. Lia was concerned that her folks could be the dead bodies.

I wonder if he has any idea just how tough this is going to be. This guy has never spent any time in the trenches, and Consumer Services has to dig out of a deep hole with consumer confidence.

"Dan, any way we look at this it's going to be tough. I'm real concerned about our ability to provide quality service to our customers if we cut bodies, and these people are working at full speed right now, or at least they feel as though they are."

"You know I want you to maintain the highest consumer service level. That's first and foremost. We could talk about it all day. Bottom line is I need you to get it done."

"Well, I'm about to initiate a series of meetings with the associates. The key will be to take a hard look at our processes and streamline or restructure them where needed. We're going to have to reach the goals through productivity, and I think they'll buy into it if they are full participants in the planning and can see it being beneficial to themselves. But, this absolutely has got to be a full team effort that includes working with the techs."

This is the perfect moment to tell Dan about my upcoming trip to the branches. I shouldn't be nervous about this, but I am.

To Lia's surprise, Dan brought it up first. "I've heard about your upcoming visits to the branches. Great idea."

I wonder who told him, and what was said. It was silly of me to think that he wouldn't have heard by now anyway.

"Lia, I'm going to share something with you. The only others who know at this point what I'm about to tell you are Don and Virginia. I'm exploring the feasibility of reducing the branch locations from six to three. We're spending a fortune to operate branches that we probably don't need, if we take advantage of the technology at our disposal to run this Division in an entirely different way. I'll probably talk about this at the next staff meeting. I'm not sure yet."

Holy shit! The branch managers are being downsized. Why have Don and Virginia been privy to information that will radically impact Consumer Service, my operation, before I am? I should ask him. No, I'd better not. Yes, I'm going to ask him.

"You said Don and Virginia know about your plans?"

"Well, I wanted to run the plan by some of the people who have been around for a while. Of course, since Consumer Service is your operation, you'll play a central role in whatever changes are ultimately made. But, it's too soon to get wrapped up in the details. I'm telling you now because I want you to have it in mind as you travel around to the branches. I want your impressions, after your return, on the operations, the people, their willingness to change, whatever else you think important."

Great, he wants me to be a spy. I just want to form some damn teams.

"Dan, my staff has advised me to be ready for all kinds of reactions on these visits to the branches. What do you think? How should I approach them?"

"Make sure you establish good relationships with the Managers; that's important. Call me when you're back from your road trip. Good luck."

Lia spoke quickly before Dan hung up the telephone. "I've heard a hundred rumors this week about the big meeting between you and Jeffries. I suppose that's where our new goals came from."

Dan apparently doesn't communicate much with his staff between staff meetings, or at least he doesn't do so with most of us.

Lia wanted to find out whatever she could about what was going on. With the exception of the telephone conversation about Lucas's departure, this was Lia's first one-on-one conversation with him since she arrived in Levale.

"Well, someone posted a graphic on the e-mail system today. Haven't you seen it?"

"No, I haven't even turned on my computer yet."

"The tag line is 'What Has Jeffries Wrought.'" Dan laughed heartily. "Hey, good luck. Talk to you soon."

He hung up. It occurred to Lia that Dan had the luxury of finding humor in the relentless march that Conallied's CEO, Jud Jeffries, was leading. He offered nothing during the conversation that assisted Lia, no advice about how to approach her road trip, and no response to her question about his meeting with Jeffries. He wanted her to build relationships with the branch managers, but didn't seem eager to forge strong working relationships himself. Lia knew she was good at what she did, but it sure wouldn't hurt to have some active guidance from her leader. She would have to figure it out on her own.

So, little miss Black girl, you think you can manage, or deliver, or lead something? Prove it! Why the hell do I have tears in my eyes? For Christ's sake, I can't have tears sitting here in my office. Anybody could walk in. This is stupid. Don't be stupid.

The beating she was giving herself irritated Lia, but she knew why. Because, after all these years, nothing was different. She was alone.

ξ

Lia started her career in California as a secretary. She was the first African-American secretary in the history of the largest downtown bank. The bank had already hired an African-American teller, but a secretary in the Trust Department was different. She would have to interact with the bank's wealthiest customers, who didn't have to bother with waiting at a teller window. Her desk was positioned just outside the elevator so the public could fully appreciate how progressive the bank was. It was Lia's good fortune that she worked for a senior trust officer of the bank who liked her and took a personal interest in her advancement. Boyd Halloran had spent his entire career at the bank, starting in the mailroom when he was still in high school. Once she demonstrated that she was bright and able, he taught her everything about the bank's operations. He also helped her deal with the often subtle, but sometimes overt, racism at the bank. A lot of people didn't want her there, and Mr. Halloran helped her learn to quietly cope with it. She learned business etiquette, and her world opened, as she had always known it would someday. Knowing how to communicate and conduct yourself in a meeting room or dining room, and in social settings, especially in the company of senior bank officials or important customers, was essential. Small indications of good training were just as important, and noticeable, as how you handled important customer transactions. Lia's relationship with Halloran repeated itself with other bosses several times over the next twenty years. Working for white men, seeking their approval, seeking inclusion, pleasing them. Lia's blue collar, working class upbringing and early experiences had shaped, but not limited, her expectations of the future. While she was growing up, eating out involved either the whole family piling into the car for a ride to the drive-in for hamburgers and French fries, or her father surprising the kids by bringing home barbecue or fried chicken from small, Black-owned, take-out places. For Lia and her brothers and sisters, these were special occasions that her parents couldn't afford very often. Even as a child, Lia could sense their pleasure with being able to provide these treats for their children. Later, she knew that lunch at the five-and-dime counter when she was shopping with her mother and sister really did not count. Lia didn't have her first formal dining out experience until she was fifteen.

Years in the business work world offered her a whirlwind of new experiences. Lia loved it all. Restaurants, upscale nightclubs, travel, training sessions, cocktail parties, and endless group dinners. Lia, though, never lost her appreciation for her mother and grandmother's down-home cooking. Their Louisiana and Texas cultural roots traveled well to the West Coast where she and her siblings were born. Funny how once new and exciting experiences can become tiresome. Funny how the quest for approval and inclusion becomes exhausting. Lia realized her inner relationship with the corporate world had become a love-hate struggle for her, and she readily acknowledged the contradictions about her feelings. She needed the professional approval to get ahead and personal approval to be included in their circles. A reality Lia learned early on was the importance of personal approval in the corporate world. Right, wrong or indifferent, the group dynamics between whites, particularly males, and minorities often played out at variance with the other. They simply were not the same because their backgrounds, cultures and experiences were different. It was clear that white men had the power; consequently, they wrote the rules for who got approval and who did not. Their world necessitated constant adjustment exercises for everyone else. Sometimes it was mild, but often the exercise required vigorous mental effort and internal fortitude. She was growing to resent the need to have their approval, to follow their game plans, no matter how misguided, to be a "team player" and go along with a course of action regardless of the personal discomfort it caused, to attend events whether or not she felt up to it, to smile, to hope they like you. Was it just her, or what? Didn't almost everyone in the work world, regardless of race, have to make old, white men happy to get a job, to keep a job, to get ahead, to be included in the group? Wasn't it just life in the corporate world? Why did she love it, and hate it, too? So, keep doing the damned thing, and do it well.

ξ

June 1963

Lonnie did not want to do this. He was crazy about Lia, and that was his only motivation for agreeing. Sixteen-year old Lia wanted to see *My Fair Lady*, the stage production, not the movie. The show was in town, and she was too embarrassed to ask anyone else to go.

"Why do you always want to do white things? Lia, I know the songs are going to be so corny."

"I don't always want to do white things. We just saw the Temptations and Four Tops two weeks ago. It was one of the best concerts I've ever been to. Is that a white thing?"

"We'll be the only colored people there. They'll point at us and say, 'look at the nice Negroes.'"

"Oh Lonnie, they won't. You know colored people down south can get lynched, or at least beat up, for going into a big, white theater or even trying to. We're lucky. Anyway, you promised we could go anywhere I wanted for my birthday."

"Yeah, I guess so. I'll bet if there's any colored people there at all, they'll be old and ancient."

"Lonnie, do you think we could go to dinner before?"

"Dinner! Where? Lia, I don't have that much money".

"Lonnie, I was going to get the tickets for the show with the birthday money my grandmother gave to me. And, if I save all my allowance next week, we can put it with your money. If we go someplace nice, but not too expensive, for lunch instead of dinner, and then the matinee show, we won't spend nearly as much money. The restaurant and theater are walking distance apart, so we don't have to take the bus between them." Lia always figured everything out.

"Another place we'll be the only colored people". Lonnie sighed.

Lia and Lonnie's special Saturday afternoon turned out great. For Lia anyway, it was pure magic. Lonnie admitted long afterward that he enjoyed himself more than he thought he would. He had been right; there was one other colored couple that was much older, or at least seemed to be, from the perspective of sixteen-year-olds. And, they did get some stares in the theater, but even more in the restaurant. It made Lonnie self-conscious, but Lia was determined not to let it bother her; in fact, she stared right back and enjoyed it when the people looked away embarrassed. She was proud of how well they did with the menu and figuring out the tip when it was time to pay the bill. Lonnie had steak, and Lia had veal parmigiana, a first for her.

ξ

September 1964

On a rainy day in San Francisco, Lia took the streetcar downtown to Woolworth's to buy Barbra Streisand's *People* album. Her neighborhood record store did not stock it. She had a stroke of luck when she finally got home. No one was there; a rare thing in a small house with six people. She put the album on, closed her eyes, and sang her heart out for over an hour before her younger sister barged in with a couple of her rowdy girlfriends.

"Good God almighty, where's Aretha!" Val was showing off in her usual style

"Why are you playing that white stuff? It's so draggy."

Without asking, Val took Lia's record off the small, portable record player and put on Aretha Franklin's *Respect*. Val, Benita and Cherri pushed the coffee table against the couch and danced around the living room floor. The three of them popped their fingers and laughed as they swiveled their hips and tried new dance steps. Lia joined in. She liked Aretha, too. Barbra would wait until later. Aretha, Gladys, and Marvin reigned for the rest of the afternoon.

ξ

Lia relayed these teenage experiences, always memorable for her, to Wanda over dinner one evening after work.

"Girl, when I was sixteen, I didn't know nothing but Motown and James Brown. How did you get into stuff like Barbra Streisand and *My Fair Lady*?"

"You know, I don't really remember. I just love Broadway show music. My father played records all the time; jazz and blues, female vocalists like Sarah Vaughn, Dinah Washington, Patti Page and blues musicians like B. B. King and Muddy Waters."

"My parents listened to that music, too."

"My father also had a lot of Frank Sinatra and Tony Bennett records, and Doris Day. He always listened to show tunes on the radio, but I never knew him to go to a concert or the theater. I don't think we could afford it, and I know my mother wasn't interested. I guess I learned to like them because I listened to records with him a lot."

The waiter brought a tray of sushi and set it down in the center of the table.

"I love this. I'm glad you do, too."

"Kanzi and I forced ourselves to try sushi while he was on a special assignment in Tokyo and, surprise, we really liked it. Of course, it was totally fresh and traditionally prepared. Tastes much better than most of what you get in the States."

"Did you like Japan?"

"No. Kanzi's project lasted ten months and I was glad when we left. We traveled around the country a little and some parts are very beautiful, but it's much too homogeneous."

"Hell, Conallied is much too homogeneous; it's overpopulated with hacks!" "What the hell is a hack?"

"Oh, it's just a silly term we use to describe ourselves. Company indoctrinated, driven by ambition, travel all the time, read the Wall Street Journal every day whether we're interested or not, think we're the smartest, the center of the universe, you know the type."

Wanda laughed. "Yeah, I think I'm having dinner with one, but you have a tan and better manners. I wish they would throw some business my way."

"How is your business doing?"

"Business is okay. I love what I'm doing and I'm making a living. But, it seems like I'm treading water. Here I am in a city with big corporations, but I've yet to get a really big contract."

"Define 'really big'?"

"I'm talking about a major campaign; logo, slogan, television, print advertising, corporate identity planning, special events graphics; there's a lot of possibilities."

"What kind of dollars are you talking about?"

"Big dollars. It depends; a hundred thousand plus."

"Can you handle a big contract if you get it?"

"If I had the opportunity, I would do whatever I have to do!"

"Well maybe I can help you down the road. I need to secure my own position first."

It would be great to work with Wanda on something related to EPD, but I'm not sure it could ever happen.

"How's it going?" Wanda looked her directly in the eyes.

"I'll be able to better answer that question after this grand tour I'm about to do. I'm dealing with some guys who are entrenched and don't think I should be here at all. But, my boss has handed me a challenge, and I'm moving forward."

"Don't you get tired of dealing with the bullshit?"

"Girl, yes. Please, don't get me started!"

"I worry about where my next client is coming from, and delivering on time and paying Ben, and business taxes, those kinds of things. But, I don't have to worry about being undermined or sabotaged. I'd become a screaming bitch."

"I'm going to try like hell not to be that, but if I end up calling you in the middle of the night, you will know I'm on the edge."

"Don't worry, though I may be tempted to help you, I'll keep you from hurtin' any white boys."

They both laughed.

ξ

Hey, Ms. EPD, I'm calling to see if you're still alive."

Keith's voice was a welcome interruption. Lia was about to leave for Boston, and Sara was going through her travel details. After no less than six telephone calls, Lia finally had a specific date and time to talk with Gunther and the technicians who all would be at the branch for training. The other five dates had been adjusted to fit around her Boston visit.

"It's good to hear your voice. I'm about to hit the road; doing six cities in two weeks, and squeezing in two days back here in the office."

"I hear you're starting to shake them up down there, firing folks and stirring up the employees."

"Damn, the grapevine is working overtime!"

"You've been around long enough to know that everything floats back to Fielding; you know that."

"I had to fire one redneck. You don't want to know the details."

"Yes, I do."

Lia recounted to Keith an abbreviated version of the Lucas Mayhew story.

"Didn't you want to slap the shit out of the asshole?"

"Keith, you have no idea. What else have you heard?"

"That's it."

"The Mayhew thing wasn't that big of a deal, or it shouldn't be."

"Yeah, but I want you to keep your eyes and ears open, be watchful of attitudes, not what people say, but how they act and what they do."

"Do you think I have a problem?"

"Lia, it was the right thing to do, but face it, you fired one of their own on your goddamned first day on the job. Gutsy, but you know plenty of them have got to be pissed."

"You know, I offered the guy a way out, a chance to explain himself and apologize. I was willing to listen. Hell would freeze over first."

Oh God, he's trying to be supportive, but it sounds like Keith, my friend, thinks I made a mistake.

"Did I make a big mistake?"

"Lia, you did what you had to do. But, don't underestimate the dynamics around the situation. They're not thrilled at your even being there, let alone having the audacity to fire one of their boys, and one who is smart and has been around a long time."

"I wonder what would have happened if I had done the same thing to Dan, or any other new boss I've had, that Lucas did to me."

"Oh please! We'd all be getting a notice that you have left the company to pursue other challenges." Keith's chuckle had no humor in it.

"Have you heard if Castle has had anything to say about it?"

"Not a thing."

Keith changed the subject. "I ran into Dawson the other day. He said you're starting a lot of exciting stuff down there. You're having some kind of special meetings with your employees in Levale?"

I miss Daw. He'd help me to feel better about all of this.

"Yes, I am. I'm laying it all out on the table, giving the associates details they've never had before, and challenging them to come up with solutions to increase productivity and hopefully make their lives easier at the same time. This is not rocket science; just breaking the mold of how things have always been done. They seem excited, and a little nervous, about it.

"It really sounds great, Lia. Corporate does a lot of talking about valuing the knowledge of employees at every level and using everyone's ideas. I sometimes want to tell them to cut the crap, because it rarely happens."

"Well my buddy, it's happening here, and we're going to get some real results from it. I've encouraged the associates to come in my office and talk to me anytime, and they're starting to do it! It's really time consuming, but I'm learning much more from them than from anyone else in the Division. Even my staff, who work with the associates every day, are surprised and pleased." Lia couldn't resist bragging a little.

"It all sounds good. Leave it to you, girl! Human resources people here are always questioning how much involvement lower level employees should really have. They think the whole concept could open a can of worms. Real progressive thinking, huh? This is why I get so pissed when they talk a good game and then panic and retreat when someone actually brings employees into the process of running an operation."

Lia's back stiffened and her head started to pound. She struggled with the reality that her approach may not be viewed positively in Fielding.

Why do I feel like this? Why not annoyed or irritated instead of these physical reactions in my body? Why are my feelings hurt?

Now, she was also angry with herself for allowing these emotions. God, she hated this. She knew that Keith was on her side, but she almost wished he hadn't said anything. She had too much to get done to worry about this pettiness. Lia tried to keep her voice light.

"Don't they have more important things to worry about than what's happening at EPD? You know, human resources is supposed to be guiding us, cheerleading us, encouraging us to push the envelope on these people issues. Instead, it seems I've always had to push them, for Christ's sake!"

Lia was not successful at keeping her voice light.

"Lia, do your road trip, knock 'em dead, make things happen, but watch your back. You're assuming the roles they have always had, and you brazen, little black hussy doesn't hesitate to take action." Keith laughed so uproariously that Lia had to laugh a little, too.

"You know what Castle needs you to get done. Go do it." Keith managed to end the conversation with some good cheer and good advice. Lia really did appreciate him.

"Thanks, Mr. Monroe, I will. I'll call you after I'm back."

Lia calmed down by the time she hung up the telephone. Keith had taken her momentary anger and worry and neutralized it, and she felt reassured. Lia, later, came to learn that it was a mistake not to worry, that what was petty couldn't be shrugged off, that it could bring her down. She didn't understand, or maybe she didn't want to understand. It was the weakness in her game.

ξ

Lia was surprised to hear Virginia's voice when she picked up her phone after 6:00 o'clock; she was working late on her notes, the main points she wanted to communicate to the employees in the regions.

"Hey Lia, how are you?"

She sounds upbeat. It's the first time she's called me. Why is she calling this late, though? What does she want?

"Hey Virginia, how are you? Things are going well. We're working hard over here, trying to keep up with what Dan wants from us. I'm about the hit the road to visit the branches for the first time. You've probably heard about my travel plan by now."

It will be interesting to learn how much she knows. It would also be good to know what's she working on.

Lia continued. "How's everything going in your operation these days?"

"Things are good. Just like everybody else, we're trying to wrestle the alligator. That would be the revenue alligator! I don't make money. I spend money. So we're trying new strategies and looking at different timing to order and manage product inventories and parts.

"Lia chuckled. "I can relate to figuring out new ways."

"Lia, I have heard all about your planned trip, and I think you should delay it."

What's going on?

"Why?"

"It's too soon. You need to slow down; you don't want to appear like you are taking over."

"I have specific instructions from Dan to do exactly that. I've been instructed to shake up Consumer Service and do whatever I think is best to achieve our revenue goals. I have revenue goals to be concerned with, too. This road trip is going to be the beginning of a major initiative that we are all excited about over here."

So, there.

"Lia, I'm on your side . . .

Lia interrupted Virginia. "Virginia, why are there sides?"

"Because that's the way it is here, and some of the guys think you're moving too fast and taking over. Gunther is not thrilled, so the rest of them are nervous."

Why is Gunther not thrilled? I haven't done anything that impacts him yet. So, why should I give a damn? I have to do my job. I called him in advance to discuss all of this.

"Virginia, I don't get Gunther. He hasn't spoken more than a few words to me since I came onboard almost three months ago. It's puzzling but, bottom line, I have a job to do and challenges to face, just like we all do."

"He's been around forever, and he is a temperature gauge for everyone. Even Dan knows that.

"Well, I have my very clear marching orders, and I have my plans. Every opportunity I've had to discuss them in detail with anyone runs me into a brick wall. You have not asked me why this trip is important, and what I hope to gain from it."

I'm getting angry now, and the last thing I want is for Virginia to think I am angry. I'd better stop.

"I just thought I would call you and put the bug in your ear. Good luck. Take care." Virginia hung up.

Well, those are mixed messages. I'm moving on.

ξ

A corporate ritual, a leader's duty, a trip to the field, the periodic duty of any company leader whose operation is geographically dispersed. Sometimes long, solitary car drives and sometimes numerous short and long airplane flights. Travel hotels and coffee shops of varying quality. The occasional treat of a five-star hotel and gourmet meal in an elegant restaurant. Lots of preparation on both ends in advance of the visit. Visits can be positive and affirmative, or stress-filled and intimidating. For the guys in the EPD regional branches, a chance to see and hear this new woman who is heading their operation. For Lia, an opportunity to demonstrate her leadership and reveal her authentic self and to convince them that their work, and its new challenges, and the work that had to be done in the future, and the success they could all share, would continue the tradition that made EDP successful for decades. She could only hope that Gunther, even Gunther, and the other division managers, Walter, Jay, Dennis, Glen and Phil, would believe it, too. Lia had never observed that a visit to the field was not a necessary thing to do, nor had she ever heard of anyone else being given this advice.

ع

Lia arrived in Boston at 12:40 in the morning; it had been typical of too many business trips. Two delayed flights, bumpy rides through bad weather, a cold, dry sandwich, a rental car whose turn signal lever didn't stay in place unless she held it, and a half-hour drive to the hotel a short distance from the regional branch location near Boston. Another travel story to add to her collection. Lia fell asleep as soon as her head hit the pillow, and it seemed it was only minutes before the telephone jangled her brain.

The hotel operator's voice was bright and chipper on the wake-up call. Lia decided to take her cue from the unknown operator on the other end of the line. As she showered and dressed, and shook off the fatigue, she resolved to make this a positive day. She was going to deliver a strong, upbeat message, encourage questions, and hopefully have a chance to talk with as many technicians as possible. Gunther had put Lia first on the meeting agenda this morning. Lia had suggested to Gunther, to no avail, that she be scheduled last to allow the questions and answers to go as long as necessary. Now, she was confined to an hour, but determined to make the most of it. Whether Gunther had arranged the agenda by design was a question Lia decided not to worry about.

She drove the two miles to the branch office location. Gunther's secretary, Louanne, "Lou" as she liked to be called, was very nice and seemed genuinely pleased to meet Lia.

"Welcome to Boston! We're so glad you're part of EPD now. Gunther's down the hall in the training room with the others. I'll walk you down there."

Lia entered the large training room and surveyed the sea of white faces standing in clusters talking. Gunther spotted her and nodded. He was a small man, very thin and not a lot taller than Lia. She had noticed at Dan's staff meeting that he was meticulously dressed, starched and pressed without a wrinkle. He stood arrow straight, legs apart, hands folded behind his back, in strict military fashion. His intensity made up for what he lacked in size, and he clearly used it very effectively through the force of his strong personality. When he did not cross the room to greet her and make introductions, Lou grabbed the closest agent, Bob from Rhode Island, introduced him to Lia, and asked him to follow suit with the other agents.

"I'll get you some tea; do you want a muffin?" Lou asked and headed toward the table in the corner where coffee, tea, and muffins were laid out. Lia was impressed that Lou knew she was a tea, not coffee, drinker. She must have spoken with Lia's secretary, Sara. Bob continued making introductions, and soon Lia was mixing with the guys on her own.

They all seem cordial enough.

Gunther called for attention and asked the techs to take a seat. Lia took a seat in the back of the room. As Gunther welcomed everyone and outlined the training agenda for the day, Lia took in the group. All male, all white, these guys were the senior workers of EPD. Most of them had been with the company twenty years plus, and knew the EPD Division inside and out. Gunther finally got to Lia.

"Let's all welcome Lia Granger. As I'm sure you all know, Lia now has responsibility for the Consumer Services operation. Now, this probably won't impact what we do out in the branches. As you've all probably heard through the rumor mill by now, Dan Castle is working on strategies for EPD and, as a member of his staff, Lia will be working along with the rest of us to improve Consumer Services and help the Division overall. She's here to meet everyone and give you an update on what's happening within Levale."

Well, he got a little of it right. My goals for this visit are much more aggressive, and Gunther knows it.

Lia felt she did well. She consumed twenty minutes delivering her message about teamwork, the necessity for the techs and associates to work more closely together, streamlining processes and procedures, the pressures in the national service delivery marketplace, many of the critical issues affecting these guys. She made a point, necessitated by Gunther's introduction, that the overall direction for Consumer Services, including the regional branch offices, comes from Levale. Lia chose her words carefully; she wanted to communicate a theme of change, with a lot of enthusiasm behind it, but not come across as preachy or condescending. Or threatening. Lia took note of the fact that Gunther busied himself with some sort of paperwork, sitting on one side of the room, while she spoke. His inattention could not have been lost on the guys in the room. Lia noticed a few sullen faces, but most of the sixty or so guys seemed to respond by actively listening to what she was saying; she concentrated on them. She noticed nods of acknowledgement, and the body language throughout the room was good. It crossed Lia's mind that she was speaking to probably the most knowledgeable consumer service people in the country. She felt their potency in her gut. She encouraged questions, and immediately got them.

"Lia, since you're in Levale, what have you heard about branches closing?"

Oh shit, I'm going to have to lie to these guys the first time they see me.

Lia looked directly at the technician.

I should try to make a joke out of this by asking Gunther if he had put this guy up to asking the question. No, I'd better not.

"I know that Dan Castle is looking at a number of options to improve the Division's competitiveness. To my knowledge, there are no firm plans to close any branches. I think if we focus on working as a team to stream-line our processes and really crunch the productivity, that's what will help EPD more than anything else."

Lia didn't exactly lie, but she assumed they would conclude "no firm plans" was not the definitive answer they wanted. She hated not giving straight answers. She prided herself on being a straight shooter, sometimes even to a fault. It had taken her a long time to learn folks don't always want to get the undiluted truth, though she didn't think this was one of those situations. She looked over at Gunther for a moment, and continued to answer questions for another half hour.

"My name's Dick. I'm keen about the things you've been saying. I don't mean any disrespect, but I hope you're not just talking a good game. This teaming idea sounds great, but who, when, where? I'd like to see us get to specifics, then the idea could really take off and get some results."

The gods have sent a messenger. I could kiss you for asking that question.

"You're absolutely right, Dick".

I'm glad that he told me his name.

"I'll be on the road for the next week, but what I'd like to do is draft you, along with a small team of techs from other branches, along with two or three associates from Levale, to work as a task force to begin to identify the work process and customer service issues that are most critical to us, and then schedule specific dates and locations to tackle the specific issues.

I might add, tackle them aggressively. You guys are critical to our future successes. Let's start with a conference call. If necessary, we'll pull the task force together in Levale. Okay?"

"Sounds great," Dick replied and settled back in his chair and nodded to the others.

"Of course, we'll have to consider our workload pressures and travel costs, but it sounds like something to think about."

These were Gunther's first words since Lia began talking.

"Gunther and I will stay in very close communication on these team initiatives," Lia said quickly. "We'll make it work."

As Gunther moved on and was introducing the training team to the assembled group, Lou peered in and motioned to Lia. Lia quietly left through the door in the back of the room.

"Gunther asked that I give you a tour of our branch office and its operations. You're joining all the guys tonight for dinner?"

"Oh! I have a 5:45 flight to St. Louis, and they're expecting me for breakfast in the morning. If I had known about the dinner, I would have rearranged my schedule to fly out in the morning. I hope Gunther will give me a rain check."

"I'm sorry, I thought Gunther had already told you. Well, we hope you will get back to Boston soon."

Lou gave her a tour of the branch, and Lia was struck by the contrast between it and Levale. While she knew it was a regional base for the Consumer Service technicians who spent the majority of their time in the field in consumers' homes, Lia was surprised at the low-tech, dilapidated, almost shabby environment. It seemed somehow incongruous that this was where an increasingly significant amount of the Division's revenue was being generated. The disparity was disconcerting, but she was getting educated fast.

ξ

Lia's experience in St. Louis and Los Angeles, the other two larger branches, was a study of contrasts. Walter Weldon in St. Louis was very cordial, and he introduced her to everyone during a buffet breakfast in a private room in the restaurant next door to the regional branch office. He was at Lia's side during the entire visit, pulling together as many agents as he could from his region. He vocally endorsed the team initiatives Lia discussed and immediately identified two of his guys to work with associates from Levale. The visit went off without a hitch, and Lia was pleased and grateful.

In Los Angeles, Jay Doane was not there, a complete no-show. A manager who reported to her. Lia knew Sara had called ahead to reconfirm her visits and itinerary, and neither of them had been advised of a change in schedule. When she arrived, Lia was told that Jay had to attend a meeting in San Francisco, but apparently Jay himself had not tried to track her down and advise her, nor had he left any instructions at his office for her visit.

I am speechless. Fucking speechless. Jay must be Gunther's best buddy.

Jay's secretary was on maternity leave, and they were getting along in the office without a temporary replacement. Freddy, one of the senior agents who happened to be in the office, took over. After a tour, introductions to the small staff group and the handful of agents who were around the branch office that day, a brief and informal chat circle with the agents, and a half-hour conversation with Freddy about general issues in the Consumer Services operation, Lia left.

Well, I was totally disrespected. How am I going to deal with this? I can't get mad.

I am mad, I just can't show it. I've got to figure this out.

Lia took an earlier flight to Denver, checked into the hotel, and ordered an early room service dinner. She was thinking about what she might encounter at the smaller branches as she fell asleep across the bed on top of the covers. Later, Lia woke with a start; she was cold. The only light in the room was from the digital clock that read 1:40 am. Lia turned up the heat, got out of her clothes and into her long t-shirt. Years of not-for-sissies business travel dictated that pajamas, gowns, robes and slippers were too much weight to carry. Lia never checked her bag. She didn't have the time or the patience to wait for it. Before getting under the covers, she stood at the window and stared out. It had been such a clear spring day that the night sky was still blue, and the full moon was huge. She wrapped her arms around herself and leaned against the window. The sensation of cold from the glass combined with the warmth in the room felt good to her. She was working on turning these solitary moments into good ones that comforted her and reinforced her strength. She withdrew into herself and let the quiet and momentary peace encircle her. The moon illuminated the outline of the Rocky Mountains in the distance -- a bonus. Lia moved to get in the bed, but turned back to the window. She stood there until the clock glowed 3:00 am, and then got under the covers.

ξ

Dennis DeLucca was a very young branch manager, and Lia spent the day watching him struggle at moments. Dennis and Lia started the day with coffee in his office.

"We've already heard about the message you're trying to commu-nicate about teaming and looking to streamline our work processes. We already practice a lot of those concepts here in Denver."

He sat back in his chair, and he and Lia stared eye to eye at one another.

"That's great Dennis; let's link the techs with the associates, pool the energy you've generated here with the energy we're creating in Levale. It will be terrific."

Okay. Here we go again. I get the feeling that he's not as tough as he's coming off. This could be an interesting day.

"Well, we'll see. Let's head down to the meeting room; the guys are gathered there".

The "guys" turned out to be the most diverse group Lia had encountered in the branches thus far; two Hispanics, one African-American, and one real, live female among the agents, who had been with EPD for only five months. Lia had very briefly discussed female technicians with Virginia right after Castle's February meeting with his staff.

"I think there are either one or two female agents out there somewhere," Virginia had remarked when Lia raised the subject.

"Is there any initiative going on to attract and retain female agents or bring the one or two we do have into Levale to discuss their experiences and how we can recruit more females?"

"Not that I know of."

I guess I'd better leave this one alone for now. Virginia seems indifferent to the issue. Dan has never brought it up. I suppose that, when you're determined to be one of the guys, you're not particularly worried about the gals.

Curiously, the Denver group was not very diverse in age. This was a very senior group, and Lia made a mental note to ask someone in Levale why such a young branch manager had been placed here. Lia had a good lesson reinforced for her on this day: never assume. When she stepped in the room, she somehow thought her message would require a hard sell. So, she sold hard. She didn't have to. The body language in the room, always the first thing she paid attention to, was very good. For the first time, she was actually interrupted with questions before she finished her message, and once she was done, there were many more.

"Most of us are older than you are, and we've been around EPD many years." This was Andy Kenner, who was clearly a leader among the techs.

"We are also aware that big changes are coming and, if we're smart, we need to be a part of what's going to happen. We need to have some goddamn initiatives of our own. We can't just sit by and let the suits in Levale make all the decisions."

Wow, I like his passion.

"And they'll make the damned decisions in a vacuum." Elmer Garwood, one of the most grizzled-looking men Lia had ever seen in her life, jumped in. He looked like a senior citizen Hells Angels biker, and she expected to see him roar off on his Harley at the end of the day.

"Nobody has asked us a damned thing, and we don't expect anyone is going to. Ms. Granger, this teaming you're talking about seems to me to be the bridge we need to build to have some say-so in what the hell happens with EPD. If it's the way you really want to go, that's fine with me."

Lia immediately recruited Elmer to the task force. He could represent the older guys; he didn't look the part, but spoke in a clear-cut tone.

Looks are certainly deceiving.

Dennis finally spoke up. "Lia, I've heard that you discussed the task force strategy at the other branch offices. Did Gunther like the idea, what did he have to say?"

"Dennis," Andy spoke up again. "You know out here in the big, bad West we do our own thinking; our buddies in the East do theirs. This teaming will bring us together, and this is a time that we damned well need to be together. We've got to show Castle, and the bosses in Fielding, that we can think. I'm guessing Lia already knows this. I like it when we have reasons to get together, because we don't do it often enough. I'm sure your old mentor, Gunther, will help all he can. But you know us cowboys do our own thing."

Whoa, baby. You go get 'em cowboy!

Lia suppressed a smile. These senior guys were deftly managing their manager, and Andy had provided her with a hint of how Dennis had ended up as a branch manager. They exhausted the remainder of the morning with more questions and discussion. Dennis had ordered in a cold lunch buffet and they all ate together.

Lia was headed back to Levale for a couple of days and had a mid-afternoon flight out of Denver. Dennis walked her to the parking lot. He looked worn out as they shook hands and promised to work together. Lia felt sure it had been an effort for him to play the welcoming host; there was a definite undercurrent she picked up when they first sat down that morning. However, he had set aside ample time for her, pulled together a large number of his techs, who turned out to be a great group, and arranged a nice lunch. Whatever his feelings, he made a good effort to see that the morning was productive. Pushed along by his troops, yes, but Dennis was the designated leader, and he had played the role.

ع

Lia arrived in Levale early evening and went directly to the office. Sara had arranged her mail and messages by priority, a ritual that Lia always appreciated. While she was thumbing through the stack of papers, Gerard stuck his head in the door.

"Hi there! How's the road show going? I'll bet it's been interesting as hell. We can't wait to hear about it."

"It was a thrill a minute. I'll tell you all the gory details at staff meeting. You're working awfully late. Everything going okay around here?"

"Going fine. The associates are buzzing about their meetings with you. You know you have the first two sessions with them squeezed in tomorrow and the day after, both at 11:00 am. These two sessions will cover some of the people who come in early and have an early lunch hour."

"Good. Then I'm back on the road to finish up in Memphis and Jacksonville. I'm a little weary, but I'm learning a hell of a lot".

"Good luck."

"Gerard, thanks. Stop in before I leave again; I'll give you a quick briefing on how the branch sessions are working out. Then, you can do some follow-up with the associates if you think it might help".

ξ

Memphis and Jacksonville, two of the smaller branch offices, were pretty much carbon copies of one another and went about as well as Lia could expect. The branch managers, Glen and Butch, were certainly more cooperative than Gunther and Dennis, but not as welcoming as Walter. But, unlike Jay, at least they showed up. The agents weren't renegades like Dennis's group in Denver, God love them, but they responded positively to her message, and Lia felt pretty good about the cooperation she could expect to get from them.

Lia felt a great sense of relief on her flight back to Levale. She had survived this first effort on the road, and felt she had delivered her message in spite of some roadblocks. She just wished the activity had not emotionally fatigued her so much. She again struggled with the question of why it had to be this way.

Do I put a screen over everything that is too negative, that clouds everything too much? I need to keep asking myself this question.

Gunther had yet to communicate with her at all, and Jay on the west coast, a no-show and no-call, apparently he felt this kind of behavior was appropriate. It apparently didn't matter that Lia was technically his boss. On the other hand, there were branch managers who had made an effort to accommodate her visit, and there was no doubt in Lia's mind that she had struck a nerve with many of the technicians. Their world was changing, and she was offering them an avenue to have some measure of control.

This is probably not the road they would choose to take, and I am definitely not the person they would choose to follow, but I'm what they've got, and I am available to them, now, when they need it.

ξ

Lia thought about the two associate meetings she had earlier in the week in her office. Many of the associates were still a little intimidated by coming into her office, but once in it they seemed to enjoy the sense of inclusion and relaxed atmosphere. Such a little thing gets a lot of mileage; no sophisticated business expertise required to simply include people.

Brenda was the first to show up at Lia's door, and she hesitated. "Good morning, Miss Granger. Am I too early? I can come back in a few minutes." Gerard had told Lia that Brenda probably would not say much, but she was a good thinker and should be included in one of the sessions.

"No, come on in Brenda; you get first choice of the muffins."

"I can come back in a few minutes," Brenda repeated.

"The early bird gets the worm; here come the others."

Lia followed Brenda over to the table, and they both sat down. The other associates started to drift in. After everyone settled in, Lia began.

"Let me start by saying I have not always headed up a big operation; I haven't always had the buck stop at my desk. I started out many years ago as a secretary and worked my way up through the ranks. I've raised a son and worried about his health and education and constantly juggled workload and family priorities like you have. I've been there. I also know what inclusion would have meant to me early on."

I don't want to patronize them; I hope they will appreciate knowing these things about me.

"I knew I had contributions to make, but I was not allowed to make them until pretty far along in my career. Well, times have changed. Frankly, I need all the ideas and energy you can give me, and more. We have got some very challenging goals to reach. Hell, if I didn't take advantage of all of the contributions you all can make, individually and as a group, then shame on me!"

Lia then laid out her plans for more communication with the regional branch offices, process improvements, repackaging and selling more service plans, and internal incentives for the associates that she and Marva were developing. The associates in the group who were naturally gregarious opened up and led the way. The more introverted folks didn't talk much, but their body language said a lot. Lia was surprised, but shouldn't have been, at the logic and thoughtfulness of their ideas and suggestions. They were feeding off each other, energizing everyone around the table.

I love this. It feels good.

To Lia's surprise, Brenda spoke up, quietly, but her tone was resolute. "You know, it's almost pathetic. Here we are on the front line with customers across the whole country. They come in contact with us on the telephone even before the technicians, and we're mostly invisible. You'd think someone would have asked us before now how to improve Consumer Services. This is the first time we've had any meetings like this. And, Marva is great. She had a lot of good ideas."

Frances Cole, one of the associates who had been around for a long time, generated a number of nods in agreement around the table when she responded with an enthusiastic "yes!"

"Ms. Granger," Thelma Scott, who Lia noticed was also very quiet, spoke up.

"Call me Lia, please."

Up and down the line EPD was an informal Division, probably more so than any other in Conallied. But, many of the associates still were not comfortable addressing executives by their first names.

"I think us getting together with the techs is so good. I just know that when we talk to each other, we'll find out we all have many of the same concerns. In the end, we're all the same people working for the same Division trying to do what's right."

Afterward, Lia remained at the meeting table, nibbled at the last piece of banana bread Frances had baked, and put her feet up in a chair. The sunlight, weak but there, warmed her legs. She couldn't help but feel the contrast between these sessions and some of the meetings at the branches. Lia was not on stage. There were few preconceived notions, no second guessing, take it on face value until proven otherwise, a blessed absence of hidden agendas. Lia's comfort level with the associates encouraged her, even provided solace.

Does this say something about me? Is something wrong that I don't feel the same way with my peers on Castle's staff and some of the branch managers? What's out of kilter that makes the experiences different? What's wrong with me? Will I always have to struggle with people wanting to keep me in what they think is my place? I need to concentrate more on the positive, on the affirmative. I just had a great session with the associates.

Dawson had always been on her case for constantly questioning herself this way.

"Why do you always beat up on yourself? It's unwarranted and downright annoying sometimes."

"Easy for you to say," Lia snapped back. "You're blessed with the assumption that you are good at what you do and deserving of what you have. I always have to prove I know what I'm doing and that I deserve to be in your world. You have no idea how exhausting it gets."

"No, I don't! Why don't you help me understand? Maybe I can help in some way."

"Oh great! It won't do either of us any good if I appear to be leaning on you."

Lia and Daw had a lot of these conversations during her time in Fielding.

More recently, she had discussed it with Wanda.

"I think it's pretty simple, Lia. You're a natural leader, and you apparently lead with ease. Mama Clara told me this many times before you and I met. It sounds to me that when you're with your staff and employees, you can be yourself. You don't have to watch every word, every expression, every gesture. This is your operation, your little sandbox. You get to plan and motivate and lead the charge. You control what's happening. Girl, you're the boss."

"You're probably right on target."

"The difference is that when you're with Castle and his boys, you're taking up space in their sandbox."

"You know, I have to confess that I wasn't sure you could really relate to what I deal with because you've always been an entrepreneur and haven't worked in corporate America . . ."

Wanda interrupted her. "My clients are corporate America, at least small-sized corporate America, so I have some understanding of the nature of the beast. I want contracts from them, but I don't want to be inside their world."

Lia had thought about this dilemma as much as she could today. She didn't want to lose the energy she had gotten from her sessions with the associates. She got up and turned on the radio, rather than her tape player, and flipped through the stations. She was looking for high energy. Martha and the Vandellas delivered. Great memories, too.

ξ CHAPTER 4 ξ

"Hey Daw, what's new and exciting?" Lia called him the next morning. She made the call on the spur of the moment, a need to stock up on friendship and goodwill.

"Jesus Lia, we really must be on the same wave length; I was going to call you this afternoon. Daw sounded distracted and stressed, very unlike himself.

"You don't sound so hot; what's going on?"

"Oh, it's the goddamn financials, what else. Jud is beating up on all the Division leaders. Muhammad is coming to the mountain; he's visiting every Division. Jud's giving no slack, the man has got serious tunnel vision. We're going bat shit crazy here. Listen, I'll be in Levale at the end of next week. It'll be so good to see you. You'll be in town, I hope?"

Your heart is beating fast. Get a grip, girl.

"I'll be here. Are you going to be able to get away from the entourage?"

Lia put emphasis on the word "entourage", because corporate usually sent a hit squad of anywhere from five to ten people for these financial reviews at the Divisions.

"Just how many hours are you guys going to spend beating up on Castle?" Lia laughed.

"Hey, you may have to sit in along with Castle's other staff members."

"I hope not. I haven't heard anything about a meeting with Jud. We've all been given our marching orders. I really don't know much about what the other EPD functions are doing in response to Dan's directives because our cross-communication down here is practically non-existent, but we're rolling along in Consumer Services.

"Well, don't worry, I'll get away. Think about what you want to do. I've got to run. Hey, I hear you're kicking up a lot of dirt; that's just what those crackers need. Can't wait to hear all about it. Bye."

At home that evening, she took the light blue velvet pouch out of the small jewelry box in her top bureau drawer. The gold charm, a whistle, was Daw's gift to Lia when she left Fielding. The gift card, still in the pouch, slipped out with the whistle. Lia read the card again. "Anytime you need me, just whistle. Daw" She had never worn the whistle and she wasn't quite sure why. Somehow, she liked the idea of the velvet pouch there in the drawer, to be pulled out whenever she felt like it. Lia decided to cook dinner for Daw. He had not seen her new home. Lia was a good cook, though she rarely did so any more.

A good home-cooked meal instead of eating in another restaurant will be nice. I'm sure Daw will appreciate it.

ξ

"Check your calendar. I need you next month". Keith sounded excited. "We're finally going to get the folks together."

"What folks are these, Keith?" Lia knew the answer, but she was teasing him.

"You know. We've been talking for months about pulling Conallied's African-American leaders together to talk about our issues in the company. Hell, we've really been talking about it off and on for years. Nothing's ever happened, but it's going to happen now. Nelson Mandela just got freed from prison after 27 years; maybe it's time for us to have this little gathering.

"Wow, now that's the truth. So, who's given us permission?" Lia was still teasing.

"No one is going to give us permission; you know that."

"Who do you have on board?"

Lia was hesitant, not because she didn't think it was a good idea and long overdue, but because she was not as optimistic as Keith about it ever happening, or being effective if it did.

"Well, I've talked to Josh, Lance, Jarvis and Mark, and now you. I just want to pull together an organizing committee at this point. I'm also going to call Doris, Jeff and a couple of others".

"Don't forget Cecelia, too," Lia commented.

"Okay, good idea. You've got to be involved for us to have any hope of getting this thing off the ground. You know, your position is probably the highest ranking of any African-American female in the company."

"Oh shit," Lia replied.

"Yeah babe, what can I say. So I'm thinking we'll call it the African-American Roundtable, for now anyway. What do you think?"

Roundtable seemed to be a theme in Lia's life these days. She hoped it was a symbol of something hopeful.

"Sounds good."

"It will be interesting; all of your brothers and sisters are not crazy about this initiative, you know."

"I'm not surprised. Where are we going to do this, Keith?"

"I checked the schedule at the Farm and they can accommodate us. We're going to make this a one-day meeting, but some of you will need a room the night before, so they are blocking off a few."

The Farm was the informal name for Conallied's national training center.

"You know I'll be there. Order some good food for us."

"Lia, how are things going? I'm hearing all kinds of stuff about first quarter results. The finance guys are in and out of meetings like mice in a maze. Jud's apparently raising holy hell all over the place. You know when he sneezes, everybody gets a cold."

"Yeah, we get those colds in Levale, too. I talked with Daw yesterday. He sounded really stressed, and you know that's so unlike him. He'll be here next week; we're going to get together. You and I can talk more when I see you in a few weeks."

"Hang in there buddy." Keith hung up.

ξ

"Hey Laura, how ya doin?"

"Hey Lia! Your one week turned into two months; hasn't it been about two months?"

"Yeah, I think so". It didn't feel like that much time had passed, and Lia could sense that Laura had been concerned.

"What's going on?"

"Oh, you know, I'm a hero and a bum."

"Sounds like a roller coaster."

"You nailed it. Actually, I think I'm doing a great job for EPD so far. As a result, though, there are those who wish I'd just disappear before too much change happens."

"Well, so what."

"I'm mandated to work with these guys even though they don't seem to be mandated to work with me."

"I'm sorry to hear this. How are you feeling about it?"

"It's just so tiring. I would really like to connect with just one of these guys both as a colleague and as a friend. It just seems to be impossible, even though there's a few of them who seem to want to see positive change happen. A lot of them are so busy resenting me, and I'm probably just as busy pushing to prove myself in spite of them. It's like we're locked in a dance together, but we're certainly not having any fun."

"I can understand why you're tired."

"I should be grateful that I have a great staff, and becoming good friends with Wanda has been really nice."

"But, I sense that you are lonely."

"I expected that I was probably going to be lonely, but it's really tough at moments."

"How are you feeling when you wake up in the morning"?

Laura always could read my thoughts before I articulate them, and apparently she can do it over the telephone, too.

"Still out of sorts, not grounded, not steady. It makes me angry, a quiet angry."

"Why angry."

I knew that question was coming, too.

"Because I'm dealing with a lot right now, so why do I have to be plagued with anger and resentment from white men, and as a result, have all these feelings inside me? I'm having stressful dreams, and when I wake up in the morning, my sense of well-being feels so tenuous, as though I'm barely holding on to it."

"Are you fearful of what's going to happen to you in Levale, at Conallied?

"Sometimes."

"It seems to me that your subconscious is working overtime to get through to you."

"What does that mean?"

"Did it occur to you that your sense of well being is reflected in the images in your dreams, whether you fully remember the dreams or not, and how you feel when you wake up in the morning is merely the mechanism to relay messages to you?"

"This is getting way too out there for me. Anyway, it's not so much the images as how I feel when I wake up."

"I appreciate that it's discomforting. But if the dreams go away the feelings will likely go away. Lia, it's all circular. There are many theories about dreams, but it is well known that our life experiences impact the subconscious, which in turn influence our conscious thoughts and actions".

"Oh good, that really clarifies it for me."

"I know you prefer the straightforward approach to everything. Anything else annoys the hell out of you. It doesn't always work that way, though, and you have to deal with that reality."

"Well, I'm sitting here on my deck in the sun. It's warm and it's healing, and I love the reality in this moment".

"It's great that you have a way to temporarily wind down, this love affair you have with the elements. You need to draw in some of that healing power and apply it to those moments when you have to navigate difficult professional relationships. Try it; at minimum you may better understand the dynamics, then you can develop a new strategy to keep working on it, just like you tackle and solve business issues.

"Maybe I should be devoting all that energy to personal relationships and not worry so much about these guys."

"Well, progress! I'm so glad to hear you make that statement."

"So, why didn't you just tell me that?"

"Because, Lia, I wanted it to come from you, and now it has. That's good. I don't want to minimize the benefit of having a good working relationship with your colleagues, but I'm interested in the long-term, in your life."

"I'm going to see Dawson in a few days. He's coming down for a financial review at EPD. I'm going to cook dinner for him."

"That's great; are you looking forward to seeing him?"

Lia hesitated. "Yes, I am; a lot, actually.

"Enjoy your time with him. It's been a long time since you've had a date, hasn't it?"

"It's not a date."

"Well, it's close enough for me."

Lia laughed.

"I just want to keep all this in its proper perspective. I seem to spend so much time trying to please people who refuse to be pleased, at least by me anyway."

"It's painful for you, isn't it?"

Lia paused. "Yes."

"So, what are your next steps?"

"Keep doing the best job I can, hit a grand slam if I can, and continue to nurture personal relationships whenever I can, wherever I have the opportunity."

"Good student; you get an "A". But, can you do both?"

"What else can I do but try?"

"You sound better than when we started."

"I am better. Thanks Laura."

As usual, Lia received a lot of comfort from her therapist and friend. Laura still felt like both to her.

Laura hasn't billed me for these calls. I'll send her a check and a thank you note.

ξ

Lia's staff laughed at her when she adjusted her chair at the table to sit in the sun.

"What a sun worshiper you are," Gordon grinned and shook his head with amusement.

"You're just a total sky worshiper. The worst hell for you would be an office with no windows."

"You're exactly right," Lia responded. She looked around the table expectantly.

Strange, I don't really want to talk about it. It's my own comfort thing. But it is nice that Gordon took notice of something personal about me.

A month had passed since Lia completed her road trip and, and soon after her return, she had met with her staff in a lunch session to share her experiences and impressions from the branch office visits and her follow-up communications with the managers. She also briefed them on her first sessions with the associates. She had wrapped up the staff meeting on a positive note.

"All in all, the technicians are an interesting mix of guys, and a couple of gals, and I enjoyed getting to know them. I feel that our team can forge a strong working relationship with them. I feel that most of them want this initiative to work just as much as we do."

"What do the branch managers think? Has Gunther made any comments to anyone?" Carl's voice betrayed the doubt he apparently felt.

"Are they ready to get behind this effort? I mean for real, not just pay lip service to it." Gordon echoed Carl's sentiments.

Try to stay positive.

"Frankly, the managers have a mixed bag of opinions, but that's okay." Lia chose her words carefully.

"Change is tough, but everyone realizes we have to go in new directions to stay competitive. I know they understand this. In the end, we all have the same goals for the Division. It's ensuring that we have a good process to reach our goals and working together toward that end. Look at it this way, we'll all have plenty of chances to do great things."

"Well, let's do it." Jerome looked serious as he clapped his hands together.

"Tell us what we have to do." Marva waved her arms and did a little dance in her seat to demonstrate her enthusiasm.

Bless them; helps me keep my own energy up.

Lia gave assignments to ensure that each of them, and the associates they supervised, were fully involved with the technicians in the task force initiative. Now, three weeks later, Lia was ready for their first status report on task force activities.

Gerard spoke up first. "The first task force is rolling right along. Frances, Donnell, Sally, plus Dick Smith, Elmer Boone and John Davis from three of the branches, have had two conference calls. They're having the first face-to-face meeting here in Levale day after tomorrow. Frances and Dick have pretty much taken the lead. Frances is really blossoming. The technicians love her. You're going to be so proud of our people."

"I know I'm going to be proud. I don't want to slow them down, God knows I don't. But I want to be sure that specifics come out of their meeting; identify how they are going to review the Consumer Services processes, how they will actually go about improving them, specific meeting dates for follow-up work with specific participants suggested, and develop a monitoring plan. This will all go for naught without a strong plan to monitor our progress. Start with end dates for reaching goals and work backwards. We're going to have to estimate a dollar figure for how much can be saved, or revenue generated, from the initiatives they develop. We must quantify our results. That's where the rubber will meet the road."

"The associates have asked me to sit in on the team meetings and facilitate their discussions; what do you think?" Marva sounded apprehensive. "I don't want the technicians to think you're planting someone from your staff in the meetings."

"I understand your concern. Actually, I think it's a good idea to have these meetings facilitated. The best thing to do is ask the full groups. Ask them to be honest and if they're not comfortable with it, then withdraw. You can handle that."

"Okay, I'll handle it that way," Marva said.

"What do you guys think? Are you okay with that approach?" Lia needed their input.

"I've been hearing from some of the technicians, and they generally seemed to be enthusiastic."

Carl's my best barometer at this point because he knows a lot of these guys well.

"I've had some calls, too." Ben spoke up. "You have as well, haven't you Gordon?"

Gordon nodded yes in Ben's direction. "There are a few technicians out there who are negative, but most are, at worst, still curious and wary and, at best, supportive. I think Gordon, Carl and I will need to do a lot of cheerleading as we talk with them one-on-one over the next several months when they come to Levale."

"Ben is right on target. This has got to be a team effort to promote what we're trying to do and provide strong leadership on this initiative. We can yield some dramatic results from our efforts. I'm confident it can work."

"I'm going to do a lot of one-on-one chats with associates as a follow-up to your meetings with them to keep a pulse on their feelings as we move forward."

"Gerard, thanks, that's great. I want you to share the feedback not only with me but the entire staff."

Lia wrapped up the meeting.

"I know it sounds hopelessly cliché, but teamwork is the key here; within this group, among the associates, between the associates and the technicians, everybody! We can do it, so let's do it!"

ξ

Lia was doing what she referred to as her "rounds." She liked to wander around the four floors and chat informally with the associates when they weren't busy with a call. She started the practice in an effort to put names with faces and to feel closer to their work in a way she could not in the group sessions in her office. It was now her favorite thing to do at the office.

The interior of the building had been remodeled two years earlier. Lia was told that it had been a real sweatshop before that, and the associates were threatening to walk out due to the unhealthy conditions. The custom-made circular modules each accommodated six associates. The blue and gray ergonomic chairs coordinated with the blue-bordered dark gray carpet. The computer hardware and software had been upgraded, and Lia was contemplating another software enhancement to allow expanded online communication between the associates and technicians with laptop computers in the field. Large potted plants were placed around the floors and some decent framed prints hung on the walls. Voices hummed continuously as the associates worked three shifts around the clock. They communicated by telephone with hundreds of customers daily across the country that used "America's Products." Lia was learning so much more from them about the daily operations. She was also beginning to identify the leaders who could help guide the associates through the change process that was beginning. She genuinely liked most of them, and felt they had a growing trust in her by asking questions and offering comments.

"Ms. Granger, I haven't been scheduled for one of the sessions in your office yet, but can I tell you an idea I have to reduce the number of calls we have to make to the branches?"

"Lia, you know what we need? We need a regular time, weekly or every two weeks, whatever you think, to get together and tell you and the staff the most common complaints we hear from the customers. Then, we could focus on those things first and get them fixed."

"Lia, can I call you Lia? Marva invited me to participate in the meeting yesterday with the techs. It was so great. We all learned a lot about each other, and we realize there's a lot to be done. I've never been involved in anything like this before, I never thought I would be. We really got a lot of work done in only one day!"

Lia mentally wrapped their remarks around herself like a warm blanket. It was all good news, beyond Lia's expectations this soon. As she started back to her office, Lia decided to prepare a written update for Dan that she would distribute to his entire staff. It was time to fill in everybody on the good start and hopefully generate some reciprocation from them.

ξ

Sara was waving at her from the other side of the floor. As she approached, Lia noticed she seemed out of breath and looked anxious, out of character for the always calm Sara.

"I've been looking for you. Gunther is on the phone. I told him you were out on the floor, but he insisted on holding while I looked for you. I don't know if he's still holding, it's been over five minutes."

Well, this is a first.

Gunther had never called Lia for any reason, and the fact that he was holding obviously meant something urgent was going on. She hurried.

"Gunther? Sorry you had to hold on so long. I was with the associates. What's going on?"

"Lia, I called to talk to you about this task force business. We have something here that's getting out of control, or close to it."

"Gunther, they've only just gotten started, and it's been a good start."

"Dick came back from Levale talking about more meetings, changing the way we work; who's going to pay for all this travel expense and who's going to say what's okay to change and what's not?"

"Gunther, I have been briefed on their initial meeting by my folks, and I directed Dick to fully brief you. In fact, I did a brief kick-off when they started in the morning and popped in at the end of the day. I can tell you they are all really charged up. It's amazing what can happen when our employees are put around the same table together. They did a nice job of getting down to specifics in the afternoon. They laid out a plan, all the participants agreed to it, they scheduled follow-up sessions to review the entire service delivery process, drew up a preliminary time frame to implement the process improvements they identify, and they put together a list of techs and associates to participate in upcoming sessions. They actually had a lot of fun together. I think both sides were apprehensive going in, but I'm told everyone was surprised at how quickly they let go of all their erroneous assumptions about one another."

I feel like I'm in a courtroom testifying in front of a judge and jury.

Lia knew she was making an effort to overwhelm him with the facts, and she probably sounded preachy, but she didn't care. This was too important. She pushed on.

"I don't think we can afford not to go forward, Gunther. My feeling is if we find that we really have an issue with the expenses, let's go to Dan for some help. I'm pretty confident he will spend some short-term dollars for the kind of long-term benefits our folks are planning to get us. They have taken the ball and run with it. Actually, I'm quite proud of them."

Now, you jerk, what do you have to say?

"Listen," Gunther's voice had a hard edge to it, "a lot of stuff is going on suddenly that none of us feels sure is going to work. We've got people who think they are going to fly all over the place, and who exactly is going to give them guidance?"

"You're absolutely right, Gunther. There is a lot is going on now, and I think we're in a situation in Consumer Services where we'd damned well better have a lot going on. I've been challenged by Dan. As far as who is going to give guidance, that's me, and I'm hoping it will also be you and the other branch managers."

Don't beg this guy, just tell him. It's my operation.

"By the way, the task force has scheduled a date to make a presentation to us, that will include branch managers, when they are a little further along in their process. In the meantime, we need to be their cheerleaders, coaches, facilitators, whatever they need."

"Look, I've been in this operation for over twenty-five years, and I know just about all there is to know about running it. Now I know that Dan is hell bent on changing everything, delivering big revenue, and that's all fine and good. I'm not going to have my branch upset by all of this, especially when we're really the ones out here who deliver the biggest piece of the goddamn revenue!"

"Gunther, it takes all of our efforts as a team to deliver revenue. But the bottom line here is really how well and how efficiently we deliver quality services to our customers. Remember them? I'm focused on it because I strongly believe if we do that better than anyone else, with the best processes in the industry, and have all our employees embrace it, the revenue will naturally follow. Hell, it can't help but follow."

"Lia, let me say this. Don't try to do too much. It won't work. We have kept this operation going for many years, and we'll continue to do so. I'm telling you now, early in the game, don't try to do too much."

Is he threatening me? Why does he think he can? Why am I here? What do they see? A professional trying to make positive changes, trying to develop some relationships, trying to do what my boss, who is ultimately their boss too, has asked me to do, and even trying to do more than he's asked? Shouldn't I want to do more, isn't that how you're rewarded in this company, am I wrong? Do they really just see a Black woman, a colored girl, out of place in their world, uninvited by them? Is that all they really see? It hurts, I hate how it hurts, I can't let it hurt; they're not worth it. Can I call Dan to talk with him about this? No, that would only make things worse. They don't particularly like him either, but they have to give him at least the appearance of respect, which probably just makes them more pissed. Dan probably knows that he can't afford to alienate these guys any more than he already has, so I have to make it work, and what would he think of me anyway if I came whining to him, what would I think of myself?

"It will be a team effort. Ultimately, what I do, and do not, try to do is up to me. Lia did not say anything else; she didn't want Gunther to be able to recount how she cursed him out.

"I have some people waiting in my office for me, Lia, so I'll hang up now." And with that, Gunther hung up.

So much for teamwork, at least from him. What am I going to do about him? I've got to figure out what to do. Don't you dare cry, you idiot.

When she was angry and tired, she cried. When threatened, she was usually dark and quiet, and steady. That's how she felt now, steady. She could not afford anger now, and she pushed back the emotion and fatigue. Lia looked out the window. The spring sky was a bright, crystalline blue, without a cloud; strong and steady.

ξ

October 1955

Lia began walking to the Broome Street branch of the public library every week when she was in the third grade. It was a long walk for an eight-year old; it took almost forty-five minutes to get there. No one was particularly worried about her; the neighborhood was safe, and people along the way knew her. The branch was small; the larger, more modern one was in the white neighborhood that bordered Lia's.

Lia loved the library; she didn't care that it was small. Once inside, she always felt warm and cozy, and it seemed that all the books in the world were there for her to choose from. She often sat there and read for an hour or longer, until she realized she'd better head home so her mother wouldn't be worried. She knew the librarian's name by the small sign on the counter that read "Ruth Sullivan". She always addressed her as "Miss Sullivan", while Lia was addressed as "little girl" or "young lady" depending on her mood.

When Lia first started going to the library, she would check out three books each week. Soon, she was checking out the limit of six every time. She would choose a mix of the thick and thin ones.

"Are you reading all of these books, young lady?" Miss Sullivan, in a very curt tone, asked Lia one day.

"Yes, I am!" Lia replied with all of the indignation an eight-year old could muster.

Lia enjoyed walking home with six books under her arm. She imagined that the adults, and the kids too, were thinking, "there goes a smart girl" when she walked past them. She felt especially good when she walked past a white adult who seemed to notice the books, smile at her and sometimes even say hello.

In a house full of people, Lia had found her own private, quiet corner where she read. The closet in the bedroom she shared with her sister was roomy, and she had cleared out a corner of the floor for herself. Her books were stacked against the wall and right next to them was the small, portable radio with a bright red plastic case and a red and white polka-dot shoulder strap that her grandparents had given her for getting all "Excellents" on her report card. She sat on an old, flattened pillow her mother was going to throw out. She covered it with a pillowcase that had faded pink and purple flowers on it that had sat unused on the top shelf of the linen closet. Lia also had her yellow baby blanket, tattered around the edges but still in pretty good shape, because it was sometimes chilly on the closet floor. She often read into the night under the bare light bulb that had a long string hanging to switch it on and off. Her parents smiled, shook their heads, didn't encourage or discourage, but usually shooed away her younger brother and sister when Lia screamed loud enough for them to leave her alone. Lia always felt her parents thought she was a strange and serious child. She couldn't explain why, but it made her feel a little proud that no one in the house seemed to understand her. She retreated to her "spot" well into her teens

Eventually, the six books Lia checked out of the library were all thick ones. She walked up to Miss Sullivan, and had a little trouble with the hefty weight of the books as she placed them up on the counter to be stamped with the due date.

"Little girl," Miss Sullivan sighed deeply, as if to gather energy for what she was about to say.

"Others use this library and want to read books, as well. I want to know if you're really reading all these books. You don't want to over-whelm yourself."

"I am not overwhelmed!" Lia was struggling between hurt and anger. She thought she knew what "overwhelmed" meant, but she was not posi-tive about it, and it didn't seem to be a good thing.

"You appear to be a good girl. Not many little colored kids visit the library as often as you do, and none of them check out six books. You don't want to take more than you can read. Do you understand?"

Lia stood silently as she stamped each book, then gathered up all six of them and stomped out. She walked home very quickly and ran the last block to her house. Lia went directly to her spot in the closet and sat there, without turning on the light or reading, until it was dark and her mother called her to dinner.

ع

"Hello Lia, how is everything going?" Virginia caught Lia just as she was preparing to leave the office.

"Virginia, hi! Things are going really well." This was the first tele-phone call she had received from Virginia since her one and only baffling telephone call warning Lia about visiting the regional branch offices. There was no mention of it now.

"I'm sure you've heard about the initiative the associates and tech-nicians are working on. Well, they're really rolling and doing some good work. It's been pretty amazing, actually. We're in the process of preparing an initial written report for everybody."

"Yes, I've heard. Look, I've just returned from a trip to Boston, St. Louis, and Los Angeles for the inventory distribution update we do every year. A bigger hassle you cannot imagine. But I'm calling because I thought you might want to know what I heard along the way".

Lia felt the tension creeping up her back.

"The branch managers, most of them anyway, are really upset. Things are changing too fast for them. They can't handle it. Your initiatives have them off balance."

Why are you really calling me with this?

"Virginia, you know as well as I do that change is going to happen here. Dan's already set the course. And, you may or may not know, I called each one of the guys after my return from visiting their offices, just to have a follow-up discussion with each of them directly. I got little, if any, feedback from them, although Walter and Dennis certainly were not negative. Len and Butch are cooperating. Gunther and Jay, well that's another matter."

"Lia, you're right about change happening. Hell, Dan hasn't even communicated everything he's planning to do, and that's making things even more difficult. But that's Dan, and this is you."

"Exactly what does that mean?" Lia was trying hard to not be angry with the messenger.

"It means that they're focusing their fear and anger on you because they sure as hell can't focus it on Dan.

Well, she's actually right about that.

He is the boss, after all; he can do what he wants. But, they say you're launching initiatives without their approval."

"Their approval? They're absolutely right; I didn't ask for their approval. It's not my understanding that I have to. But, I have asked, repeatedly, for their advice, ideas, suggestions and gotten little or nothing. Most of the techs, on the other hand, have been great."

"Lia, I know that's all probably true, but in the end it doesn't make any difference."

"Well Virginia, I'll tell you what does make a difference. The work that's being done by the associates and techs, that's what. This thing is going beyond our expectations, and it's great. Here we are able to show positive results in the first quarter, after only eight weeks of effort. We weren't expecting any results to report until mid-year. The employees have been empowered, they're loving it, and the Division is benefiting from it."

"These guys are not big on empowerment. They've had total control of their own little kingdoms for too many years."

"Well, then I'd say they have some adjusting to do. We all do to some extent. Managing an empowered workforce is a whole new ball game; it requires more from us as leaders. I'm sure you know that."

I'd better give her some credit even if I'm not sure she deserves it.

"Lia, I've seen the branch managers band together and crush people. They're good at it, and they'll do it to you if they think they have to."

"What do you want me to say Virginia?"

"You don't need to say anything to me. You just need to learn to play the game. That's as important as anything else here. Just play the damned game."

Don't scream.

"What am I supposed to do? I can't make the goals Dan has given me without these service and productivity improvements, and, damn it, they're starting to do it!"

"Lia, you'll have to work it out. And, if you try to run to Dan, they'll really circle the wagons."

What makes her think I would do that?

"That's the last thing I'd do," Lia shot back. She was angry now and made no attempt to hide it.

Virginia took a deep, audible breath.

"There aren't many women here, and I think we need to be careful not to bring negative attention to ourselves. They've never accepted us one hundred percent, you know that, and I don't want them using all this as an excuse to minimize us. We have to be careful about rocking the boat."

She's trying to protect her own position, her own ass.

Lia couldn't believe she was hearing this. She didn't know what to say to Virginia and, at this moment, didn't know what to do. She was disturbed by the tone the conversation had taken. Virginia had not given her one word of support or acknowledgement of the good work that had already been done or the potential that was there. It was as though she didn't want to believe that their efforts and results were legitimate.

"I've got to go. Bottom line, these guys need to be settled down; just be real careful from this point on. EPD is their division."

"Bye Virginia." Lia was more than willing to bring the conversation to a close.

ξ PART II ξ

Spring

ξ CHAPTER 5 ξ

January 1987

Mitch Boyce's invitation took Lia by surprise. The relationship between the two of them had apparently come a long way. They had been like oil and water from the moment Trisha Lyman introduced them in Fielding about a year after Lia joined Conallied, and assigned them to co-lead a special project team for her. Serving on special project teams for senior officers were highly sought-after assignments in the company. They usually offered high visibility and, if the outcome was successful, could ensure a promotion or desired transfer. The project, to look at the current process of how and what Conallied's divisions report quarterly statistics to corporate and to recommend a simplified, speedier alternative, was important and could impact the entire company. Many special projects required a full-time commitment, and team participants were often taken out of their regular jobs temporarily. In this case, Trisha set it up as a part-time effort. Lia figured that Trisha wanted to keep the effort as low key as possible to avoid having the Divisions getting nervous about corporate poking into how they do things. The result, though, was to place a tremendous amount of pressure on Lia and Mitch to balance both the project and the responsibilities of their regular jobs. Mitch was quite a bit younger than Lia, but held a position that was close to the equivalent of hers by virtue of having been given a seat on the fast track express early in his Conallied career. Not the most pleasant person to be around, he was arrogant and loud, but Mitch had a brilliant mind. They spent close to three months traveling to all the Division locations, meeting with Division leadership, facilitating process flow charting sessions, gathering and assessing data back in Fielding, working weekends to keep up with the demands of their jobs, and all the while intellectually pushing, shoving and sniping at one another. While Lia was glad the project was nearing its end and assumed Mitch felt the same, a grudging respect had developed between the two of them.

"Let's give ourselves at least a week to put the final presentation together before we ask Trisha to set a presentation date." Lia turned toward Mitch and noticed that he looked very tired. They were seated side by side in business class on a flight back to Levale. Lia was sipping on a cranberry juice; plane rides and alcohol didn't quite agree with her, and Mitch had his usual gin and tonic.

"Yeah, you're right. Trisha will have everybody and their grandmother there to hear this. I think we've got some really good recommendations, at least I hope the hell we do."

"We're fine; don't worry about it."

"Why are you always so cool and calm. You pretend that nothing ever worries you." Lia could hear both annoyance and envy in Mitch's voice. He was always primed to pick a fight, and Lia had pretty much gotten used to it. But tonight she was too tired to get into the kind of long, jousting conversation that he enjoyed.

"Mitch, stay calm, okay. We've done some good work, we're almost done and we're headed back to living a sane life again, thank God."

"I'm always worried, it comes with the territory."

"Well, that's true."

"No, I mean I have it coming and going. I get it at work and away from work, too".

Is he talking to me about personal problems?

"I'm the first in my family to graduate from college, or go to college for that matter; I went to Cornell on a scholarship. My father and his brother both retired from Conallied plants, my oldest brother still works in a plant, over fifteen years, my wife's father, the same."

"Jesus," Lia said quietly. She didn't know Mitch's wife, but was aware that she, too, worked at corporate headquarters as a programmer in corporate information technology.

"I'm the first white collar in the family. And, now they're expecting that I'll make it into the executive level soon. It's all my father talks about; I know he feels that I owe it to the family, all of them. You know, I make more money now than my father was making when he retired. Even Jud Jeffries once made a comment to me about my Conallied family. I should have been flattered, but it just added to the pressure."

Mitch grimaced fiercely to control his obvious emotions.

I don't know what to say. I'll just listen.

"Trisha put you on this project, Lia, because she brought you into Conallied as a special hire and she likes you, everyone knows it, so you don't have to worry".

"And exactly why did she ask you to work on it, Mitch? Lia's tone was sharper than she intended, but she could feel herself trembling. "Isn't it because she likes you too, Mitch, and thinks that you can handle it?"

Mitch looked at her blankly and didn't respond.

Even when he's vulnerable, he's a jerk.

"Trisha is way too politically astute to put a project like this in the hands of anyone who couldn't handle it. She wants a home run, a long one, and she'll get it from both of us. She gets experience, youth, diversity and results. We'll all look good. You're young and you're smart, you will be okay. We're in this boat together, so let's row together to the end."

Mitch closed his eyes, sighed heavily and reclined his seat. Lia wanted to tell him to get a grip and shut up, but it was the wrong thing to say at the wrong time. She had to swallow the fact that Mitch had attained in five years what she had worked hard to reach in close to twenty years.

Now here she was, months later, staring at the invitation to a "celebration of Mitch's promotion to the Executive Level of Conallied Company." Why the hell had she been invited? They led a successful project together, but had not seen or spoken a word to one another since their final presentation. Her first instinct was to call the number listed on the invitation and politely decline. But Lia's curiosity won out, she accepted, and planned to make a brief appearance.

ξ

It was a cold, gray day with light snow just beginning to fall as she pulled into the circular driveway to Mitch's house. A teenage boy bundled in a heavy jacket and cap, clapping his gloved hands together in an effort to keep warm, waved her to a stop.

"Hi," he said cheerily. "I'm Bobby, Mitch's nephew. My brother and I are your valet attendants today. We'll park your car for you."

He opened the door for Lia, and she got out and headed to the front door. Bobby had rolled her car out of the driveway and parked it behind the long line of cars that stretched down one side of the narrow road Mitch lived on. The front door opened just as she approached and an attractive, older woman smiled broadly and spoke in a disarmingly thick, Irish brogue.

"You must be Lia. I'm Fiona, Mitch's mother. Please come in and warm yourself."

Mitch looks just like his mother.

Lia could hear music and loud conversation inside the house. A younger woman approached the door and held out her hand.

"Hi! I'm Heather, Mitch's wife. I've seen you around headquarters, but we've never met. Mitch is so glad you accepted our invitation. Come, let's get you a drink."

The house was a typical, upper middle-class corporate executive's home. All brick, it sat on a beautiful lot, Lia guessed about two acres, that backed up to a thick stand of trees. The entry hall was spacious and filled with decoratively wrapped boxes and fresh flowers, most of them obviously congratulatory gifts for Mitch. Lia didn't bring a gift; it hadn't occurred to her that one would be necessary or expected. She was led past nicely furnished rooms to the back of the house into a huge family room filled with people. The room was furnished with several pieces of deep green leather furniture. In the far corner sat the biggest pool table Lia had ever seen with four, stained glass light fixtures hanging over it. All the requisite video, audio and computer equipment sat on a mahogany unit that covered the length of one wall. Liquor and food covered long tables set up on the other side of the room. Three large windows looked out to the trees that were just starting to shine from the dusting of snow. The big tree nearest the house twinkled with small, white lights. It was a warm, beautiful scene.

This is lovely. Conallied executive lifestyle at its best. And, he just made executive level. We've all bought into it, I guess.

As Lia followed Heather through the room to the bar set up in the corner near the windows, noted that she was the only African-American, or person of any color, in the room. Mitch rushed up to her.

"Lia, welcome! Good, you have a drink. Please, make yourself at home. There's some Conallied people here that you probably know, but most of the people here are family and friends. Have fun, this is a real Irish party; there's plenty of drink and cheer. Oh yeah, we eat a lot too," he laughed.

It all felt strange to Lia; she and Mitch had not communicated at all since the project ended months before. He was talking to her as if they were old childhood friends or worked together every day. A heavyset man with salt and pepper hair and a thick mustache, along with another man and woman, walked up to them. The heavy-set man put his arm around Mitch's shoulder.

"Lia, this is my father, Cullen, and my aunt and uncle, Maureen and Blaine.

Could this possibly be more Irish?

The three of them greeted Lia cordially. Mitch's mother, Fiona, approached the group and grasped his hand. Mitch was the center of attention and the very obvious object of everyone's pride. Cullen set his drink down and clapped loudly. The sixty or so people in the room stopped talking and someone turned off the music.

"Raise your glasses, one and all. A toast to my son, Mitchell, the first in the family to graduate college, ivy league mind you, and the first to make the executive level at Conallied. A son to all of us. His grandfather, who toiled forty years in the plant, smiles from heaven. And, let me not forget my beautiful daughter-in-law, Heather, and their beautiful new daughter. We're so proud of you, Mitchell. You are our hero."

Cullen drank from his glass, everyone followed suit, and the activity and noise rose again.

Cullen spoke to Lia. "Mitch speaks highly of you and how much you've helped him."

Well, you just never know.

Fiona laid a hand on Lia's arm. "It's wonderful of Mitch to have colored people here in his home. Mitch says they're doing it at the company now, so we're delighted he's doing it too. I must say, you seem to be different and handle yourself like such a nice lady." Fiona put extra emphasis on the word "you." She had said it with clueless ignorance.

Lia, not quite believing what she heard this woman say, gave her a polite smile, excused herself, and headed out of the room.

I guess I could just take it and swallow it. No, not today. There's just no excuse. It's the 90s for God's sake. If you're going to welcome me into your world, you have to know better.

She felt a hand on her elbow and turned around to face Susan Sherwin. Susie handled executive compensation at Conallied. She had been with Jud Jeffries since early in his career, and Jud's ascension to Conallied's chief executive officer included Susie in his inner circle. She had a subservient demeanor and many of the numerous tasks she did for Jud seemed to fit that image. Lia had heard smirking comments about her, but she had Jud's ear and therefore no one in corporate dared to cross her. Lia once asked Dawson about her and he shrugged and said Jud liked her and that she was a high-paid, but very efficient, "go-pher."

"Lia, I didn't expect you to be here! Great party isn't it? You and Mitch are friends?"

"Well, we worked on a special project for Trisha. It was pretty intense."

"Oh yes, that's right. You're really getting around, aren't you? How do you wrangle it? I see you everywhere these days."

"Well, not everywhere, but I didn't want to disappoint Mitch. Excuse me, Susan, but I have another commitment. You take care." Lia managed an exaggerated, extra sweet smile to match that of Susie's.

She made her way to the entry hall to collect her coat, and left Mitch's house. As she drove home, with the sound of Billie Holliday's *Billie's Blues* filling the car, Lia thought about the high school graduation party she attended given by a wealthy, white classmate where she was one of only two Black kids invited. The two of them were invited because they were identified as different, as the smart, nice ones. They were told this outright without any understanding of the effect on the psyche. Now, over twenty years later, she felt exactly the same way.

ξ

Dusk was Lia's favorite time of the day. The diffusion of light, the reds and golds of the setting sun, the browns and grays when an overcast day turns to night, the passage from the bustle of the day to the calm of night. There was something comforting about the dark settling in around her. Maybe it was the knowledge that she had made it through another day. No, it was nicer than that; she always felt cozy and content when dusk settled over the day. It was dusk as Lia sat staring out of the window, rocking backing and forth in her desk chair, still replaying her last conversation with Virginia over and over in her head.

"*. . . I've seen them band together and crush people. They're good at it, and they'll do it to you if they think they have to.*" Lia recalled her words, and willed the last warmth from the disappearing sun to drive the chill from her body. She pushed back the negative thoughts that were creeping up from behind and pouncing on her.

"Lia?" Gerard interrupted her reverie. "Is everything okay"? He could see that she was distracted and looked very tired. Gerard was taken aback by the contrast between her present demeanor and the energy she had displayed and spread around earlier today in one of her sessions with the associates.

"I think I need to reassess," Lia answered Gerard, continuing to stare out of the window.

"Reassess what, Lia?"

"Oh, maybe everything."

"What do you mean?"

"The branch managers are very upset about the initiatives the associates and technicians are working on. Things are changing too fast for them. I've got to think about what I'm doing." Lia sighed heavily and turned her chair to face Gerard.

"This is crazy!" Gerard yelled. Lia had never heard him raise his voice before.

"The employees are feeling as good about themselves as they ever have. You can't go back now that everyone has started down this road. This is a good road to be on, Lia!"

"I know, I know. Can we please talk about this tomorrow? Let's talk about it tomorrow."

"Okay Lia; go home and get drunk. You deserve it. I'll see you in the morning."

Lia pulled out of the parking lot just as the last light slipped behind the horizon. On this evening, dusk was not comforting. The colors were cold and so was the impending darkness. Maybe she would discuss it with Daw. She was cooking dinner for him the next evening and she concentrated on planning the menu. What she needed now was some warm music, something to warm the impending darkness. She fumbled through her cassettes looking for something in particular. Lia slipped Gloria Estefan's *Into the Light* tape into the player. She leaned back against the headrest and tried to relax.

ξ

The following morning was perfect; brilliant, deep blue sky filled with big, puffy white clouds. They seemed thick enough to lie on, and it made Lia feel calm and peaceful. She decided it was a good omen and thought about seeing Daw later that evening. At mid-morning, he surprised her by showing up at her office door.

"Found you!" He laughed and walked over to take both her hands in his.

I'm glad I wore this dress; he likes it. I remember he complimented me on it. Seems like a hundred years ago.

"Daw! When did you get in?"

It's really good to see him.

"A gang of seven flew in on the jet early this morning. You look great. I'll give you a hug later. We have to maintain a level of decorum; don't want your employees wondering about you and your low-class corporate buddies."

Cynical as ever; I love it.

"I'll see you later. You have the directions to my house?"

"Yes, I do. See you at seven."

Seeing Daw immediately lifted Lia's spirits and sustained her throughout the day. She hardly thought about her conversation with Virginia, and that was fine with her for now. She didn't want to be reactive and realized she needed to take a little time to come up with a strategy to deal with the branch managers. She resolved not to let all the negativity ruin her evening.

She had toyed with the idea of trying to pull the six branch managers together for a meeting somewhere, probably not in Levale, to try to talk things out and develop common goals. She intended to discuss the idea with Gerard. His help would be beneficial in this situation; maybe she would ask him to facilitate the meeting. But, Lia didn't cross paths with Gerard all day, and she was somehow relieved. She would discuss it with him tomorrow.

Lia left the office at four o'clock. She had decided to cook her favorite shrimp Creole dish and was picking up fresh shrimp flown in from the Gulf that she ordered at the fish market. She prepared it with a spicy kick, and like Lia, Daw enjoyed spicy food. She also had to pick up the wine. The weather had stayed beautiful and warm all day. Lia decided to set up dinner on the deck. At ten minutes to seven, Lia was putting her crystal goblets, filled with strawberries and cream, in the refrigerator to chill for dessert. She heard a car pull into her driveway, and she went to the door to let him in. Any group from Fielding always had limos waiting for them when the jet landed at airports, so she wondered how he was going to get to her house. He was driving what appeared to be a rental car, or he could have borrowed a car; she didn't ask. One way or the other he made it there.

He immediately gave Lia a big, lingering hug and a quick kiss on her lips. That had been the extent of their physical intimacy in the past, and since they had not seen one another in more than four months, Lia hugged him back tightly. Lia and Daw's professional relationship and close emotional connection had come quickly and with ease in Fielding, but they had both abided by unspoken limits for a long time. He had been a good mentor and had given her just the right advice when she had issues to resolve during her assignments in the company. Lia regularly shared her varying degrees of angst with him during the last year of her marriage and divorce from Rob. He was always available for her. She had listened to him express regret about decisions he had made in his past and his struggle to decide what he wanted to do with the rest of his life. They had shared many cups of coffee and tea, lunches, and dinners. It had, though, been a Monday through Friday relationship. It occurred to Lia only today that this was the first time their dinner could be even characterized as a date. Daw had been divorced almost ten years from his wife, Anne. He told Lia he had simply outgrown Anne and had felt smothered by her dependency on him for everything. He had two daughters, Miranda, now married with a baby girl, and Meredith, a junior in college. There had been another woman, Bonnie, at one time. However, after Daw's divorce, they never lived together and three years later, Bonnie was gone. Daw had been vague about what happened between him and Bonnie. Once she got closer to Daw and really got to know him well, Lia figured it out. She believed Daw had no regrets about his divorce, but he had never totally cut the cord with Anne. He still helped her through seemingly never-ending crises and, as far as Lia could tell, the woman had never worked a day in her life and still didn't. In many ways, Daw and Anne seemed to be somewhat co-dependent, and she concluded that Bonnie got tired of it and gave up. Listening to him talk about it, it felt to Lia that he had not fallen apart when Bonnie ended the relationship.

"I am so glad to finally see you!" Daw gave her another quick kiss.

"You saw me earlier today, remember?"

"This is different, and much better. Your place looks great; it looks like you."

"Wander around while I get you a glass of wine. We're eating on the deck. I'll also get the salads. Isn't it a great day?"

Lia found Daw in her bedroom when she handed him a glass of wine.

"Well it sure is cozy in here."

"Yeah, I like it a lot."

"Are you ever lonely here."

"Yes, sometimes."

Most of the time.

"Let's go out on the deck."

Dinner turned out well. She called upon her good cooking skills to make everything special, and Daw responded by eating heartily.

"That was delicious. You're a great cook."

"Dessert is pretty light. So enjoy it, too." Lia poured them both another glass of wine.

"I'm going to be stuffed, but I'm enjoying every minute of it."

"So, how did it go today? Did you guys rake Castle over the coals. Am I going to have to bail out the entire Energy Products Division with the revenue we generate in Consumer Services?"

Daw laughed. "Yes, and yes! Today went fine. It was a little tense at moments; you know how Jud is. Today was the first time I've seen him and Dan go at it seriously. Jud now wants me to come down here at the end of each quarter for the rest of the year to monitor things."

"You didn't whisper that suggestion in Jud's ear, did you?"

I'm teasing, and I'm flirting a little, too.

"No, but I should have. Okay, no more shop talk tonight, all right?" Daw clearly wanted to switch gears to a personal conversation.

"Okay, how've you been?" Lia smiled and looked directly into his eyes.

"I've been okay, but I have really missed you."

"How's Anne?"

Why am I asking about his ex-wife? Do I really want to know how connected to her he still is?

"Anne is fine. She's decided to go back to school to finish her degree. She's taking two classes right now."

"How are your girls?"

"They're just fine, both doing their own thing quite successfully. Their old man is proud. How's Jordan? You must be getting excited about his graduation, coming up soon, right?"

"Yes. Jordan is great. He's so glad the end is near. He says he wants to make some money; he's tired of being a poor student. He wants to wait and go to graduate school in a couple of years. Poor babies, they don't know how good they've had it."

"So Lia, how are you? Really, how are you? I know it can't be easy here. EPD is a very tough environment. After sitting through the meetings today, I think it's going to get worse before it gets better."

"I'm doing okay, Daw. Things are going really well in my office. My staff is great. The associates are responding to everything I've asked them to do. Now, they're working with the technicians from all the branches to improve the processes, and they're progressing much faster than we all thought it would. It looks like it's going to be a real success. But, guess what? Success has created big-time problems for me."

We're talking shop again.

"The branch managers are on the warpath?"

"Yes, how did you know? Did you hear something today?"

"No, didn't hear a word today. Lia, you forget, I know these guys. I've crossed paths with them many times over the years. I don't even know all the details, but I know you, and I know how you go after a goal. I can imagine they're probably threatened as hell. You've brought together the two groups at the bottom of the Consumer Services totem pole and, by the way, the groups I would guess are probably the most knowledgeable about what needs to be done. To you, it seems perfectly natural, and progressive, and enlightened. Shit, now it's necessary, too! But, the branch managers have been the EPD heroes and now here you are trying to be a hero too, a bigger hero."

Lia had always been impressed with Daw's ability to quickly grasp a situation and put it in perspective.

"I'm not trying to be a hero for myself. I want all of us to be heroes. I'm just trying to get the job done."

I sound defensive.

"Yes, you are. You love being a hero. You're used to being a hero. That's okay, Lia. There's nothing wrong with it."

"Daw, I have asked these guys for input on more than one occasion and have gotten nothing. My visits to the branches were a real experience. They ranged from really pleasant to an embarrassing disaster in Los Angeles. I've been thinking about trying to pull together a meeting with all of them, but I'm just not sure how much good it would do. But I did strike a nerve with the technicians and, for the most part, they responded. They've been great actually."

"Bingo! Therein lies your problem. Their people are following you on this initiative, and you're getting results from them on top if it! You know what this is about; it's not hard to figure out."

"I sent Dan a written report the other day, and I copied the entire staff. I got it back from him with a note that said, 'nice work, keep at it', and noted he was passing along a copy of the report to Jeffries."

"Oh boy! Now add on the fact that you have gotten kudos from Castle. You can bet that one way or another, they'll know about that."

"Shame on me for getting something done," Lia snapped.

I refuse to let the emotion well up inside me this evening; defiance, yes, but emotion, no.

"Hey, absolutely no more shop talk, okay? Let's go inside. I'll help you with the dishes."

She put on a Barbra Streisand album, her favorite, and she knew Daw was a big fan, too. They loaded the dishwasher and cleaned the kitchen without much conversation. It was quiet except for the music from the living room and the clink and clatter of the dishes. It was easy and comfortable. It was very different from being with Rob; this quiet was warm and cozy, not cold and empty. When done in the kitchen, they wandered to the living room, and Daw plopped down in the corner of the sofa. He smiled at Lia, leaned his head back on the cushions and closed his eyes.

"God, what a day. This is really nice here; you've made a nice home."

"I have to nest, or I feel like I'm not connected to anything."

Lia sat beside him and, without thinking about it, turned her body, put her head in his lap and stretched her legs out across the sofa. It was the most intimate contact they ever had.   *Jesus, what the hell am I doing? How needy is this?*

If Daw was surprised by her move, he didn't show it.

"Umm, you feel good," he said softly.

"I'm exhausted," Lia admitted.

"You should be; you've had a lot on your mind. You know, you're going to have to deal with the guys in EPD. I'd like to help you, but I'm not sure what you need me to do."

"Daw, I can't have you helping me out. I don't want that. I've got to work it out on my own somehow, but I am so tired of always having to work things out with guys like Gunther. He's their ring leader."

"You mean guys like me?" Daw's voice was thoughtful and quiet.

"Daw, you're not like them and you know it!"

"Maybe not, but I've certainly grown up professionally in the same system, and I understand it."

"And I didn't grow up in the system because, until recently, I did not have access to it. It seems no matter how hard I work, or how successful I am, I'm never going to be part of it."

Lia sighed and closed her eyes.

"It seems that we have had to do all the work to belong . . ."

Daw interrupted her. Who is 'we'?"

"It's Black folks like me, and other minorities, too. The people in the system, white males, I'll just say it Daw, don't feel they have to do anything to encourage inclusiveness. They don't bother to try to learn or adjust at all. Why should they? There's no obvious benefit or reward for them. Only a threat; that's how they perceive it. Every time I discuss this, I feel like I'm whining. I don't want to talk about it any more. I'm not a whiner by nature, and you know I don't have any patience with anyone who is."

"God knows that's true," Daw laughed.

Lia adjusted her body to a more comfortable position, and Daw sank his body deeper into the sofa cushions.

"Let's try, again, to forget about this work stuff for a while. What about you personally? You and Rob have been apart a while now. Are you okay? I've asked if you're okay about five times, you know."

"Hey, I'm alive and kicking."

"But, are you okay? You don't want my professional help, so what can I do to give you personal comfort? I want to, you know."

Lia didn't answer because she wasn't sure what she wanted from Daw. Several silent moments passed.

Why can't I just admit that I'm not sure, that I don't know? I think maybe I'm afraid to know.

"You know, Lia, I've never felt as close to anyone in the way I feel close to you. I don't want to sound sappy, but I consider our friendship a gift in my life. I'd like to return something if I could.

"Okay, buddy, make me an offer."

Daw sounded sheepish, even embarrassed. "Okay, here goes. Lia, I couldn't help but notice that great whirlpool tub in your bathroom. You're so tired and tense. Why don't you to fill it up, get in it, and let me wash your back, massage your neck and shoulders, or whatever. I'd be lying if I didn't say I'd love to be in that tub with you; but that's okay, don't panic." He laughed softly, almost to himself, different than his usual hearty laughter.

This is as bold as he's ever been, by a long shot. So, what's wrong with me?

Lia sat up, kissed Daw lightly on the lips and laid her head on his shoulder. She was not ready for that kind of intimacy with him, and she knew it. Daw must have realized it, too, because she didn't move, and there was no further conversation about it. They sat quietly that way for a long time, the Streisand album playing on and on. Finally, Daw sat straight up.

"I'd better get back to the hotel. I told the others I was seeing old friends for a while."

"Let me get your jacket."

Daw was already at the door as she retrieved his jacket from the hall closet. He suddenly seemed to be in a hurry.

"Great dinner, fantastic company; you're a hell of a woman, my dear friend."

"Thank you, Mr. Manford; I'm glad you enjoyed yourself."

They were both keeping their voices light. The atmosphere had changed; the intimacy was gone.

"Lia, I notice that you have on the whistle charm tonight. You know what it means.

Any time, any time at all."

He kissed her quickly on the lips twice and left.

ξ

Lia turned out all the lights, went into the bathroom and turned on the water in the tub. She added her favorite almond scent to the bath. She undressed, letting her clothes drop to the floor, and got in. The swirling hot water shocked her skin. She sat very still with her eyes closed and let it burn rather than adding cold water. Why didn't she let Daw take care of her? She certainly could have used it.

I'm very fond of Daw, and I long for his friendship, his presence. I feel real affection for him. He is a good man.

She leaned back and made an effort to turn her mind off so she wouldn't have to think more about or define the feelings she had for Dawson. It was well after midnight when she climbed out and got into bed.

ξ

June 1967

Lia always felt the single dumbest act, or moment, in her life was the last day of final exams during her freshman year in college. She had completed her world geography exam more quickly than she anticipated, and felt pretty good about her answers. But, now, she didn't know what to do. Ken was sitting hunched over next to her, still working on his exam. She felt funny, just getting up, leaving without saying something to him. It was two weeks before her nineteenth birthday. Ken was thirty-three years old, worked at night, and had returned to college to complete his bachelor's degree. He began talking to her on the first day of spring semester classes. At first, she was put off by his friendliness and wondered why this older, white guy always wanted to talk to her. Soon, Lia relaxed because he seemed to be a good guy, and she enjoyed their conversations when they ate lunch together in the cafeteria after class twice a week. She became a little nervous and unsure again when he asked, and she agreed, to have lunch on the lawn area surrounding the outdoor campus grill and then at close-by, off campus places. Eventually, he suggested they go to a movie or dinner, and even spend a weekend day on the boat he owned with his older brother. She declined each time, but the invitations continued.

The attention from Ken distracted Lia. She liked talking with Ken and was comfortable passing time with him on campus. But the pangs of apprehension would not go away when she let herself think about accepting one of his invitations away from the campus area. One day near the end of the semester Ken pushed very hard as they sat alone in class before anyone else arrived.

"Lia, please, I'm asking you to spend some time with me away from here. Please come out on the boat with me. I'm not asking you to go for the entire weekend; how about just for the day on Saturday?"

He put his hand on her shoulder and squeezed it with what Lia felt was just a touch of urgency. Lia didn't think he was trying to be disrespectful or threatening, but the pleading tone in his voice startled her. Students began wandering into the classroom, and she avoided having to answer him. When class was over, she quickly left ahead of him, breaking their habit of leaving together and having lunch. Lia was relieved that she wouldn't have to see Ken for almost a week. Finals were approaching, and they had no classes together for the rest of the week. Lia didn't sleep well that night, worrying if she was doing the wrong thing and hurting his feelings. She thought about calling him to apologize for being rude, especially after he had opened himself to her. He had given her his telephone number a while back to call him anytime she wanted, but she had never used it; she didn't have a reason to use it. She didn't call him now either, because she simply did not know what to say. After two or three days, Lia's preoccupation with the Ken situation subsided, but it remained in the back of her mind as she studied for finals.

Now, here she was wondering what to do. Lia began to feel conspicuous, sitting there doing nothing. She gathered her things, walked to the professor's desk, and handed in her exam. As she opened the door, her body was trembling. This wasn't right; Ken had always been nice to her, and she had to say something. Holding the door open, she turned around. Ken was staring at her with a look of almost panic on his flushed face.

"Sorry. I'll be working at California National Bank on First Street this summer, on the third floor. Come and see me if you're downtown. Have a good summer."

The dozen or so students still in class, and the professor, all looked at her and then over at Ken. A few students exchanged knowing smiles, but most of them displayed dumbstruck expressions. Ken's face turned beet red. Lia let go of the door and ran.

How stupid! Talking out loud to him in front of everybody! But, I couldn't sit there doing nothing. I totally embarrassed myself and Ken, who simply wanted to go out with me. What was I thinking about, talking to him out loud like that in front of everybody! I can't believe I was so dumb. Stupid, dumb girl.

She went directly home, closed herself in her room, and started to cry. She was confused and angry.

How could I know how to react? I know about Black guys my own age, but what am I supposed to know about a grown-up white man? He doesn't have my telephone number, and calling him is out of the question; he would probably hang up in my face. Thank God that was my last final and I don't have to go back to campus until September.

It took two weeks, after Lia had started her summer job, to stop thinking all the time about what happened. After a month or so, she hardly thought about it at all. Then, she met Rob.

Throughout the years, Lia occasionally thought about Ken and a hot flush of embarrassment covered her every time.

After all this time, I'm still telling myself that I didn't do anything wrong!

ع

On Sunday morning, Lia walked twice around the small lake located in the center of her development. Spring was in full bloom, summer was not far away, but it was a cool day and the sky was a diffused light blue. She had spent all of Saturday in the office, and felt like a freed bird this morning. Wanda had invited her over for brunch, so she headed home to shower and dress.

Lia always enjoyed driving down Wanda's street. It was lined with large houses and huge oak trees. Levale's early well-to-do resided in the area before urban creep sent them fleeing to the foothills a generation ago. The homes were still well cared for and a few of them had official historical designation. Professional, white "urban pioneers" had discovered the neighborhood in recent years and were scooping up the old, stately homes. Just about all the first wave of African-American inhabitants to populate the neighborhood had either died or sold out when lured by money they never dreamed their property would be worth. Wanda inherited the house when her mother died and was one of only three African-American households remaining on her block. Lia climbed the stairs and, as always, admired the large front door that Wanda herself had designed when she refurbished the house. The original glass panes had been replaced with leaded stained glass squares that she individually designed and made. The bordering wood had been stripped, stained and polished to a deep, rich shine. Wanda opened the door before Lia rang the bell, and they hugged after she stepped into the square foyer. Wanda had maintained all the original hardwood and moldings throughout the house. Her modern furnishings and artwork provided an interesting and striking contrast.

"Hey there! Give me your jacket. I've got someone I want you to meet."

Wanda had lowered her voice, and Lia wondered what was going on.

"How lucky can I get; two beautiful women to keep company for brunch."

Lia turned toward the deep, melodious voice and smiled at the very tall, very black, very handsome man. He was thin, but a muscular upper torso was evident under the light pullover sweater he wore."

Damn, where did Wanda get him?

"Lia, I'd like you to meet my friend, Oscar Bennett. Oscar and I met while I was doing some work for the school district. He teaches music at Levale High and is also the assistant principal."

"A man of many talents," Lia remarked as they shook hands. While the three of them moved into the living room to sit down, Lia gave Wanda a quick thumbs up.

"We're having mimosas; I'll pour you one."

Wanda filled a champagne flute from a large, glass pitcher.

"Wanda has told me so much about you, I feel I already know you. She brags about you all the time."

"Oh God," Lia laughed. She immediately felt at ease with Oscar and could see why Wanda was attracted to him.

"We've been trying to team up with Conallied to involve their local executives in some of our programs at the high school. The process has been slow. I'd love to get you involved and maybe you can help push it along".

"Well, just let me know; I'll see what I can do."

The three of them chatted a while longer. Oscar played saxophone in a jazz quartet, and Wanda talked about the previous evening when she went to hear him play. They eventually went out to the enclosed porch to eat. Wanda's eggs and hot smoked sausage casserole and fresh fruit salad were delicious. They sat at the table talking and laughing for a long time.

"Well folks, I've got to run." Lia planned to spend the rest of the afternoon in her jacuzzi, reading a new novel, and she figured Wanda wanted to spend some time alone with Oscar before he went to the club. His quartet was playing an early Sunday evening set.

"Oscar, it was a real pleasure meeting you; I'll look forward to seeing you again soon."

"Me, too. Today was real nice. You'll have to get Wanda to bring you to the club."

Wanda was excited. "Absolutely! Lia, let's go sometime soon."

As Lia drove home, she felt a twinge of envy of Wanda's life, but stubbornly refused to let herself dwell on it.

ξ

"Well, what do you think?" Wanda called Lia just as she was getting into bed.

"I like him. You've done well, girlfriend. That is one good looking man. How long have you known him and why haven't you talked about him? Has he been married? Kids?"

"He's been divorced for years. He has twins, a boy and girl. They're seniors in high school and live in Little Rock with their mother. Oscar is so proud of them. His son has been accepted to Princeton and his daughter is going to travel in Africa for a year with a church group. I may put her in contact with Kanzi. He's my ex, but he might be of help to her group. I'm surprised he didn't talk about them this afternoon."

"Well, I didn't talk about Jordan either. I'm sure we'll both get around to bragging about our children."

"Lia, Oscar has a good friend that he wants you to meet. He thinks the two of you would be perfect for each other. His name is Ellis, and he plays keyboards in Oscar's quartet. I've met him, and he's very charming."

"Well, it might be nice to meet someone. But, girl, Oscar is the one who seems to be perfect.

"I've only known him a few months. I didn't want to talk about him too soon; not until I felt there was going to be something there."

"I'm so glad it's working out for you, for both of you."

I've had enough false starts that I don't want to talk about something that isn't."

"Well honey, he definitely is!" They cackled like two hens.

ξ CHAPTER 6 ξ

The following weekend Lia headed to the Farm, Conallied's executive training center.

"Hey, Ms. EPD! I'll see you tomorrow morning?" Keith had called her the day before.

"Keith, don't call me that, especially this week."

"Uh, oh. Sounds like we need to talk. I ran into Dawson yesterday; he said he saw you last week and you were doing great."

"Well, you know Dawson; he's my buddy."

"I've arranged sleeping rooms for everybody tomorrow night. We'll start with lunch at noon and go as long as we need to. I've told the staff there that we'll probably have dinner late. We've got the Gazebo for dinner. I don't know what meeting room we'll have; it'll be on the board. I'm really looking forward to this. I'm so pumped that it's finally happening."

The group had decided to hold this organizing meeting on a Saturday. There was still plenty of sensitivity among Conallied's African-American executives about getting together and how it would look, and they didn't want to use a workday for this purpose. Lia didn't care one way or the other about the meeting being scheduled on a Saturday. Like Keith, she was just happy that it was taking place.

ξ

It had been a strange week of contrasts for Lia before she left for the Farm. The silence was deafening. Nothing happened. She didn't talk with anyone all week, not Gunther, Virginia, Dan, or anyone outside her building. She hadn't even had the follow-up conversation with Gerard about the situation with the branch managers that she had promised him, although she knew he was concerned. But, there had been a session that week with a group of associates and technicians. Gordon, Carl and Ben had come together to her office at the beginning of the week to review the schedule they had prepared for various associates to participate in upcoming sessions. Carl's voice was excited; he slapped both palms on the tabletop.

"I've personally gotten real positive feedback from a lot of the technicians. I called a few, but most of them called me. I think a lot of them were trying to feel me out on how things are going in other regions. Once I share the feedback, I've gotten from someone else they know, they seem to open up with me. We're doing great so far."

"A couple of the older agents have called me", Gordon said. "Carl has worked with a lot of the younger agents, so he should continue to be a good channel of communication for us."

Lia felt some of the tension leave her body. Things were going well between the associates and technicians.

God, I needed some good news, some successes right now to hold onto.

"Oh goody! I can put a bow on this present," Marva spoke up in her uniquely animated style. "Gerard and I have talked to more than half of the associates as a follow-up to their meetings with Lia. We've gotten so many comments and suggestions, a lot of thoughtful stuff. We're going to have to sort through it all; I think a lot of their ideas are really good. And, we need to make a big deal out of what we use, highlight the technicians and associates. They tell me that some associates have even stopped at your door, Lia, to chat."

"Yes they have, and I love it."

"They can tell that you enjoy them," Gerard said, smiling warmly at Lia. "They can sense when it's genuine or not."

"Nothing negative, you guys, nothing at all?"

"Not so far, it seems," answered Gerard.

"Yes!" Lia said it with emphasis and then let out the breath she had been holding.

"You know Lia, we should put together a presentation for Castle, a big-time dog and pony show, with a selected group of associates and technicians involved, and let's really trumpet the results these guys are getting."

Gordon's idea was excellent, and Lia was glad he communicated it in the presence of the others. Among her staff members, she had felt Gordon harbored a little of that old-school hesitancy about the whole idea of teaming the associates and technicians.

"Great idea, Gordon. Do it! I'll call Dan's secretary, Valerie; I'll try to get two hours on his schedule for us."

"Lia, we should probably invite Castle's full staff if it's okay with him. They are all going to reap benefits from the work that's being done, too, so we want to be sure they hear the story firsthand from us."

"Thanks, Ben, absolutely," Lia replied.

This presentation will provide me with a chance to communicate in person to all of them together what I haven't been able to do one-on-one.

"We can already produce some real numbers to show the savings generated just from the initial easy process changes that have been made. We'll get Jerome to put together some flashy financial charts. We want to demonstrate what we're doing is not smoke and mirrors and will have a positive impact on EPD's bottom line. You all know that is what will really count."

"You're exactly right, Carl. It's what will count with Dan. Let's keep the whole thing simple and straightforward. Plus, we want to give the groups some additional time to work together so we can have even more results to discuss in the presentation. We'll get together with Jerome, Marva and Gerard to strategize our message; all of us need to participate in the presentation. We can highlight a number of elements: customers, employees, critical processes, current and projected savings. We'll have a really good story to tell. Just keep cheerleading your associates."

The guys were excited when they left Lia's office, and she let herself feel good about it.

Today, I have to give myself permission to feel good.

ξ

Lia slept through her early morning flight north, and the ride in a hired car along the winding river road to the Farm put Lia in a relaxed mood. It was a beautiful, almost-summer morning, and she kept a window down in the back. She soaked up the fresh air and the woodlands bursting with greenery and a palette of pinks, purples and yellows along the roadside. The Farm, so-called by that name because the acreage was formerly farmland Conallied purchased in the 1950s, was situated on a high ridge above the river. It had the appearance of a small college campus; two old and massive red brick buildings covered with thick ivy on beautifully manicured grounds. There was also a nine-hole golf course and basketball and tennis courts. One of the buildings housed the sleeping rooms, a fitness center and dining rooms, and the other contained a variety of meeting and training rooms and a small auditorium. Individuals and teams from Conallied's Divisions throughout the country regularly traveled to the Farm for management training sessions and meetings.

The propaganda is laid on thick and heavy on us here, but this is a beautiful place.

In fact, Conallied's management training center enjoyed an excellent reputation in the corporate world; the Company compared its curriculum to the top graduate business programs in the country.

This group of Conallied's African-American executives really needs to make a commitment and do something meaningful about the retention and development of other African-Americans in the company. Conallied's track record has been dismal. This gathering needs to mean something. We're so overdue; we're the ones who have to take some action, or stop talking about it all the time. Now that I'm almost there, I realize that I've been yearning for this. I need the companionship of others who were going through, or at least can relate to, my struggle with layers of white men – old and young – who resent my senior position and want so badly for me to fail. I just need to be around some other Black folks - easy conversations, sharing "horror stories," raucous laughter, and the comfort of just being myself for a while without the constant tension.

ξ

Lia arrived with just enough time to check into her room before the meeting started. She walked over to the education building and found the meeting room number posted on the information board under the benign listing of "Cross-Business Forum." The Company's top African-American executives were seated around a long table, and the meeting was just getting started. When Lia entered the room, Keith, her best friend in the company other than Dawson, got up from his seat at the far end of the table, walked to the door and embraced Lia.

"Hey, here she is! How ya doing buddy?"

"I'm good now that I'm here, and you must be good too because you sure look it."

Keith laughed. "You sure know how to greet a brother! We're just getting started. Come sit next to me. There's food on the side bar if you're hungry."

The bar ran along one side of the long, narrow room, and it was covered with platters of sliced cold meats and cheeses, along with an assortment of salads, rolls and desserts. Cold beverages and three silver pots with regular and decaf coffee and hot water for tea sat at the end of the bar. China and silverware bearing Conallied's logo was stacked at one end of the bar. On the opposite side of the room a large window looked out to the woods surrounding the Farm. The midday sun splintered among the trees and poured into the room in beams and criss-crossed the conference table. Lia exchanged enthusiastic greetings with other colleagues, some with hugs and kisses and others with handshakes.

Well, everybody showed up, even Lance. Keith must have really worked those phone calls.

The cast of characters was varied and interesting, and Lia was closer to some than others. The were all professional in demeanor, generally self-assured, relatively attractive, clean-cut, appropriately dressed in varying degrees of "business casual" attire, though no dress code had been communicated, and alternately comfortable and wary of their presence in the luxury and privilege of the Farm. Lia considered the strengths and weaknesses of her colleagues, as she knew or heard over the years. She was still the newest member of this group, even though she had been with Conallied for over seven years.

Lance Tolliver was the senior member in the group. He was the number two man in Conallied's Insurance Services Division, and it was rumored that he would soon be promoted to lead the Division. If Lance got the promotion, it would be viewed as a watershed event in a company that had been historically very slow to hire and promote African-Americans at any level. However, Keith had repeatedly made the astute observation to Lia that allowing Lance to head the business presented little or no risk for Conallied. The man had grown up in the business, knew its operations inside and out, and the promotion was long overdue, anyway.

I've got to do an attitude adjustment about Lance. He's here, after all.

Lia grudgingly admired Lance's ability to play the corporate game cleverly. From time to time, she had observed his interactions with the company's senior management at corporate headquarters. He knew just when to laugh with them, agree with them, and strategically disagree on minor points in order to appear to be an independent thinker. Based on comments Lia heard over the years, Black folks in the Conallied had very mixed feelings about Lance.

Jarvis Addison was on Lance's staff. He was a clone of Lance, and he, too, was very knowledgeable about the company and its politics. He craved Lance's approval, and it seemed to her that his every act was directed to that desire. Nonetheless, Lia liked him.

Josh Coleman, one of the company's senior information technology executives, unlike Lance, was genuinely well liked. He was low-key, but very smart. He, too, expertly played the corporate game, but was not perceived to have sacrificed his African-American identity, as Lance had, in the process. In the presence of company leadership, he laughed loudly, initiated debate, and he was always articulate and right on target in his down-home manner.

Eddie Ballard, outgoing and well liked, was the marketing guru in the group. Eddie seemed to be as visibly excited about the meeting as Keith was.

Doris Wade and Lia worked on a project team together at corporate headquarters, although their paths rarely crossed otherwise. A little older than the rest of the group, she had a reputation as "mother hen" to everyone – listening to problems and dispensing platitudes and hugs – a historically acceptable role for an African-American female in Conallied, especially out in the Divisions.

Cecelia Hampton, the youngest of the group, was an up-and-coming human resources executive, very smart, who had been with Conallied since she was a high school intern.

Mark Douglas, a star in Conallied's finance group, was moody, analytical and had a sharp sense of humor when he chose to display it.

Jules Sampson, a product development expert, was charming and a really sweet man. Lia had once heard him declare that he was a male feminist, and she was glad he was there.

And, of course, there was Keith Monroe, Lia's friend and confidant. This effort was very important to him, and clearly, he had devoted a lot of effort to arrange it.

Jake Wallace should be here, too. It's too bad.

Unlike Lia, who had been recruited to Conallied at the executive level, most of the group had been recruited right out of college, or shortly thereafter, and had grown up in the company. They were not immune, however, to the same issues of acceptance that Lia faced every day.

I am very fortunate to be here today. They accept me as one of them; it feels so good.

By early evening, the group had discussed, debated, cursed, laughed about, reached consensus, and drafted an organization structure around a concept that was originally conceived by Keith.

We got loud a few times, but we got it done. Loud is okay.

The group of ten would act as the leadership council of a new, company-wide, initiative called the Leadership Roundtable, dedicated to recruiting, retaining, developing and promoting African-Americans in Conallied. Each of them would take personal responsibility to inform and secure support from the leadership team in their individual Divisions about the plans and goals of the new initiative. Those in the same Division would team up. After each of them felt comfortable they had the necessary support, something that would be challenging for some of them and downright torturous for a few, the details of the initiative would be communicated broadly to the Division's African-American employees through a series of local meetings that hopefully would be endorsed, even if not wholeheartedly supported, by the leadership of the Division. They put together the first draft of a five-page presentation to be used during the meetings with Division leaders.

Josh and Lia agreed to refine and finalize the presentation and distribute the final version to the others. It was an extraordinary day's work.

I am very proud to be part of this group

ξ

Keith had arranged dinner for the group in the Farm's gazebo, a free-standing structure perched on an ornate, raised base. It sat on the grounds outside the main dining room, and it was used for small, private gatherings. The group was served the Farm's always-delicious gourmet dinner by the solicitous dining room staff -- cornish hen and wild rice entree with crème brule and fresh strawberries for dessert -- and settled back to relax for the first time since noon. The night sky was bright enough to illuminate its deep blue color and countless stars. The half moon hung low in the sky. The lights in the Gazebo had been dimmed, and it seemed to float in space as the Farm's other buildings receded into the night.

I feel so cozy and safe tonight. Why can't it always be like this? Oh, please, Lia, get a grip on yourself; that was an immature and unrealistic thought.

"Okay, you guys, what's the real deal with Jake?" Mark's voice, sounding urgent and tense, was out of sync with the mood of the evening.

Jake Wallace, absent from the day's gathering, held an influential controllership position in the company; but Jake had always displayed a streak of arrogance that he couldn't control, and it ultimately led to his undoing. He apparently had been called into a top-level meeting earlier in the week and unceremoniously fired, seemingly out of the blue. The rumors had been flying all week about which specific straw broke the camel's back, though it must have been bad. But Jake knew where a lot of the company's financial bodies were buried, and it had gotten out that he demanded and received a very hefty separation package.

"The real deal is that the brother forgot!" Doris, too, was clearly angry and frustrated about Jake.

"Forgot what? What does that mean?" Lia asked, both confused and curious.

"Forgot he is a Black man, forgot he couldn't raise hell, forgot he couldn't flaunt his upscale lifestyle, forgot he couldn't screw around with whatever white women he wanted; forgot that he couldn't do what they do all the time and get away with it!"

You go, Doris. Bless her heart; she says what's on her mind.

"Take a breath, Doris. Why are you so angry?" Keith responded, putting his hand on Doris's arm.

"I'm angry because he fucking knows better. He's a hell of a smart guy, with tons of talent. Why was he so damned stupid about this? It just makes me crazy!"

"I heard he was building a house, right down the road from his boss, for God's sake. How stupid is that? Did he really think they were going to be okay with that? The brother already had a fabulous house, anyway." Eddie shook his head in disgust. Lia noticed that

Lance remained silent and feigned ignorance about any of the details of Jake's departure.

"Oh, c'mon Lance, I'll bet you know every gory detail."

"I've heard the same things you all have heard," Lance responded.

Josh also had a close relationship with Jake, and he spoke up. "Hey folks, I talked with him yesterday, and you all know Jake will land on his feet. He said you guys won't have to hold any telethons for him."

"So, his frame of mind is good?" Keith sounded doubtful.

"Well, I could sense his regret. You're right Doris; he didn't understand that he had to be careful around the white boys. They can go from tolerance to resentment in a heartbeat. Jake forgot that."

"He got too caught up in it all; he lost his soul." Doris' declaration settled in the Gazebo like a thud.

Oh boy, did he ever. He's an idiot for not picking up on the bad vibes that had to be coming from the people around him. I want to put in my two cents, but I don't want Josh to think I'm piling on the arrogant jerk now that he's gone. And, anyway, am I doing the same thing by ignoring the obviously bad vibes I'm getting from Gunther and his cronies, and what it could mean for me?

"You know, talking about staying in your place brings to mind something my father-in-law did many years ago that I didn't understand at the time, but I've certainly come to understand and can totally relate to it now." Mark leaned back at an angle against the gazebo's tall, plate glass window, his legs stretched out in front of him, both hands in his pockets.

"What was it?" Cecelia and I both asked simultaneously and looked at one another with a grin.

"Back in the seventies, he bought a Cadillac Seville, when the Seville first came out as a new model. Remember how good it looked? His was light gold, kind of a champagne color, with tan leather interior. That baby looked good! He surprised my mother-in-law and all the rest of us when he drove up in it one Sunday afternoon. A lot of the family was there for dinner. His brother, Reuben, let out a whoop, 'Good God almighty, my brother done gone crazy, and I damn sure love crazy!' The rest of us just stood there with our mouths hanging open. I later asked him if he was excited about showing it off to his co-workers. I knew he had a lot of good friends at work; he had been the supervisor at a factory for many years, and they all loved him. He emphatically told me that would only drive his beat-up old Toyota to work. Now, this was a man who had no shortage of vanity, so I knew he would have loved to pull that Seville into his space in the parking lot near the front door of the factory. He told me in no uncertain terms that he would never let his boss, an old white guy who had run his family's business forever, know that he had a new Cadillac, let alone ever see it. My mother-in-law nodded her head in agreement. He said that he had a good relationship with the man for over twenty years and had gotten good Christmas bonuses and lots of free merchandise. But, he knew him well enough to know that the relationship would turn on a dime if his boss saw him driving a brand new Cadillac. The fact that he had worked hard many years to get it would be irrelevant. Well, it blew me away. I was all young and naïve and indignant and felt that his thinking was old-timey. I know better today."

"Yeah, old-timey and new-timey." Eddie laughed and continued talking.

"I'll never forget when my Mom died. After the funeral, my Dad was all worried when my aunts set up the dining room with Mom's good china, crystal, flatware, and tablecloths. She had collected those things over the years and really loved that stuff; she loved the holidays and special occasions when she could use it all. I think my aunts felt they were honoring her memory by laying it all out to be used by visitors. My Dad thought his white co-workers who were coming by the house would think we were putting on airs and we'd better not show off in front of them. I was too emotional to even respond to him. But his cousin, who is like a brother to him, told my Dad that he damned well better be proud that he had a wife who displayed grace and class and created a home with nice things and to hell with those 'honky, ofay, white folks.' That's a direct quote, and that was the end of that!"

"When I get back home tomorrow, Patsy and I are going to spend the afternoon having an economic summit conference." Jarvis, leaning back on the rear legs of his chair sipping a beer, changed the subject.

"An economic summit conference?" Doris repeated Jarvis' phrase. "That sounds like President Bush talking." Everyone smiled, but Jarvis was serious.

"Yes. We've decided our lifestyle is out of control. We're going to pay off all our bills, maybe sell our house and buy a smaller one, and get rid of some cars. It's getting ridiculous. We've decided to face the reality that I could lose my job in an instant if one of these white guys with influence decides he doesn't like me or want me around anymore. I could come in the office one day and not be a team player anymore. I certainly wouldn't be the first person to be dumped for not being a so-called team player. I want to be prepared if that happens."

Oh, shit.

Lia was truly stunned. Jarvis was probably the last person around the table, except for Lance, who she expected to make that statement. It was disturbing to her because Jarvis seemed to have excellent relationships with all the white guys.

Lia responded, "You know, it's strange you say that. I did the very same thing right after my last assignment transfer. I paid off all my credit card debt, and now I put more in savings and investments each month. I don't quite know what's driving me, but I definitely feel a need to do it."

"Well, you're doing a smart thing," Jarvis said.

"It's a scary proposition when they can simply decide on any given day to toss you aside, and then set about doing it." Jules sounded grim.

"You guys are always talking about 'they.' You all sound like the end of the world is coming." Lance's voice had a mocking tone, yet betrayed an edge of anger. "I think you all worry too much about 'they.'"

"Lance, please, be real. You know damn well that we have to worry all the time." Mark sounded exasperated. "'They,'" Mark said the word with exaggerated cynicism, "don't have to work as hard as we do to prove themselves, and they constantly get opportunities that are not available to us or, at least, not to the overwhelming majority of us. And, they don't have to worry about all of this corporate political crap; well, okay, certainly not to the extent we do."

"Do you really believe that?" Lance shot back at Mark.

"Look at Mr. 'Golden Boy' Dan Castle," Mark said with cynicism fairly dripping in his tone, based on the strength of his example.

Oh God, they're going to talk about Dan. He's my boss; damn, I should be able to defend him. It would be really nice to feel as though I could. Do I owe Dan loyalty at this point? I don't know the answer to that question.

"It's expected that after he runs amok in your Division, Lia, he'll be sent to Asia for a key international assignment in some huge, emerging market where he can't lose. They don't give a shit that Castle takes credit for work that others do and does not know how to interact with his workers right here in the U.S. He won't know what the hell to do with foreign workers, for Christ's sake!"

It's all probably true.

"Well, look at Matt Franklin in my Division," Cecelia cut in. "He's being groomed for big things, too. Corporate thinks the guy is just great; he's definitely one of the golden boys, too. I'll tell you something that I happen to know, and I won't say how, so please don't anybody ask me. Matt's last annual assessment contained very negative comments about his ability to lead a group and his tendency to leave his staff behind while he's demonstrating his so-called genius to make a deal. They now realize that people who work for him really hate the guy. So what are they doing? The company is hiring a special consultant to counsel him. Trust me folks, this counseling is costing the company a fortune."

"Can you imagine what would happen to one of us if word got out that we were hated by our staff? We'd be out so fast it would make your head spin. Counseling? Please! I tell you, though, everyone is in his face smiling, regardless of how they feel about him, because they know he is being groomed, and he has power." Eddie's comments caused heads to nod around the table.

"I think that very thing is a serious shortcoming among us. We have a hard time doing that." Josh was speaking quietly. "It's a cultural thing. It is very difficult for us to look in your face, laugh with you, and socialize with you, if we don't like you. We can work with you if we have to, but we have a real hard time faking it, and I think it can show. I hate to say it, but it works against us. Their culture teaches them to do whatever is necessary, if it involves business and profit. It's not considered wrong or immoral, it's just good business. The truth is we struggle mightily with that concept."

Lia spoke up. "Sometimes I wonder if we really have anything in common with them. Professionally, I assume we want the same things, but our process of getting there seems to be so different. I think my most frustrating issue is that I don't respond to situations the same way white males do. Why should I have to?"

Am I sounding too defensive? If I whine too much here, will they think I whine all the time?

"Last week was a good example." Lia continued on. "One of our process improvement teams, which I asked to focus specifically on specialized products, was not working together well and not meeting the goals they set for themselves. I called them all into my office, put the issues on the table, challenged each of them to voice their thoughts about the issues, and to offer possible solutions. I assured them that it was going to be a no-fault meeting. It was a difficult session, but a useful one, because the team eventually agreed on a new plan of action that was actually more effective, and everyone supports it now. But I had to reassign a couple of the agents on the team. We did it all very openly. I just happened to briefly mention it to Dan, and he wanted to know why I didn't meet with him first to discuss who we should remove from the team and do it quietly, as though we really could. Dan had absolutely nothing to do with selecting the people on the teams in the first place. We hardly ever talk, but he was bothered by the overt directness of my approach. Secret meetings to screw people are what these guys do well. Instead of appreciating an open and different perspective or approach, they see a different style or approach as a problem."

I'm too embarrassed to tell them that Dan was annoyed with me and described my approach as "taking matters into your own hands." I've got an impressive title and a ton of responsibility, but I'm in a constant battle for authority.

"Lia, the problem with your approach is that it made just too much sense," Keith chuckled.

"I've wondered about this many times, and I'd like to think it's not true, but I truly believe that many of these white guys feel that African-Americans are fundamentally not as good, not as smart, or intellectually thoughtful, as they are. No amount of civil rights or social pressure is ever going to change that." Cecelia's voice betrayed her deep anger. "Even with our education and experience, they feel we're here in their precious company on a free ticket."

"Lia, Cecelia, how many times have you held a meeting with white guys who don't know you, and even some who do know you, and they direct their comments to your white male subordinates and never look directly at you?"

Cecelia and Lia both laughed at Jules' question.

"I'm lucky enough to have a staff that helps make it clear who the final decision maker is when they see that crap happening," Lia said. "But, it makes me sad. Then, I get mad at myself for feeling sad about it."

Sitting there among her colleagues, Lia recalled that Ben on her staff made a comment after a long meeting the week before with three of the Conallied's telecommunications experts and two outside consultants who had come to her office to discuss upgrading the aging national communications equipment at Consumer Services.

"That must really piss you off."

"What?" I asked.

"When guys ignore you and direct their comments to me or Greg as though you're not even here."

"Yes, it pisses me off, but whenever it happens, I generally think of something very direct, but diplomatic, to say to let them know who's in charge."

"Yes, I've seen you in action." Lia remembered Ben had laughed heartily.

"You know, I don't think we get much credit for developing young staffers, either." Lia was on a roll. "It's the kind of leadership role they envision for themselves, but not us. After all, most of the staff we manage is white guys! We do what good leaders are supposed to do, develop our people, and don't trip on who people are. I had a guy on my team in Fielding last year, his name is Mack Danowich, a very smart guy, and he was languishing in an entry-level supervisor position. He was refreshingly straightforward, his staff really liked him, and he shared a lot of valuable information with me when he didn't have to. I asked him to lead a couple of projects for me, really stretched him, and he delivered big time. When a promotion opportunity developed in your Division, Cecelia, that I thought was perfect for Mack, we talked about it, he asked me to support his application, and I lobbied hard for him. He got the assignment and a year later won a summit award. He called me the day after the award announcements. I was really proud and happy for him."

"Oh God, let's not even talk about those damned summit awards." Cecelia threw her hands in the air.

Her Division awarded an annual "Summit Award" to its top-performing employees. They received a cash award and a trip for two to a destination they could choose from a list of exotic places. The African-American employees in the Division continually complained among themselves that the award process was obstructed by politics and cronyism, and they were generally excluded from the award.

"The real issue is that there are so few African-Americans in positions where there are responsibilities and special assignments that are eligible for the award."

"How many Black folks got a summit award this year," Eddie asked.

"One this year, none last year. Hey, a one hundred percent increase!"

They all laughed at the irony of Cecelia's remark.

"This experiment, and I use that word purposely because I think that's how they still view it, of diversifying corporate management has basically failed because the effort has been one-sided only. We've done all the work; we've done all the changing, all the adjusting. Think about it, you guys, they haven't changed one iota. They don't feel that they have to." Eddie first sounded somewhat defeated, then resigned to the reality.

It's not only me, this angry-sad thing.

"We've tried to fit in, adapt to their traditions, their terminology, their way of doing things, and it's a struggle because many times it goes against our grain. You know, when you're going against your grain, it exhausts you. We keep doing it anyway, though."

"We're not quitters," Doris said. "That's why we have survived."

Eddie continued. "But, to finish my point, what have they done to adopt any of our culture or way of doing things, or understand that we react to situations differently? Nothing! It hasn't happened."

Lance spoke up as he banged his hands palm down hard on the table in exasperation. "We've got to face reality here. It's their game, and we have to play by their rules. And, you know what? It's always going to be that way. Once you accept that reality, all you have to worry about is getting the job done."

The response to Lance's comment was silence. A couple of sighs wafted through the momentary silence in the Gazebo.

"I think the thing that I have the hardest time dealing with is the quiet, low-key, pseudo-civilized way in which they do their dirt. They'll calmly discuss and rationalize someone's career while manipulating it in such negative ways. I've been witness to some pretty cold-blooded shit while they're moving the pieces around on the big chessboard. I've asked myself, more than once, what I'm doing here, why am I a part of this? The truth is that we are all pieces on Conallied's chessboard. Sorry, Lance, that includes you, too." There was a discomforting quiver in Keith's voice. He spoke of a reality that gnawed at all of them, and he was quietly challenging Lance's view of the world in front of the group.

"Hey man, white people could make some of the same comments, they deal with some of the same bullshit." Lance's voice bordered on real anger now, but as the senior member of the group, I felt sure he wasn't going to allow himself to lose his cool.

"That's true, but we experience it so much more often. For them, it's the exception and not the rule, and you know it, Lance."

Lance did not respond this time.

Mark spoke up. "They continually change the definitions and use these goddamn codes and phrases, 'team player,' 'all the right tools,' 'loyal soldier,' 'displays our values.' That's their values, of course. 'Change agent' is another favorite, but it's only the changes they want made, of course. Then, the bastards discard the damned code, or any part of it, at will! I have to admit, though, that it's a damned good strategy; it's designed to keep you off balance and it works like a charm. And, hell, I realize it's not just us that have to adhere to their code; a lot of people do. It's just we're always the first ones to get picked off. I guess that's why this goes beyond simple anger," he said again quietly. "It wounds your soul. I'm more often questioning why I continue to do this to myself. Then I question my internal fortitude, take a deep breath, and keep on going. But, it hurts. This crap hurts."

The Gazebo was quiet again, but the silence was filled with shared experience and feelings left unspoken; too painful to talk about, too painful not to talk about.

I want to say something; I don't know what to say. No one else does, either.

Keith broke the silence. "What I can do is the best I know how and hope they ordain me, based on my performance, just like the others."

It sounded as though he had said all he would on the subject; his voice seemed to completely run out of steam.

"They have a culturally inbred need to dominate. There's centuries of documented history that cannot be denied no matter how much they'd like to. The corporate cabal has simply perfected the shit into a more sophisticated form." Cecelia's proclamation hung in the air.

Either her opinion is ridiculously untrue or devastatingly true.

"Folks, we do say 'they' a hell of a lot. We're talking about white men, so why don't we just say the words?" We say 'they', we say 'white boys,' as slang, but we rarely say exactly what it is, white men." Lia liked the way Jules put it right out on the table.

"You can't exclude the women," Doris interrupted. "They can be just as racist, more so sometimes, but in subtle ways."

"Hey, I think we're talking about both white men and women, in upper management and middle management, and that's a whole hell of a lot of people. A few exceptions among them try relate to our issues, but I'd still categorize the vast majority of them as 'they.'"

Jules continued. "I asked the question because I wonder if it's always going to be 'they' and 'us'?'"

"I've actually had a few days when I've said to myself, 'I belong here, I really do belong, I'm one of them. I'm one of the team.' I want so much for it to true, for it to last. Then, there are too many other days when I feel like a complete outsider, and I get caught in this vicious circle of feeling inadequate, then angry at myself for allowing my self-esteem to be shattered by all this shit, then anger at them for creating the whole thing in the first place, then I question why I'm here and what I'm doing, just like some of you, and around and around I go. This corporate derangement screws with the mind." Lia had been hesitant about making such a strong and personal statement, but felt okay after she said it.

Jesus, little flashes of light are dancing in front of my eyes; it's tension. That shouldn't have been so difficult to say out loud.

"It really makes me angry the way they pat themselves on the back when talking about those of us sitting around this table," Doris said. "They opened the door a crack and let a few of us into upper management. And, Lia, you had to be brought in from outside the Company. The small group of us leaders here, out of a hundred thousand employees, is pitiful. And, you know what? We're stagnating. Why? Because those of us here, and the one or two others who aren't here, are quite enough, thank you very much. I had a guy tell me in so many words that Conallied's African-American executive quota – he actually used the word 'quota' – has been met. What made it so galling is that he is a young, arrogant jerk who is in a key management position, and he has a fraction of the experience of any of us."

"Keith," Lia said, "Remember when I hired those four, young Black guys on my last assignment? Summer interns, for God's sake. A lot of the hundred and twenty-five white people in my group at corporate headquarters were all hot and bothered by it. At an all-staff meeting, I put together a pie chart showing the race and gender breakdown on an overhead transparency and included it as part of an organizational overview. The tiny sliver of the pie that represented African-Americans was so ridiculously small, I never heard another word about it."

"If a person only relied on the headlines and photographs in Black magazines, you'd think we had totally integrated the executive ranks of corporate America. But the number is so ridiculously minuscule when compared to the total," Keith added.

"You sure hit a sore spot with me, Keith," Doris responded and continued. "You've got to look at the kinds of positions most of those brothers and sisters are holding. God bless them, but very few have operational positions with important clients to serve, big budgets to be responsible for, or revenue to generate. Look at the titles; many are professional support roles, like attorneys, and way too many are cultural diversity or community relations jobs. They love to fill up those slots with us. All visibility and no power."

"Speaking of who is not here, where is Jeff Williams?" Josh asked. "We all expected him, didn't we?"

"He initially said he would be here," Keith answered. "But, he called me yesterday and said that he supported our effort and would do whatever we needed him to do behind the scenes, but did not want to be out front."

"Well, we have to respect that." Lance stood up and leaned against the glass, sipping a scotch and soda that had been brought to him by one of the staff.

"Why?" Mark asked. "I mean, I like Jeff, but we're all going to be out front; we have careers to worry about, too. Jeff will show up after all the work is done and make some grand show of support. You all know it's true."

"Look at us. We're having this meeting on a Saturday, using our own time, because of sensitivity to how *they* will view us using a business day to discuss these issues."

"Well, I think it's a legitimate concern. Come on, let's be honest. A few of us around this table felt more comfortable having this meeting on a Saturday."

Why is Jarvis sounding so defensive? The tone of our conversation has changed; it's starting to feel different now.

"In fact, I'll admit I even questioned if we should have it here at the Farm rather than completely away from Conallied, at a hotel somewhere or even at someone's home."

"Oh, Jesus Christ," Doris shrieked, "Jarvis, you have got to be kidding." She said each word very slowly.

Lia jumped in. "Jarvis, don't you think what we've started here today will be of great benefit to the Company? If we do what we say we're going to do, we'll help African-Americans be better prepared to make significant contributions to Conallied. I don't mind meeting on Saturday, but I sure don't think it was necessary."

Seems to me like we're letting Jeff off the hook.

"But, we do have to be careful how all of this is perceived," Lance commented. "I'm sure most of the guys at corporate think I'd be the last person to be part of this kind of initiative. They don't realize all that I see and hear about who makes it in this company, and who doesn't, and why. I get disgusted sometimes, too."

It sounds like Lance is trying to redeem himself among the group, balance some of his earlier comments.

"Does anyone know how Clark Blackburn is doing? I haven't heard a thing," Eddie asked, looking around the table.

Clark Blackburn left the company almost a year earlier after a short, but splashy and ultimately ugly stay at Conallied. Lia came in contact with him only once and felt, while he was friendly enough, he preferred to function and socialize only at the very highest levels in the company. He had served in the administration of the state's former governor and was highly thought of in political and business circles. Clark had to be given his due, because he was the person who firmly connected Conallied with the African-American political and community activist leadership around the state and, to some extent, on the national level in meaningful ways. Conallied was one of the last corporate giants to acknowledge the importance of developing and sustaining relationships with minority groups. Prior to Clark, the company's "community outreach programs" had been limited to the arts and local cultural events sponsorship, the country club stuff.

In Ohio, an Conallied employee at the Health Services Division, Lester Sampson, had initiated a mentor program at a high school that had a large minority student body. He started it on his own as an outreach project at his church, and recruited his Conallied co-workers, mostly African-Americans but some whites as well, as mentors. After a year of success, he persuaded Health Services to make a small donation to the program. The following year the donation was increased. Eventually, the program became identified as Conallied's. Senior management, including Jud Jeffries, the CEO himself, used the program over and over again for photo opportunities as an example of the company's commitment to community involvement. It became a running joke among African-Americans in Conallied, often repeated by Lester himself, that the community outreach program had become Conallied's fruitcake; there's only one in existence but it continually gets passed around so there appears to be many of them. Now, every time a reference is made to the mentor program, especially by Jud, the Black employees just shake their head and laugh, or sigh.

During his first few months, Clark Blackburn staged a number of high visibility symposiums, roundtables, dinners and the like that created some great photo opportunities for Jud and the other senior executives. All style with little substance. But, Clark had a plan. He anticipated using his initial efforts as a launching pad for the company to make a major commitment to a series of programs targeting inner-city communities. He knew he was in trouble when, after presenting his long-term plan, the startled executive group decided to take the matter to the full board of directors for discussion and approval. Then, there were repeated postponements in putting the issue on the agenda of the quarterly board meeting agenda. Clark pushed. Why couldn't the plan simply be blessed by Jud, who made much bigger decisions every day, and was known to have almost total autonomy from his board of directors? After another few months of inaction, Clark very quietly left Conallied. The circumstances of his departure had been locked down tight. Lance didn't know. Daw didn't even know the details when Lia inquired about Clark, and she was confident he would have told her if he had known.

Jarvis responded. "He dropped out of sight for a while. I heard about a month ago that he had gotten some kind of lucrative consulting contract with one of the countries on the African continent. I don't know what country, but that's right up Clark's alley."

"I'm sure Jud's boys feel like they dodged a bullet, but I think the most relieved person was George Anderson. Clark made him nervous. He wasn't ready for Clark. Hell, Conallied wasn't ready for Clark." Mark didn't make much of an effort to restrain his bitterness.

"Hasn't George Anderson seen a lot of the same things you have? He's been around corporate headquarters for a while now. And, why isn't he here, too? You understand, of course, that these are just rhetorical questions." Doris threw her hands in the air for emphasis. "We all know the answers."

George Anderson had been hired almost two years earlier as Conallied's Corporate Diversity Manager, with oversight across the entire company. Conallied had filled the position three full years after announcing it would do so. The sad fact was that it seemed as if George didn't even exist; he had little or no visibility in the Conallied or credibility with the company's African-American employees.

"They go out and hire someone who is totally non-threatening and looks just like them; George can damn near pass for white," Mark said.

"That would be a grossly unfair statement, Mark, if it were another fair-skinned person. But, in fact, George has no guts and that is why he is so useless for the purpose he was hired," Josh responded.

Jarvis jumped in. "The guy was born and raised in Wyoming, for God's sake, and then spent twenty years in the military taking orders. He's been in a very structured environment doing exactly what he was told to do. Perfect profile to break new ground and push for some fundamental changes, huh?"

"I talked with George briefly about this meeting, and he said that he didn't think it would look good for someone in his position to be part of this group," Keith said. "He also didn't offer any moral support, or even ask me to fill him in when I return to the office on Monday."

"Keith, just what the hell does he do?" Jules asked.

"I sit right down the hall from the guy, and I have no idea. He's hardly ever there. But, what's telling is that I never see any African-American, or any other person of color for that matter, in his office talking with him."

"It's a perfect match; they don't care and George doesn't care." Eddie didn't hide his disgust.

"We can't worry about George; he's irrelevant. All of us have to be conscientious about the attitude we display in connection with the Roundtable. If we show arrogance, or anger, we'll lose important public relations points." Josh's voice took on its usual, reasoned tone that was respected by everyone.

"Okay all you big egos around this table, no arrogance or anger!" Eddie stood up as though he were going to make an announcement. "Heaven forbid if we should ever be arrogant!" We laughed because there was nothing else to do.

"You know," Eddie said, apparently feeling the need to switch gears, "in America, financial success is endowed with spiritual resonance. That's all they really care about. It's downright religious for these people. Now, making money is okay with African-Americans, too, but it for damn sure is not spiritual. It's that cultural thing again; it's just different."

"Speaking of cultural, I had my saddest experience in all the years I've worked at Conallied right here at the Farm," Doris said. "I was part of the initial focus group trying to determine if and how the subject of diversity should be incorporated into training classes at Farm. The group leader put us through several exercises. One involved all the whites going into a room and all the minorities going into another room. They were going to ask us a series of questions, and we were going to compare answers of the two groups. Well, there were two Asians participating in the big group. Six of us minorities were sitting there in the room waiting for the Asians to show up. Well guess what? It took about ten minutes before it dawned on us that they had gone in the room with the whites.

"I would have loved to have been a fly on the wall in that room and watch those white boys trip out on that situation." Jarvis chuckled.

"Our group couldn't decide whether to be mad or sad. I personally felt sad, for myself and for the Asians. We discussed confronting them and decided not to do it. I guess, in some twisted way, we understood their need to be one of them. I thought about that afternoon for a long time."

"The training here is top-notch, but a lot of time is wasted, too. It's that cultural thing, yet again. They love to play games and create silly competitions around damned near everything. We prefer to build teams by more direct, face-to-face kind of interactions, you know, sitting around the table, like we're doing now, talking through issues and knowing more about one another on a very personal level. Do you guys think I'm way off base here?" Jarvis asked.

"No," responded Jules. "But we participate and play the games their way so that we are not tagged with that old 'not a team player' label."

"I say it again, it's their game and their rules; get used to it." Lance stared out the window he was leaning against, almost talking to himself.

The group sat silently, again, as a bowl of fresh fruit, brought in as a late snack, was passed around the table.

"I guess I'll take the banana since I'm with you guys," Keith said.

"What does that mean?" Eddie asked the question that was on everyone's lips.

"Well, I wouldn't eat the banana if I was with a group of white guys." Keith made this statement as though it was totally reasonable, while everyone stared at him.

What! Keith has never shared this with me. I guess he couldn't admit it, until now.

"Hey guys, I can't help the way I feel. I know that if I sit in front of them eating a banana, they're going to think about and visualize a monkey, an ape, a gorilla."

"I heard it, but I don't believe it," Lance said, shaking his head.

"Well you enjoy that banana, brother Keith," Mark shouted. Our loud laughter was punctuated with clapping and foot stomping.

God, this feels good.

"You know, folks, we have to be really careful about some African-Americans who are just fine with the status quo and feel okay with these white guys being in charge of everything, as long as they personally get treated well." Everyone looked in Doris's direction; it was evident she had more to say.

"I had a very unpleasant experience a couple of years ago that still disturbs me. I don't talk about it much. My boss, Joe Campbell, embarrassed me, and other staff, unnecessarily in a staff meeting; I'll spare you the details. I was practically in tears, confronted him in the hall after the meeting, and asked for an explanation. Well, just for asking the question, he told me, a grown woman, to watch my mouth, and I pointed my finger at him and responded that he should watch his mouth and be aware of how he talks to his staff. He walked away without listening any further to me. I went to my office, gathered my things, and left for the day. The entire confrontation between us in the hall was witnessed by a co-worker, Janet Tinsley; I don't think any of you guys know her, but she's Black. The two of us had been on very friendly terms. She has worked for Campbell for many years, he takes her with him after every promotion he gets, and she cleans up various messes for him. After that day, she never looked me in the eye again. I'm sure she didn't approach me to talk about it because she didn't want to know any details. I've always felt she knew her situation was comfortable, and she was not about to put it at risk. It was her choice, but I'd bet she won't openly support our new initiative."

Jules responded. "We all know who they are. They are content with old-school thinking. Hey, some of us are old school, too, but we're determined to see changes. Some will eventually support what we're trying to do, and some won't. Sadly, not much can be done about it."

Doris looked around the table. "Nobody has mentioned Lily Godfrey, either. Why haven't we talked about her? Hell, she epitomizes everything we've been talking about all evening."

"Maybe that's why we haven't talked about her," Jarvis said.

"What you do mean," Doris stared hard at Jarvis.

"I think it's hard to talk about Lily because it touches on so much stuff that's sensitive to all of us. I mean, she did have a large operation to run, over seven hundred people . . ."

"Seventy-five percent of her employees were Black . . ."

"So what?" Jarvis raised his voice over Doris' comment. "It was a big job at an important assembly plant."

"Oh, come on, Jarvis. I'm not saying it wasn't a big job, but she didn't have profit and loss responsibility like Lia does now. We all know she was sent there just to keep the natives from revolting, to keep 'yo people' in check. The union was sniffing around, and they were about to have a revolution on their hands; everybody knew it, and Lily was given a big promotion and was sent to suppress the rebellion. They figured all those black folks, most of them relatively unskilled women, would be so glad to see a Black woman in that corner office, they would stay calm for a while. What they didn't figure on was that Lily wouldn't stay calm! When she tried to make a real difference, suddenly all the important decisions were made from the Division's main office. Lily never got to make one damned decision about how to run that place that really mattered."

It was Jarvis' turn to bang his hands on the table. "The whole mess was insulting to Lily and to all of us, too. We were all so proud when she got that job. She was totally sandbagged. I can understand why she quit only a year after accepting the assignment. I liked her a lot. It's Conallied's loss."

Cecilia spoke up. "We all know that the real beneficiaries of affirmative action are white women. They're climbing the ladder to the executive suite faster than any group. It's true in other occupations, as well."

"I just wish they would, for once, acknowledge this truth. Too many white women try to attach the "affirmative action" label on Black folks, when they are the ones who have benefited the most. I think Trisha Lyman is a textbook example of this attitude, because she's always talking about the importance of affirmative action in reference to Blacks." Doris threw her hands in the air while making her statement.

Keith responded. "I can tell you many of the white men in Fielding resent her. They think she's not that smart, but she has been promoted to the senior executive ranks with lightning speed because Jeffries likes her. You know her best, Lia, what do you think?"

"Keith, I have a little story about Trisha. Just before I left Fielding last year, she took me to lunch at The Crescent."

"That's pretty rich, even for her expense report," Lance chortled.

"Well, we were standing at the curb waiting for Trisha's driver to pull up. Two elderly, East Indian women approached us, long saris, veils, the whole thing. They were trying to communicate something to us. Trisha let out a little shriek like she was afraid, waved her arm at them, and said 'no, go away' without even trying to understand what they were saying. I smiled and made an effort to communicate with them. It turns out that one of the women badly needed a restroom, for God's sake, and they were hoping that other women could help them. I led them into The Crescent and pointed out the ladies room. It helped that it was located in the front just off the waiting area of the restaurant. Trisha didn't say one word to me in the car all the way back to the office."

"It bothered you," Keith said with a look of understanding of Lia's disillusionment.

"Yes, it always has," replied Lia.

"You know, one of the brightest, most promising young African-American men in this company suggested to me the other day that we, the people around this table, were more part of the problem than the solution. He says we sold out a long time ago and, I'll tell you, the other young people who were with him all nodded in agreement," Josh sounded frustrated and perplexed.

I don't know why Josh sounds so frustrated. These young people aren't going to be the good Negroes like we've been.

Cecelia nodded and added, "It's scary, because these young folks are not going to put up with the barriers for as long as we did. These kids are very impatient, and they are going to demand what they've earned."

"Well, I'll watch it all from the safety and distance of retirement," Lance had a tone of relief in his voice.

Cecelia raised her hand like she was in a classroom asking for permission to speak. "My sister, Lanie, is a college professor. She listens to my stories about experiences in the corporate world, and laughs. She says the politics and racism among administrators and faculty on college campuses is the worst, especially because it's shrouded in intellectual phoniness. She thinks college campuses are just as hostile, or more so, and the so-called 'liberal' environment on college campuses is a myth. She's constantly talking about the phony liberals on her campus. She says certain professors are chosen for the best teaching assignments, committees, conferences, and then nurtured by the college; some are not, and it's not based on who is the best educator. Does that all sound familiar?"

"It's so sad. Higher education and learning, huh?' Lia sighed loudly.

"I'm sitting here asking myself if we are bitching and moaning too much. I mean, we're sitting here, enjoying the all the ambience and hospitality and good food that the Farm has to offer, being waited on just like everyone else, so now I'm asking why we are whining so much?" Jules' expression as he looked around the table seemed to beg for somebody to say something profound in response. No one did.

"Okay, I guess I can answer my own question. The problem is that it's all so tenuous. We have precious little history here, no solid foundation, and I'm afraid we'll never have the opportunity to build one."

"Why do we stay? Should we leave Conallied? Hell, leave corporate America entirely!" Keith, too, seemed to be pleading for a satisfactory answer, something that would make it okay to stay.

"I've thought about this a lot, too much," Lia responded.

I really want to address Keith's question and have a discussion about it, maybe for purely selfish reasons.

"I think it's a number of things. Let's be real; there's a lot of status and perks that come with a leadership position in corporate America, even when you're just starting out in the management ranks. When I tell folks where I work and my position, there's always a reaction. From Black people, it's surprise and pride, and I almost always get an encouraging word or outright pep talk. But when I tell white people, I get shocked silence or a tight smile and an 'oh' most of the time."

"I know exactly what you're talking about, and either way, it makes me feel good. I admit it. I'm proud of my title."

Lia continued. "It's also the perks. We get paid well, nice bonuses at the end of the year, or at least I hope that's the case for everyone, great benefits, the best training, business-class travel, car service, the Farm, Latimer House, and all the rest. I have the perfect story. We had an early snowstorm in Fielding last year in November. It was a Friday, and I was scheduled to fly down to Washington for the weekend to meet an old friend. Right after I got to the Merring County airport, it grounded all the flights and closed. It was packed, it was a zoo, as it usually is on any Friday night. People were frantic, standing in line for phones to try to call home, get to one of the larger New York airports, find a hotel room, or whatever. I simply walked back to my car in the parking lot and headed home. About halfway there, I knew the snow was coming down too hard to continue. I was only one turnoff from Conallied, and I turned off there and went to Latimer House. I checked into a room, had a nice meal, and went to bed. I was very aware of my privilege that evening as an Conallied executive, and I really liked my access to everything Latimer House offered. The snow had stopped when I woke up in the morning, I scraped off my car, and drove home."

"Latimer House is nice; I've only stayed there once," Mark said. I think another hard fact is that we are the first generation of African-Americans where all of this is available to us. We are desperate not to fail. Maybe I should only speak for myself . . ."

"No," Jules interrupted him. "Desperation is a good word."

Mark continued. We are finally at a time in history where a few of us can squeak through and be in the management ranks of corporate America, and only a very few at the highest levels, and we don't want to disappoint or blow it. It's a lot of pressure. We put it on ourselves, but there's also external pressure especially from family, but also from friends and professional colleagues. I suppose there are white guys who feel the same way, but it has long been an expectation of them, whether they came from poor or more well-to-do families. For African-Americans, our families never thought this would ever be a possibility for us, and now that it is, the pressure can be brutal. It's all a crazy, mixed bag of angst."

Someone else is feeling the word "angst" too.

"We've all worked very hard to get where we are, and I think you'd all agree with me that we've earned whatever stature we have in Conallied because it has been hard earned, and we've paid an emotional price for it." Doris couldn't hide from us that this was a deeply personal statement for her to make."

Josh responded. "Let's face it. Conallied is no better or no worse than any other big corporation. This is America's problem, not necessarily just Conallied's."

Well, that's a good, logical answer, but it sure doesn't provide much comfort.

"Hey folks, wait a minute. Are we really just a bunch of whiners?" Lia put the question on the table again.

Cecelia stood up and leaned forward across the table, hands on her hips. "Lia, honey, let me tell you this much. The women in this company view you as just about the last person who would be caught whining."

"Well that's nice of you to say, but I think I do a lot of whining in my head," Lia responded. The whole situation makes me want to scream sometimes."

Lance's tone was very firm. "I'll say this; if we ever, at any time, whine in their presence, or lose control of our emotions, we can forget it. In this company, emotion means you can't handle the situation, you don't have control. Get emotional and you're out of here."

"We are not whiners. We are just the opposite." Mark responded, stood up, and walked around the table as though he was about to make a speech. He drained the glass of beer he had in his hand, set it down, and dug his hands into his pants pockets again. He was illuminated by the moonlight, and it made him look even taller.

"Uh oh," laughed Eddie, "I feel a sermon coming on."

"Speak brother!" Doris encouraged Mark.

Mark continued. "I think the fact that we're meeting here as Conallied's African-American leaders, that we're successful in our careers while dealing with this hostile environment, that we still have some measure of loyalty to the company in spite of it all, and that we have sat here tonight for hours nurturing each other, speaks exceedingly well for all of us. I will state unequivocally that we certainly are not whiners and, in fact, we're a damned strong group and I'm damned proud of all of us. We are survivors, and that, my friends, is our victory."

"Amen!" Josh said. "Do you guys know it's after midnight?"

"Thank you, one and all," Cecelia bowed deeply from the waist in an exaggerated gesture. "I don't know about the rest of you guys, but this day has done me a world of good. Sometimes I think I can't make it, but now I feel like I can."

Thank you, Cecelia my friend, for saying that out loud.

Lia smiled in appreciation at Cecelia for openly expressing what she had been thinking. Lia realized that, although her own style was to keep her true feelings inside and not appear vulnerable, she had shared a lot this evening. Cecelia's statement gave her another opening.

"Hey, me too. I really needed this day, more so than I realized. This was a good day of fellowship for me, professionally and personally, and it was just what I needed, too. It was good for my soul."

"This was a nice respite for all of us, even me." Everyone halted the activity of gathering personal items and looked at Lance with expectation.

"Look, we all needed this. We're scattered all over the country. Even those of us who work in the same Division rarely see or talk to one another. I know the isolation is hard to deal with. But, we're about to do something important; it's going to be viewed as revolutionary by some. Let's draw energy from one another and use it to go out and play the game, their game. Let's just be sure we play it harder and smarter."

"We'll all see one another again this fall; hang in there folks." Keith wrapped it up as he slid open the gazebo door.

I'm exhausted, but I could sit here and draw strength from my colleagues all night.

They exchanged handshakes and some hugs and kisses, and left the gazebo. They walked across the lawn together, through the deserted dining room, and headed for their rooms. Cecelia, Doris and Lia huddled when they got to the lobby, promised to communicate more often, and said good night.

ξ

Lia slept in late the next morning, and she didn't see anyone else in the group when she checked out at noon. The group experience had been special, and Lia felt she had been given sustenance to continue her fight, the good fight. As Lia's car drove away, she rolled down the windows on both sides in the back and let the midday sun bathe her. The radio was playing Ray Charles, and as he seemingly had done forever, mellowed her mood. The light and warmth completed the nurturing process.

ξ CHAPTER 7 ξ

I'm not going to try to organize a meeting with all the branch managers. It's just going to be an exercise in futility, especially with Gunther in the room. They'll be too intimidated to fully participate and openly speak their minds. Now that I think about it, Gunther probably wouldn't show up anyway. It doesn't matter that his boss has scheduled the meeting, since he doesn't acknowledge me as his boss. Or, he may show up just to ensure that nothing gets done no matter how I present it. He can get away with this attitude, and he knows it. I'd fire him, too, but it would only backfire on me. At this point, I think I'm better off avoiding the stress and not putting myself through running in circles trying to turn a tense meeting into an upbeat, congenial gathering. But, really, it does feel like a cop-out. Listen to yourself, Lia. Stick by your decision. So many positive things are happening, and you should focus only on them. I'll use the upcoming presentation to Dan and his staff to justify the initiatives my staff and I have put in motion. The branch managers will have to be there, and they can hear it for themselves. They don't dare disrespect Dan by not showing up. I'm sure their techs have given them at least some positive feedback, but none of it has been passed along to me. It doesn't matter; my team has some great early results to report. And, I haven't gotten any more telephone calls from anyone expressing concern about how the teams are working together.

"Your staff is in the conference room waiting for you." Sara interrupted Lia's internal conversation with herself, laid a stack mail and messages on Lia's desk, and then smiled.

"They also asked me to tell you to keep an open mind."

"About what?"

"I don't know what they're up to."

"Uh oh," said Lia, "I'd better get in there."

Lia walked around the corner to the conference room.

"Why are all the blinds closed?" she asked immediately and began opening the blinds around the room.

"We hadn't noticed they were closed," Marva replied, smiling.

"Now, isn't that much better; the natural light is great, and doesn't the sun feel good?"

"Yes, Lia." All six of them replied in unison and then burst into laughter. It occurred to Lia then that they had closed all the blinds in the room.

"If you guys want me to keep an open mind, you've got to stop laughing at me."

Lia enjoyed the good-natured exchange and appreciated the growing comfort they had with one another.

Any impact Lucas Mayhew's past influence may have had on any of them seems to be gone.

"We've put together the first draft of the presentation for you to review. The charts look great, especially the financials." Jerome was excited as he started the meeting.

"The associates and technicians have done a fantastic job and they're still rolling. I've put together two very simple charts showing the real dollar savings that we have gotten as a result of the productivity improvements made by streamlining many of our processes. We can show the increase in customer call response times, time spent by associates on the telephone, and the techs in customer homes. We can show almost $70K in savings now and comfortably project $195K by the end of the second quarter, all of which should fall right to the bottom line revenue. With the work everyone is doing now, and additional process initiatives that they have identified for the short- and long-term, we should see a very nice cumulative effect each month. If we extrapolate that number over the balance of the year, we may even get to the $500K that Castle wants, as optimistically crazy as that sounds."

"Great! Jerome, you're wonderful. Your charts are perfect; simple, visual and easy to digest," Lia responded. "What about the details of the specific process improvements"?

Gordon spoke up. "That's covered on the first four pages; we think you'll like it. We'll talk about the rationale for how the teams were formed, so no one will question how those decisions were made, and then highlight a couple of the early process improvements that have produced good results. With your blessing, associates can now directly authorize a technician's repair estimate up to two hundred and fifty dollars; this will allow them to reduce authorization wait time by a whopping sixty-five percent and to increase their answer rate by twenty percent because they don't have to make the authorization call to the branch offices, and they wait for someone to call back, which happens a lot of the time. The customers love it, so we'll make a particular point to emphasize customer satisfaction. And, associates can now requisition a part right from the plant and have it sent directly to the agent in the field rather than to the branch office; this will avoid someone having to drive or mail the part to the agent or the agent having to drive in, sometimes over a hundred miles, to get it. It has already increased agent productivity by close to twenty percent. They had set twenty percent as a year-end goal; hell, by year end they'll be at the thirty percent productivity".

I knew this could happen, and still I'm amazed.

"You know Carla Mariucci, one of the associates in my department. She worked with me to develop a simple online format to track movement of the parts inventory from the plant to the field, so the associates can advise callers about availability right away and the techs know that they'll have the parts locally that match their appointment list each day. Not everyone understands that we don't manufacture every part for every product here in Levale; we outsource a lot of it. Believe it or not, Virginia's group doesn't have anything we can use; they only track parts from the vendor to the plant here in Levale. This eliminates each branch office having to track it, which they were doing manually, believe it or not. We now have one national report that will be copied to each of the branch managers every month so they are better aware of the flow to their regions. Unaccounted-for parts inventory has been one of EPD's biggest expenses. Hopefully, after the presentation, we can pull in Virginia's staff to work with us."

Oh God, Virginia's going to love us talking about a process that she should have already refined. Well, this was the result of the team's good work; I didn't send them in this direction. And, it will help everybody.

"We need to promote Carla to senior associate soon," commented Gerard. "She's so bright and works very hard; we've really underutilized her in the past."

"Not any more." laughed Gordon.

"I want all of you to keep an eye on associates we should promote. Nothing will keep them more energized and motivated than to see that there really are opportunities to shine here."

"Music to my ears," the usually even-tempered Gerard had emotion in his voice.

"Great!" Lia leaned in, rested her elbows on the table and spread her hands flat on the table to emphasize the point. "Let's highlight those improvements, but we've got three or four others we want to be sure to talk about."

The group spent two hours reviewing the six-page presentation in detail, making revisions and corrections and wordsmithing to highlight the positive impact not only for Consumer Services, but also for the Division as a whole. Lia wanted the underlying message to support empowering the associates and technicians although the political importance of the presentation was critical to her, too.

"Lia, how about inviting one associate and one agent to participate in the presentation. It's a nice touch and it adds credibility; not just Lia and her staff bragging."

Gerard's suggestion is right on target; bless him.

"Let's do it. After all, the associates and technicians are the folks doing the work in the trenches," Lia answered.

"Has a date been scheduled yet?" Carl asked.

"Dan's secretary, Valerie, called me and indicated that she could carve out an hour on the agenda at his next staff meeting, which is already scheduled for week after next. Two hours is not possible but, on second thought, an hour is better for our purposes. We'll be upbeat and very focused. She's going to call me back to confirm."

"I think we should invite Frances and Dick to represent the associates and agents who have worked on the initiatives. They're both articulate and energized; I've spent a lot of time with them and they'll be great." Marva had sat in on every associate-technician session, and Lia trusted her judgment.

"Who else will participate," Ben asked.

"I want all of you there. I'll open and close the presentation, but I want each of you, plus Frances and Dick, to deliver the meat of the presentation. We want it to go smoothly without a hitch, so let's run through it a couple of times in advance."

As Lia walked back to her office, Sara was just hanging up the telephone.

"That was Valerie. You guys are confirmed for one hour at Castle's staff meeting on the 20th. You'll be the last item on the agenda."

Lia was not worried about being last on the agenda; Dan was very rigid about his scheduling, and everyone was intimidated into staying within their allotted time. Lia wanted his agenda to end with a bang.

ξ

The presentation was a home run, a grand slam. The staff meeting had been long and tense, almost totally focused on EPD's financial situation and the progress being made by Dan's staff to meet their new cost reduction and revenue goals. The results were mixed around the table, and efforts to justify why goals could not be met generated some unpleasant exchanges. To Lia's amazement, there was little or no discussion during the meeting about any of the critical customer service issues and their direct connection to the financial results. When Dan asked Lia for a report, she responded that her progress would be covered in the presentation later in the meeting. No one visibly reacted.

They took a quick break while Lia's staff and Frances and Dick joined the group. The presentation had been set up on slides, and a full color photocopy was passed out to Dan and his staff, all the branch managers who only periodically attended staff meetings in Levale, and other staff who reported to various members of Dan's staff who had been included in the meetings.

Here we go.

Lia stood at the end of the long conference table opposite where Dan was seated. Her staff was standing to the side and a bit behind her. She began by stating that they would be happy to answer questions at the conclusion of the presentation, then summarized the initiative and its key elements: enhanced consumer service, cost savings generated process improvements developed by the joint efforts of the agents and associates, revenue gains realized through productivity, and the impact of employee empowerment. Lia made sure she talked about her road trip and underscored the fact that the process teams idea had been discussed in advance with the branch managers and many of the technicians during her visits. Then, her staff stepped forward, and Lia stepped back. Frances, one of the star associates in Levale lightly touched Lia's arm when they shifted places and mouthed "here we go" in Lia's direction.

They went through the first four pages of the presentation, highlighting the specific process improvements. Frances and Dick, who were overdressed in their Sunday best, actively participated, and they were terrific. They were both a little nervous being in front of Castle's staff, but their energy about the work they had done, and the customer service issues they were planning to tackle in the future, came through powerfully.

"I've never done this kind of thing before, but I hope I was able to demonstrate how excited we are about the way we are working." Dick made the statement and then stepped back nervously and glanced at Lia. She smiled at him.

Jerome wrapped up by going through the two pages of financial charts showing the costs savings and revenue generated by the initiative thus far and projections for the rest of the year. He had done a nice job with the graphics, and the projected savings were effectively highlighted; the revenue and costs savings stood out like a neon sign. Lia's wrap-up was brief.

"Well," the first comment came from Dan. "I want Jud to see this presentation. What can we do to accelerate the initiatives you've started?"

Yes!

Lia responded, "Dan, we have to step up coordination with the regional branches to ensure that they have adequate coverage and can control travel costs so their people can actively participate."

"Aren't the numbers Jerome showed us net of all related expenses?"

"Yes, they are, and we plan to monitor them closely."

"Then, if we can continue to get savings like this, let's not lose any sleep over a few extra dollars in travel costs."

"Lia, right now all the technicians are buzzing about the meetings that have taken place. Do you think we can sustain their energy at this level throughout the year?" Phil Barnes, the Jacksonville branch manager, raised the question and Lia thought it was a good one.

"May I answer that question," Dick asked. His confidence was in high gear now.

"Sure," Lia responded.

"The technicians and associates who have participated so far have gotten to know each other much, much better; we're beginning to be a real team all across the country. And, we're all excited about it. I think the primary reason is that the process improvement work is making all our lives easier. We're streamlining and improving service delivery and can already see that customers are much happier. If our work saves money and increases revenue, that's great too. We all want to keep the Division healthy so we can keep our jobs. If I may be frank, we don't always feel that you folks completely appreciate the value of customer satisfaction because you don't have day-to-day interaction with them. We do. The task force wants to continuously expand to include more technicians who are energized about this and are really focused on the customer."

Hooray for Dick!

"We think it's possible to make the customer happy and make money too. Lia keeps preaching that to us, and we believe it." Frances added the comment, and her voice was strong.

They both said it better than I could have. It sounds more authentic coming from them.

"So far, the process improvements have been easy to go along with and relatively easy to implement. What happens when it gets more difficult?" Don Harmon had asked a sensitive question in a non-threatening way.

"Thanks for your question, Don. I have been so pleased with the logic and common sense the participants have used thus far, and I think they will continue to do well. If they do recommend something that radically changes how we deliver service or requires a significant expenditure of funds, I'd like to get the branch managers, and whoever else may be appropriate, on a conference call and make a decision. We don't want to be the ones to bog them down."

"My understanding is that a small group from the full task force wants to informally report to all of us periodically, maybe by conference call." Glen Casey, Memphis branch manager, pointed out.

Thanks for the softball, Glen.

"Yes, that's true," Lia answered. "And, we'll try to keep the number of conference calls to a minimum; we know everyone is very busy."

"Sounds great," Glen responded.

Dan jumped in again. "Let's keep this ball rolling. The dollars speak for themselves. It's been a long day guys; let's wrap it up."

Most of the staff did not ask any questions, which was not particularly surprising to Lia. She decided not to let silence from Gunther or Virginia worry her. She didn't want to imagine intrigue where none existed, at least not on this day. Dan said he wanted Jud Jeffries to see the presentation, and he wouldn't do that unless he was impressed by it and could reap positive benefits from it. Lia assumed it would be positive for her, as well.

Lia's spirits were high as she drove home. She didn't have to fumble through her cassettes. Whitney Houston delivered the goods as soon as Lia turned on the radio, singing *I'm Every Woman*, Chaka Khan's old hit.

ξ

Sara interrupted Lia just as she had settled in and focused on writing an unsolicited follow-up report to Dan. She planned to summarize, in writing this time, her road trip to the regional branch offices, the feedback she had gotten, and also include a narrative, along with the graphics included in the staff presentation. She was furiously banging out the first draft and talking out loud to herself.

This is a blatantly political report. I'll own up to it right now and save myself from questioning my motives. It will provide Dan with more documentation of the ongoing, successful initiatives that he can use if he wants to.

"You have a call from a Dana Jenkins; she says she is an old friend. Apparently, she was given the plant's main number, and the call came in to my desk."

"Oh, my goodness, Dana. Transfer the call to my line." Lia had not spoken with her old friend in over two years, now that she thought about it. Lia and Dana had been friends since the very first day of high school. Their group of friends, five of them, had hung together in a tight circle as part of a small minority of African-Americans in an all-white high school they were forced to attend when the school district boundaries changed during the summer after junior high school, and their friendship continued into adulthood, marriage and parenthood. All, except Lia.

"Dana Jenkins! Girl, how are you? It's been way too long."

"Your mother still has the same phone number. I called her to get your number. She brought me up to date on where you are and gave me your home and work numbers. I left a message on your home phone; I think your Mom had it confused with your work number, and I ended up calling information to get the main number."

"I'm so glad you tracked me down."

"Lia, it's good to hear your voice, too, but I'm calling with sad news. Gracie passed away last night."

ξ

September 1955

"What kind of sandwich is that? Why is it on that brown bread?"

Lia looked up from her sandwich into the face of a dark-skin girl with a wide smile and long ponytail that Lia instantly envied.

"It's wheat bread," Lia answered weakly. "My mother fixes my sandwiches."

"Only white people eat brown bread," the girl said with a toss of her head, and walked away with two other girls who had stood silently on each side of the dark-skin girl and mimicked her every gesture. Lia looked at the unknown white girl sitting next to her.

"That's Gracie," she offered to Lia without the question being asked.

Lia looked down at her bologna and cheese sandwich, thought about putting it back in her lunch box, but continued eating instead. It was the first day of the third grade in a new school. After her teacher, Mrs. Lee, introduced the three new students in Room 6, no one said a word to Lia. When the class was let out for lunch, she found a seat on a bench in the far corner of the schoolyard and sat next to a tiny, frail-looking girl who was also in Room 6. They did not speak at all until Gracie walked away, and they did not speak again after the girl revealed Gracie's name. Seven-year old Lia was not sure she was going to like the new school, but she felt she had to try hard because her parents had moved the family into a new house a month earlier. Even at seven, Lia knew her parents were very happy to move from the projects to a house in an all-white neighborhood because they talked about it all the time with family and friends. Lia liked the house, too, and had fun fixing up the small bedroom in pastel pink and green that she shared with her younger sister.

On the second day of school, Gracie sat down next to Lia on the same bench that Lia had chosen the day before. They had the same Superwoman lunch box.

"Hi! What kind of name is Lia?" Without waiting for a response, "My name is Gracie, Grace really. My father calls me 'amazing Grace." Again, without waiting for a response, she went on.

"You want a piece of my tuna sandwich?" Gracie held out a sandwich with two, thick slices of white bread stuffed full of tuna salad.

"No, thanks," Lia answered with as much energy as she could muster under Gracie's intent stare.

"Okay, keep eating that nasty brown bread. You want to play jump rope after we eat?"

That invitation was the beginning of the circle of friendship that remained intact for Lia until she left California in search of success as she had defined it.

ξ

"Oh my God, I didn't even know Gracie was sick."

I didn't know anything. I don't know anything. How could one of my oldest and best friends be sick and now dead, and I don't know about it. God, this is too awful.

"Gracie was diagnosed with liver cancer only seven months ago. She had been suffering from bad back pain for months and had gone though all kinds of medications and treatments. The pain only got worse and, finally, she got mad. Really, it was George who got mad and went ballistic on the doctors and demanded a CAT scan and then an MRI.

George has loved Gracie since the 11th grade.

"The doctors were treating the symptoms and not the cause, and they treated the symptoms too long. The MRI showed some spots on her liver, and now, seven months later, Gracie is dead. George is a mess; Georgie and Gina came home last week, so they're here. I feel so sorry for Mrs. Baker; she's still living, you know. She's lost her husband and now her daughter."

All these months, I didn't have a clue. I haven't talked to anyone in such a long time. Too long.

"Lia, I knew you would want to know."

Well, of course, I want to know!

"Dana, I'm shaking. Gracie, my friend." Lia tried to stifle a sob, but it escaped.

"I know; we're all devastated. I think Gracie's death has shaken all of us much more than we anticipated. You know she was our core, our compass, our sense of humor. At the end, she was in pain that I can't even begin to comprehend, but I saw her three days ago at the house, propped up in a chair, very weak, cracking jokes."

"That's our Gracie," Lia whispered into the phone. It was all she could manage to say.

Our Gracie; I can't believe I didn't know she was sick. No one called me to let me know she was sick. They didn't think to call me early on so maybe I could come to see Gracie. Why would they? I haven't called anybody. Dana had to track me down.

"They're working on the funeral arrangements. It looks like the service will be on Friday; I'll call you back with the details."

"I'll be there. I'll make reservations on a Thursday evening flight."

"Are you going to stay with your parents?"

"Yes, probably."

I haven't seen them either; it's been over a year. Maybe I can see Ruthie, too. What am I doing? Why haven't I seen, or even called, the people who love me? Why do I care more about people who would like to see me fall off a cliff?

"It's good to talk to you, Lia; it's been way too long." Now it was Dana's voice that cracked.

"How have you been doing?" Lia asked.

"I'm fine, just struggling over Gracie. I talked with Gregory last night. He'll be there on Friday."

"How's he doing? What's he up to?"

"He's good; you know Gregory is always going to be okay; he loves Southern California, the whole Hollywood scene. He actually lives in the Hollywood hills."

I'm probably the last to know about Gracie's death. Maybe I deserve to be the last to know.

"Dana, I'll see you at the end of the week."

ξ

After staring out of her office window for a while, Lia picked up the phone and called Dan. Valerie, his secretary, answered.

"Hey, Lia. Dan's out of the office; he's spending the day at his kids' school."

Lia took a deep breath in a struggle to keep her voice even.

Why don't I want her to know that I am going though something emotional?

"I just wanted to let him know that I won't be around for a few days at the end of the week. You know how he likes us to be on call 24/7. One of my oldest friends passed away last night, and I have to travel to California for the funeral."

"Oh, I'm so sorry, Lia. Was your friend ill"?

"Yes, she had been ill for several months."

"I know how hard it is when a friend or a family member is dying; I can imagine it's been difficult for you with everything else you have on your plate. I've been through it. You take care of yourself."

ξ

"Mama, hi."

"Hi honey." Dana called me yesterday looking for you. She told me about Gracie, poor Gracie. You know how I always felt about her. Have you talked to George?"

She remembered George's name. Why wouldn't she; we all hung out at the house when we were kids, teenagers, practically into adulthood.

"No, I thought I would wait until I see him on Friday. Dana told me he's a mess right now, and he's surrounded by family. I'm going to fly in late tomorrow night, and I thought I would just stay with you and Daddy for a couple of days."

"I should go to Gracie's service, but it's so hard for me to get around now with this arthritis. It will be nice to have you here. How long has it been since you've been here? Over two years, I think. Your daddy really misses you. You know, your old room is still the same although we keep saying we're going to convert it to a TV room.

Time to go home. It took a death.

"Should your daddy pick you up at the airport?"

"No, I'm going to rent a car. When's the last time you talked to Ruthie? I'd love to drive down to Monterey to see her, maybe on Saturday."

Ruthie is probably just the person I need to talk with right now.

Ruthie, her father's younger sister by seventeen years, was not only Lia's favorite aunt, but also probably her favorite person in the world.

"Ruthie's doing real good. She and Dalton are at a conference in London. She called us the day before they left to let us know where they would be. She said they were going to try to take a quick trip to Paris for a few days afterwards since they would be so close."

I feel twice as bad now. I have too many things to feel bad about. Will I ever feel happy and content again?

"I'll get there very late; don't wait up. Believe it or not, I still have my key."

I have never really talked to Mama and Daddy at length about any-thing. They never quite knew what to do with a little girl who spent hours at a time closed up in her closet, sitting on the floor reading, and then talking about all the things she was going to do and places she was going to go. I spend all my time talking to people who don't give a rat's ass about me. Why do I do it? I wish I could see Ruthie. I wish I could see Gracie.

ξ

Gracie's funeral and burial were exactly what Lia anticipated. Short, both excruciatingly sad and humorous, and lovely. Sherri, the younger sister of Sharene, also one of Lia's oldest friends, sang with such beauty and emo-tion there wasn't a dry eye among those gathered to celebrate Gracie. A perfect reflection of Gracie.

When Lia walked into the church where she and her friends had spent so much time, in as many social activities as religious worship, the sight of the ivory-colored casket covered every inch by yellow roses, made her shake. She grabbed hold to the nearest pew as she felt her knees buckle. At that moment, she saw Dana, who was sitting near the front, wave at her. Lia also saw Sharene and Thea, their circle of friends, sitting in the same row.

There they all are.

Lia took a deep breath and made the way to her friends, acknowledg-ing with a nod the familiar faces she saw along the way.

God, the faces are all familiar, but I don't remember most of their names.

"We saved some room for you," Dana said, as Lia moved down the pew giving and receiving comforting hugs. Gregory sat next to Dana; Sharene's husband, Cornelius, who everyone called Corny, had his arm around her shoulder and was almost imperceptively rocking her side to side; Thea's new husband, Darryl, was gently patting her knee.

I am the only one who is alone. Who would come with me? Who am I connected to? My friends never knew Rob very well, and they've only seen Jordan four or five times in his life. So, here I am. C'mon, get a grip. Gracie is the one who is dead.

They all sat in the second row directly behind George, the kids and Gina's husband, and Gracie's mother. Other family members sat in the first row on the other side of the aisle. Lia touched George's shoulder, he turned around, smiled at her through teary eyes, and started to say something, but could not.

"We'll talk later," Lia said. "We're all right here, and we love you."

ξ

They were all scattered around the family room in Gracie and George's spacious home overlooking the under-appreciated delta side of the San Francisco Bay. Mrs. Baker, Gracie's mom, a tiny woman who had always seemed genuinely curious and interested in Lia's travels, had sat with them for a while, not saying much, but smiling at all of them with memories reflected behind eyes clouded with age and heartbreak. She then excused herself.

"I need to lay down; I'm so tired," she said in a low voice. Three of the men immediately leapt to her aid, and it was Corny who held her arm as she walked down the hall to the guest bedroom.

Lia could sense everyone was more relaxed now that they were here among close friends and family. The public ceremonial grieving process was done, the repast in the church activity hall, with an enormous amount of delicious and comforting soul food, prepared by Mrs. Baker's friends at the church, was done. Now they could just be with each other. George sat in his big, leather lounger looking through a thick photo album that had been filled over the years. That photo album was a fixture in their family room. The kids were sitting with their friends just outside by the pool.

"Young marrieds," Lia said, looking out at them.

We were all young marrieds when George and Gracie were the first to buy a house, and then they were so proud when they upgraded to this house and had the pool installed. There have been a lot of pool parties at this house. They were all young marrieds first. I was the last one to get married; then, I moved away and married Rob, outside of the group. I've been the absent one.

"The church ladies outdid themselves with the repast; I haven't had good old Southern cooking like that in a long time. Somebody really stepped in those greens and ham hocks. I have to beg for that kind of food now."

"Oh please, Darryl," Thea interrupted, "I still cook that kind of food sometimes."

"You women don't honor y'alls kitchens anymore." Darryl looked around the room at all of the women with a mischievous smile on his face. "A brother has to go down to Mabel's and get take-out soul food." Darryl's comment drew howls from the men and good-natured sneers from the women.

"Hey man, these women spend their time at salons, spas, and on cruises," Corny chipped in.

"Wait a minute; if anybody was trying to find one of you knuckleheads on a Saturday afternoon, they'd have to know where all the golf courses are, and as I recall, you boys had a hell of a good time on our last cruise."

"That was a great cruise; Mexico was a lot of fun last year, but nothing can top the Mediterranean cruise. I can't believe that was five years ago; I still think about it. We should go back to that part of the world someday."

"Brazil is next," Dana said. "Sharene and I are planning our little butts off. Carnivale in Rio sounds so exciting; I'm told that carnivale is spiritual and decadent at the same time. We've talked to folks who have been there, and we have so many suggestions for things to do; we're going to try not to wear out everyone. I'm so looking forward to taking in the Brazilian culture."

"I'm looking forward to taking in the culture, too," Corny said, as he outlined a woman's figure with his hands.

"Gracie was always talking about keeping her figure together so she could compete with the Brazilian beauties in their little bikinis." It was the first time George had said anything since they had arrived at the house and gathered in the family room.

Gracie was the prettiest one among us, always was; she had a great figure. Now I know she was down to eighty pounds. I have to believe that she is somewhere in a blessed existence; I've got to believe it.

"George, I know you're still going to travel with us, aren't you? You deserve it." Thea's comment was half command, half question.

George sighed, shrugged and became absorbed in the photo album again.

"Lia, you should come with us." Sharene's remark was drowned out when Corny laughed and said, "After all the christenings, birthday parties, scouting activities, baseball, football and basketball games, recitals, graduations, picnics, camping trips, pool parties -- have I forgotten anything -- we shared with our rug rats over the years, we deserve all the traveling we've done and are planning to do. We earned it."

"Lia has really traveled the world; girl, you've been everywhere. I'll bet you have racked up so many frequent flier miles that you'll never have to pay for an airline ticket again. Have you been to Brazil? We haven't seen you in so long; you should try to go with us."

Yes, I've traveled the world, prior to and since I went to work for Conallied. I've gone to an endless number of Conallied meetings, presentations, conferences and training classes around the world. I've had breakfast in London, lunch in Paris, dinner in Stockholm, vodka in St. Petersburg, sake in Tokyo, rode an elephant in India, stood trembling at the Cape of Good

Hope on the trip of a lifetime to South Africa, stood at The Wall in Berlin, climbed the ruins in Costa Rica, and damned near everywhere in between, but I didn't have these experiences with old friends, with people I'm connected to, people who care about me. Almost all of my experiences have been with people who I've tried to please and tried to like, and tried to be one of them, longed to be one of them, and I hate them, and all of it, and I hate myself.

Tears welled in Lia's eyes, and she battled to hold them back. Everyone would think she was welling up because of thoughts about Gracie. Today, it didn't matter.

Don't you dare cry. Gracie is dead and buried, George and their children are devastated, everybody is grieving, and you're going to sit here and cry about your life? They chose lives of stability with connections that are true. You're pathetic. Where are you now? In Levale, a big deal in Conallied's world, but of absolutely no consequence to the rest of the world, trying every day to cope with redneck white boys, trying to please white boys.

Lia realized Thea, and now Dana, too, was staring at her. She gave them a smile and a shrug.

"Brazil sounds like it's going to be a great trip. I'll let you know."

George isn't going; there's no way. I'm not going, not alone, when my friends will all have a spouse or boyfriend to share the experience, to love them. I have severed, or at least neglected, my ties to my home, my friends, relinquished my right to be comfortable in the world.

"So, are you dating anyone, Lia? How is Jordan? How's Rob doing; where is Rob? Do the two of you still talk?"

"Damn Thea, girl, is that enough questions?" Dana gently rebuked Thea, who had always asked everyone too many questions, even when they were young.

"Jordan is great; he's graduating next month. I can't believe we all have kids who are college graduates, and married, too. The years have gone by so quickly."

"None of us are grandmas yet, but that will change soon enough, though all of us are too young, and too fine, to be even thought of as grandmothers." Everyone chuckled at Sharene's remark, while nodding in agreement.

Thank you, Sharene, for taking the conversation in another direction. There was not much to say about Rob, and Lia was not up to talking about him. They only spent sporadic time with Rob during the first few years of our marriage, and they've seen Jordan grow up mostly through photos. Jordan barely remembers the few parties and camping trips we took when he was a very young boy.

All the men, except George, had wandered out to the pool area, and they were talking to the young folks. Glen leaned over and touched George's knee on his way out. Without a word, Dana got up and sat on the arm of George's chair. She put her arm around his shoulders and quietly laid her head on his shoulder. Wordlessly, each of the girls, the women, their unbreakable friendship group, went over to George and hugged him, or kissed him, or rubbed his arm, passed on their love for Gracie to the man who had loved her until death parted them.

"Gracie loved y'all so much," George choked out.

ξ

Much later, after Lia had returned to her parents' house, she sat with them for a long while over a cup of tea, and told them all about the services, recited who all were there, and brought them up to date on her friends and their children. Lia asked about her siblings.

"How's Rosalie and Henry? Where are they? I haven't talked to either of them in a long time. Henry did call me from Germany when he heard I had a new assignment and was moving from Fielding to Levale, and I called him back. We played phone tag for a week and never talked. But I know he wanted to send good wishes my way. Rosalie and I haven't talked in almost a year; she hasn't called me, but I haven't called her either, so I can't complain."

"Rosalie and Isaiah are going back and forth to Fresno all the time; Isaiah's mama is sick, diabetes and she's losing her eyesight. They'd move her up here, but she doesn't want to come. I can't say I blame her; nobody wants to leave their home. You know Isaiah is an only child, so it's all on him. Rosalie told me she and Isaiah finally want to start a family, but they don't want her to get pregnant with all this stress in their lives. So, we'll see. Jordan's a grown man, and he's our only grandchild. We haven't seen him since he graduated from high school; that's a shame, Lia."

"I don't see Jordan that often. Y'all know he's graduating in a few weeks. I'll talk to him; maybe the both of us can come out here together for a visit."

"That would be wonderful." Lia's father, who was a man of few words, surprised her with the soft, but clear emotion in his voice.

"Henry has only two months left on his post to Germany, then he thinks he will be posted to North Africa somewhere. I think he has a girlfriend, someone he met in Germany. That's all we know. I asked him how much longer he was going to stay in the Air Force, and he said he was thinking about it. He promised he'd come home for a visit before his new assignment begins.

I didn't do that before I moved to Levale.

"Send us a photo of Jordan on graduation day. You've got a jewel of a son."

"I know," Lia replied. "I'd better get to bed so I can get a few hours of sleep. I have an early-morning flight. I love y'all."

"You know we love you, too. Always."

Before getting into bed in her old room, which had not changed at all except for a stack of file boxes in the corner, Lia peeked into her old closet where she had spent so many hours. The closet was now only half filled with some of her father's clothes and her mother's collection of three long, formal dresses. It still had the little two-shelf unit that she had bought with birthday money from Ruthie where she stacked her books in alphabetical order by the author's last name. Only a pair of her father's old work boots sat on the bottom shelf. Lia climbed in the bed, sank into its cool comfort, and immediately fell asleep.

ξ

Before light the next morning, she roused her parents just enough to move around to each side of the bed to kiss them and say goodbye.

After she settled into her first-class seat on a 6:00 AM flight, she did not eat breakfast, couldn't quite get comfortable, and fell into a fitful sleep. She dreamed about Gracie. They were sitting together in an outdoor restaurant in the warm sun. Gracie got up to go the ladies room and didn't come back. Lia felt confused and anguished, and struggled not to panic as she frantically began looking for Gracie. She couldn't find her. She awoke with a start and glanced at her watch. They had only been airborne about an hour. Lia managed to stifle a sob, which she did not feel coming, without waking the passengers sitting close to her or drawing the attention of the flight attendant. Wailing out loud, that's what she longed to do.

I have to stop ending up crying on airplanes.

Lia changed per position and pulled the blanket up under her chin in an effort to comfort herself.

I came all the way to California and didn't get to see Ruthie; she is in London with her love, Dalton.

ξ CHAPTER 8 ξ

Lia and Wanda sat at a small table for two just to the right of the stage at Club Beale. Oscar had arranged in advance for the cover charge and drinks, and the waiter was attentive and amusing. The quartet was scheduled to begin their last set in ten minutes. Lia sat back and took in the quiet, easy ambiance of the club. In the fine tradition of jazz clubs, it was located in the basement of a downtown factory that had been redeveloped into shops and art galleries. To enter the club, they descended twelve steep stairs rather than ride down in the big, wooden freight elevator that Lia noticed was lined with posters. The club occupied a small space filled with maybe twenty dark wood tables of varying sizes, and the bar running along the back wall was lined with red, leather-upholstered stools. The obligatory autographed photos of various jazz greats almost entirely covered the walls. The bandstand rose about two feet from the floor and could barely accommodate a quartet of musicians and their instruments. The club offered two food items, a gigantic cheeseburger or chicken breast sandwich; both were served, according to the little menu placard on each table, with "the works." Both Lia and Wanda were on perpetual diets, so they decided to split a chicken sandwich. Lia liked the atmosphere and felt very comfortable.

"I like this place already. It feels so relaxing."

"I knew you'd like it." Wanda patted Lia's hand. "With all you've had going on, and Jordan's graduation coming, up, you need an evening to just chill out."

"You got that right! I am getting excited; my baby is actually about to become a college graduate. I can't believe its about to happen; it seems like he just left home, and it's been four years. It's nice to slow down, though, even if it's just for an evening. Speaking of slowing down, doesn't Oscar get tired between his responsibilities at school and pursuing his music? His schedule must be very busy, too."

"Yeah, he does. But he loves playing so much. I think if he were younger, he'd devote full time to it. He says he's gotten too comfortable now, but I think he still dreams of performing in places like the Blue Note in New York City."

"Well, speaking of hopes and dreams, I've got something for you to look at."

Lia reached into her purse and pulled out six pages stapled together and handed it to Wanda.

"This is an EPD request for proposal. It was posted today and sent out to our standard list of vendors. From what I understand, the Division wants to maintain the logo it's always had, of course, but Dan Castle wants the printed images to be modernized on all our products, packaging and paper. It sounds exciting; this could be a major big deal. I thought you might be interested."

Wanda quickly read through the document, looked up and smiled at Lia.

"Girl, thanks. This is just the kind of contract I'd love to get. I just need a chance to demonstrate my capabilities to a big company like Conallied. That's all I need, one really big client. It would pave the way for me to approach other big companies after that."

"Your business has always serviced small and medium sized firms. How would they feel about you taking on a big company? I would think some might be concerned that you will give priority to your big client and their needs will be neglected."

"I've thought about that a lot. Small firms have been my bread and butter from the beginning, and I don't intend to abandon them if I get one or two big ones. I will just have to restructure my business to serve all of them. That would be a nice challenge to have!"

"Yes, I suppose it would. Well, let me know if you need me to put in a good word to someone."

"I'll be up with the birds tomorrow working on the proposal and putting together a sample portfolio of my work. Lia, thanks again."

The waiter set down a small carafe of the wine they were drinking and the sandwich, which was served in a red plastic basket lined with waxed paper. Just then, Oscar and the other musicians in the quartet, all of them good looking and about fortyish, give or take a few years, entered from a side door and stepped up on the stage. "Oscar Four" sat at their instruments and went through their individual tuning and warming up exercises.

"God, Wanda, they're all good looking."

"You'll meet them later."

"That won't be hard to do!"

They settled down and turned their attention to the music.

ξ

Forty-five very nice minutes later, Oscar Four took a break. The four men filed out through the same door they entered, and the lights in the club were raised a bit. A few minutes later the four reappeared and came over to the table where Lia and Wanda sat. Wanda introduced Ellis, Johnny and Wayne.

I haven't been around this many Black men in a non-work social setting in so long, I can't remember how long. It feels good.

Johnny and Wayne joined in the chitchat for a few moments and then returned to the stage. Oscar and Ellis pulled some chairs over and sat down at their table.

This Ellis guy knows how to do the eye contact thing. He's got very nice, very piercing light brown eyes.

"Wanda has told me so much about you, Lia, I feel I already know you." Ellis looked directly into her eyes and did not drop his gaze.

"You're wonderful on the piano and the other keyboards. I've always admired the kind of gift you have; makes me regret that I didn't stick with my piano lessons when I was a girl."

"Wanda tells me you're kickin' ass regularly over at Conallied. I know several people who work at the plant; they've all been there for years. You all need to find a way to meet each other."

"I hope to be doing exactly that, soon I hope. A small group of us from around the country will be organizing the African-American employees in each Division to promote training and promotions."

I can't seem to look away, but neither can he.

Ellis Denny was a striking man with a soft voice. His wide, handsome face was open and earnest. He had very smooth, very light brown, almost white, skin, a full but neatly trimmed mustache that was practically all gray, and a thick head of softly curling, graying hair that was brushed back from an inexplicably receding hairline. He was not a particularly tall man, maybe around 5'10", but his presence was magnetic; an interesting combination of quiet intensity and laid back ease with himself. Lia sensed that he was very aware of his charm without flaunting it.

This man seems to be very comfortable in his skin.

Wanda, who was clearly crazy about Oscar, nevertheless saved some of her fawning for Ellis, too. She leaned into him as they talked, comfortable in the room he made in his personal space for her, and he lightly touched her on the arm and shoulder during their exchange. Ellis then touched Lia's hand and pulled her into his magnetic circle as he asked her if she was comfortable.

"I'm good." Lia asked, "What do you do during the day when you're not making beautiful music?"

"I'm a radio engineer." Ellis shifted his body toward Lia.

He smells good.

"What does a radio engineer do?"

"I work at WGAZ radio. I engineer a couple of the regular daytime programs and occasionally the Sunday evening jazz program. I handle timing, placement of commercials, maintain the equipment, and whatever else needs to be done to produce a good program. Keeps me out of trouble."

"It sounds interesting, and fun."

"It is, most of the time. I've been doing it for a long time. I also teach an occasional class at the community college."

Lia had thought for a moment that Ellis, like Oscar, was a full-time educator. His tweed jacket with suede patches on the elbows had given him a decidedly professorial look. She noticed that he performed with his jacket on, and she wondered how he could keep cool under the lights in the close quarters on stage. Oscar wore a light-colored linen shirt on stage, and the other two were similarly dressed lightly.

Maybe he's just too cool to perspire.

"I think the saxophone is my favorite instrument. All my favorites seem to be saxophonists. It's so soulful, and it's revealing. You play it beautifully."

"I'm appreciative of the gift. The gods smiled on me," Oscar replied, smiling.

"I think the gods often reveal themselves in music; it's one of the ways they allow us to feel what we can't always articulate."

"I like that sentiment very much." Ellis touched Lia's bare inner arm with just his forefinger and gently brushed it back and forth.

He's pretty forward. But, Jesus, it feels good. It's been a long time.

"It allows me to continue living out a dream even at my old age." Ellis' eyes played with Lia's while he spoke and she smiled at him.

What is it that he's revealing to me? Something? Nothing?

Oscar stood and put his hand on Ellis's shoulder, and the lights in the club dimmed.

"We've got to go ladies." He bent over and kissed Wanda on the cheek.

As he stepped up on the stage just a few feet from their table, Ellis looked over his shoulder at Lia.

"Enjoy."

I hope I'm not smiling too much.

ξ

Rob waved at Lia from across the wide lawn that was covered with hundreds of white wooden folding chairs. Rob was a tall, distinguished looking man, growing older very nicely with touches of gray at his temples and in his mustache. Lia assumed he had been working out and dieting because he looked more fit and trim than she'd ever seen him. Always a meticulous dresser, he looked particularly dapper in a navy blue suit, white shirt and red tie. They met in the middle, briefly embraced, and selected good seats just as the rows were starting to fill up.

"Hi there, how are you"? Rob kissed her on the cheek. "When did you get here?"

"I'm doing okay; got in late last night. I haven't even talked with Jordan. Can you believe that this day is finally here?"

"I haven't talked with him today, either. I got in a couple of hours ago. We're lucky that Jordan granted us dispensation from yesterday's endless social activities for parents. I can't believe this day is here, but I'm glad it is. I don't know what I'm going to do with my money now!"

"Oh, I'll figure out something to do with mine." Lia answered him laughing.

"I'm a very proud Mom. Jordan's been a good kid in spite of all the moving around we've done over the years and what's happened with us."

Rob crossed his long legs, revealing navy socks with the college's insignia, just small enough to be tasteful, at the ankle. "Lia, we just split up two years ago; we were always there for him, supporting and encouraging him."

Lia bit her tongue. This was not the time or place to point out to Rob that he had rarely been there for Jordan. But, Lia had to give him credit for regularly coming through with his half of Jordan's very expensive college tuition.

"You remember my friend, Gracie? She passed away recently; liver cancer. It was beyond sad."

"Yes, I remember her. A funny lady. I'm so sorry."

"Thanks. It's been hard."

"It's a great day. Wow, I know this sky makes you happy."

Rob was long used to Lia's preoccupation with the sky and used it to change the subject. It was a gorgeous day graced by a deep blue sky and brilliant sunshine; the kind of sun that most of the guests shaded from their eyes but Lia let it beam down on her. The stiff breeze kept a very warm day mild, and the burgundy and gold bunting that hung around the portable stage flapped briskly up and down. Lia was glad she didn't wear a hat; the women who did were having a hard time holding on to them.

The band started playing, and everyone's attention turned to the large area behind and to the left of the seating. Various faculty and staff in full regalia, with the graduating class assembled behind them, started the procession down the wide center aisle that separated the rows of chairs.

The burgundy tassels hanging from their caps danced in the breeze. The white, gold trimmed, graduation gowns they all wore billowed wildly in the wind and created the effect of a white, floating island with glitter around the edges. The whole scene appeared magical in the bright sunlight, and Lia's mood soared. The graduation speakers were inspiring; good schools were able to get great speakers. Lia was anxious, as she knew everyone else was, for the program to get to awarding the degrees. When the name Jordan Granger was called, Lia's heartbeat quickened. She and Rob looked at one another and smiled when he was named among the group graduating with honors. Jordan was a bit taller than Rob and just as handsome. He shared both their features, so he looked like himself, not too much of either Lia or Rob. Lia prided herself on raising a young man who was strong, sensitive and fiercely independent. He was a kid who had made it through high school and college fighting off girls from many backgrounds, including a few who wanted to get very serious. She was glad that he was able to maintain several close friendships with women, in addition to his male buddies, but Lia was relieved that he wanted to wait a while before making a serious commitment.

Jordan was a political science major, and it seemed to Lia that he was still wrestling with what he really wanted to do. He had mentioned graduate school once or twice, but had not pursued it yet. Lia never had any inclination at all to encourage him toward one career or another and felt no need to push him now. He had always been extremely gregarious and self-sufficient. Lia and Rob waved as Jordan left the stage and headed back to his seat. Jordan spotted them, held up his degree and gave the black power salute with the other hand. They both laughed; count on Jordan to do something to attract attention. The program ended with the usual cheering and tossing of the graduation caps high in the air. Lia and Rob worked their way through the crowd until they saw Jordan waving for their attention as classmates hugged and kissed him. Lia took out her camera.

"Well I did it, I'm done!" Jordan was exuberant as he hugged first Lia, then Rob.

"You guys stand there by the tree, let me get this snapshot". Lia marveled at the two of them standing together as men.

"Okay, now I'll get a picture of you and your mother," Rob said to Jordan.

Lia and Jordan posed by the tree with his arm around her shoulder; he towered over Lia. It occurred to her, for the first time really, that her son had truly grown up. Jordan introduced them to several friends, one of whom volunteered to snap a picture of the three of them. Standing there between them, Lia felt a nice sense of accomplishment. There were no longer any lingering feelings toward Rob, and she chalked it up as a good thing.

"Your mother and I would still like to take you to an early dinner; remember we talked about it last week? I made a reservation at LaBelle. Have you made any plans with your friends"?

"Not until later this evening. A bunch of us are going out. And, Kayla Harrison has invited a few of us to spend the long weekend at her parents' place on Cape Cod. We're going to drive up tomorrow. Our last fling before we face the real world. I've got to go back to the dorm to turn in this cap and gown and put the last few things in my car. Why don't I meet you guys at the restaurant. I'm looking forward to dinner; poor college students can't afford to eat at LaBelle!"

Lia and Rob drove separate rental cars to the restaurant. They sat in the bar and ordered drinks. The dark, quiet atmosphere was just the opposite of the bright, noisy celebration they had just left.

"I've decided to run for that county council seat; remember I mentioned it to you a while back?" Rob made his announcement just after their drinks had been served and the waiter quietly moved away. Politics had long been his avocation, so Lia was not at all surprised about his decision.

"That's great, Rob. Do you think you can win?"

"Well, I wouldn't run if I didn't think I could win, and do some good. Money is the issue; it always is. We've already had two, small fundraisers that were pretty successful. I've opened a small campaign office in Fielding on Lowe Street. I have one, part-time staff person, Laurie, at this point, but I've also got several good volunteers lined up to do some of the early work. Guess what? Caroline Devore is going to host a fundraising reception for me at her little abode."

Caroline Devore was one of the community's social butterflies and had a lot of political clout via her late husband. She lived in a gorgeous mansion that was more than a hundred years old. Hosting a reception for an African-American candidate at the Devore estate would make for an interesting event. Lia almost wished she could attend just to people watch.

"Well, la de da," teased Lia. "You've got the temperament for politics; it would drive me crazy."

Rob laughed. "You could never put up with any of the bullshit, and there's plenty of it. I know you have it in your corporate world, too, but in the public arena, it gets pretty damned crazy, a different, more visible kind of crazy. Let's face it, the folks who have the power, and those who are after it, create a lot of shit."

I've surely got my share of shit, too.

Jordan entered the lounge and walked over to them. He looked mature and drop-dead handsome in his blue blazer and tan wool slacks. Lia secretly hoped he wouldn't overdo the "buppie" thing, though he certainly looked the part.

"The maitre'd says our table is ready."

They left the bar and were escorted to their table. As soon as they sat down, Jordan made his announcement.

"Mom, I won't be coming to Levale this summer like we discussed a while back. I'm going to stay with Dad and work on his campaign staff. I won't make very much money. . ."

"You got that right," Rob interrupted.

"After the election in November, I'll make a firm decision about what I want to do and dive into the job market."

Both Jordan and Rob looked at Lia, waiting for her reaction. She was surprised at their attitude. They clearly expected her to be angry, or sad, or something. Actually, Lia was quite pleased. Rob and Jordan had never been particularly close; she and Jordan has always been a team of two. Lia never doubted that Rob loved Jordan, but he was always too busy becoming a success to give much time to his son. She had carried almost all of the child-rearing load and managed to advance her career at the same time. Lia supposed Jordan was maybe feeling this was a major moment for cutting the apron strings.

"I think that's wonderful. You and your Dad have never worked together. You guys should have a great summer and fall together. I'm sure the political game will be a real education for you. You can come to Levale at any time. Ultimately, you never know where the perfect job opportunity will be. But you know wherever I am is home, and you'll always have a room ready."

Lia, you're a great mom." Jordan loved calling Lia by her first name at special moments like this. He had done it since he was a little boy.

Rob didn't say anything; he was intuitive enough to let the moment pass between Jordan and Lia.

"One more thing", Jordan continued. "I want to formally and officially thank both of you for my college education. I know it cost a fortune, and I did my best to get the highest grades I could. I'm twenty-two years old and beginning to really appreciate my parents in an adult way."

"Well, will wonders never cease!" Lia put her hand across Jordan's forehead in a mocking move to check for a fever. All three of them laughed.

They had a very nice dinner and talked about Rob's impending campaign and Lia's job at EPD. She didn't talk about her challenges at EPD; this was Jordan's day.

"I'm pretty sure I'll eventually want to go to graduate school, but I want to spend some time in the real world first and earn some money."

"I think you're doing the right thing," Lia said. "Just don't let the real world bite you; it tries to do that sometimes."

They finished dessert and coffee, and let Jordan off the hook so that he could join his friends. He hugged them both.

"Try not to do too much damage tonight, or on Cape Cod," Lia admonished jokingly.

"Dad, I'll see you next Tuesday; Mom, I'll call you. Both of you have safe travels."

He was gone. Rob paid the bill and walked Lia to her car.

"Well," Lia sighed, "we've done our duty and he's his own man now. I've got to run; my plane takes off in a couple of hours. Good luck with the campaign. Give 'em hell."

"My flight is later tonight. Good luck to you, too. Hang in there, and don't let the bad guys get you." Rob kissed Lia on the forehead and was gone.

As Lia drove to the airport, the bright, clear day made for a lovely twilight, her favorite time of day. Stars twinkled in a sky that was still light. They helped her tremendously.

This was a lovely day, a great day. But, I feel empty.

ξ

June 1965

Lia's high school graduation took place on a Thursday. On Friday night, her mother cooked a huge dinner and invited the extended family over to celebrate her oldest child's graduation, and with honors, too. Lia enjoyed the big crowd in the house; the abundance of good soul food, the staple of every good celebration, kept them there until very late in the evening. On Saturday night, Lia was invited to a graduation party hosted by one of her white classmates. Barb McIntyre lived only a few miles from Lia, but her neighborhood was a giant leap up the ladder from Lia's working-class neighborhood. The invitation surprised Lia, but it never occurred to her not to accept. She and Barb always liked one another and talked a lot in classes they had taken together, but had never hung out as friends. White kids hung out with white kids; colored kids hung out with colored kids. There were no real problems between the groups; it's just the way it was. Lia wore her best dress and spent a lot of time on her hair and the little makeup she wore. She didn't want to be the first one there, so her father dropped her off in front of Barb's house at twenty minutes after seven. He let out a long, low whistle as he pulled their station wagon into the circular driveway.

"Look at this place; these white folks got everything. Now, Lia, you look real nice. I know that you know your manners. Ain't no big deal just because it's white people in a big house. I'll pick you up at eleven o'clock. If anything changes, you find a phone and call me right away."

Lia jumped out of the car and walked up the long path to the door. She was more curious than nervous as she rang the bell. Barb answered the door.

"Lia!" I'm really glad you came. Come on in. You look fab." "Fab," a word Black kids would never use. Lia was introduced to Barb's parents, who were hovering in the corner of the gigantic foyer of the house. They looked like nice people. Barb's mother shook her hand; her father just smiled stiffly.

"Hello Lia. It's very nice to meet you. Barb has told us many times how much she likes you and what a smart girl you are. Your parents must be very proud of you."

"Thank you, it's nice to meet you too." Lia relaxed.

"Lia, let's go in the recreation room; that's where everybody is".

Barb grabbed her hand and led her to the right side of the foyer and down four carpeted stairs. The room was huge, furnished with three brown leather sofas and a variety of chairs. The far wall was all sliding glass doors that led out to a large patio. The doors were closed because it was a chilly night for mid-June. A wall-length bar was on one side of the room and was partially covered with at least a hundred soft drink bottles, glasses and ice. A pool table sat in one corner of the room, and a big, brightly lit jukebox in the other corner was blaring music. Lia couldn't believe that someone would have a jukebox right in their house. A long table had been set up next to the bar, and it was covered with food. Kids were eating and talking, and a few were dancing. One guy was at the pool table hitting balls. Lia recognized most of the faces, but didn't know everyone in the room by name.

"Hi Lia," "Glad you came Lia," and similar greetings from around the room welcomed her. She was surprised that they all seemed to know her. She returned the greeting to several of the kids, and Barb introduced her to a few that she had never met. Lia felt relieved that her peach satin dress looked just as nice, or nicer, than most of the other girls' dresses.

"Grab a plate, and get some food; my mom went overboard as usual."

Lia went over to the table and picked up a real china plate. She had expected hot dogs and hamburgers. There were more than twenty different kinds of foods, most of which Lia had never tasted before. She had eaten the little hot dogs, Swedish meatballs and few different cheeses before. The barbecued shrimp on skewers, scallops wrapped in bacon, chicken salad piled on miniature rolls, some sort of Chinese dumpling filled with meat, and a big hunk of really rare roast beef and a huge roasted turkey sitting upright, being sliced by a small, Black lady in a maid's uniform, were first-time experiences for Lia. At the end of the table sat a large cake that Lia thought was almost too pretty to cut. Lia took her full plate and sat at the end of one of the sofas. Everything tasted delicious and she wanted to remember it all so that she could tell her parents about it. John Walker, the only other colored person among the forty or so kids at the party, walked over and sat next to Lia. John and Lia had classes together over the years and he always got "A's" like she did, but they didn't hang out in the same clique of Black kids. In fact, it didn't seem that John hung out with any particular crowd. He was very quiet, and Lia always thought he was just a little weird.

"Hi Lia." He lowered his voice. "I'm glad there's somebody else here."

"I didn't know you had gotten an invitation." Lia said to him, her voice also a little low.

"Mary Hardin was invited, too. She said she didn't want to be around all these white people and they don't know how to throw a good party, anyway."

Mary Hardin was also an honor roll student, and she had hung out off and on with Lia's crowd. Neither girl had mentioned the invitation to the other, which seemed a little strange to Lia.

"Only a few of the Black kids got invitations, the smart ones. I guess they were afraid to invite any of the others."

Lia didn't respond to his comment and continued eating.

"This house in unbelievable, isn't it? I wonder what it looks like upstairs."

"Yes, it's very fancy. The jukebox is nice." Lia tried to sound complimentary, but not overly impressed.

Lia and John didn't talk much more as she finished eating; just sat and watched the others. The maid walked over and took Lia's empty plate and told them both to help themselves to more food and soda if they wanted it, and mentioned that the cake had been cut. Lia began to feel conflicted about being at the party. She couldn't verbalize how she felt about maybe being a token guest at the party. It probably wasn't true, anyway.

"Lia, would you like to dance?"

She did not notice that Mike Sullivan had walked over to her. She loved to dance, but had never danced with a white boy before. John stared at her with a questioning look on his face. Lia was afraid to say yes, but more afraid to say no. She didn't want anyone to think she couldn't handle dancing with Mike.

"Sure," she said; he took her lightly by the arm and led her to the center of the room where the other kids were dancing. It was a pretty awful three minutes. Mike was a terrible dancer, his movements totally out of sync with the beat of the music. It wasn't a good record for dancing, anyway. At the end, he asked if she wanted a soda, and they walked over to the bar together. After they got the sodas, Mike thanked her for the dance and started talking with some of his buddies. Lia returned to the sofa, where John still sat. During the rest of the evening, Lia shared one, awkward slow dance with John, and she was Tony Petrocelli's partner in a line dance with the whole group that was kind of fun.

Lia's father rang the doorbell at eleven o'clock sharp, just as the party was starting to wind down. One other parent had showed up, but most of the kids had cars or were riding together. She said goodbye to John and Tony. Barb thanked Lia for coming and surprised her with a hug.

"Have a great summer, Lia; stay in touch."

"Thank you, Barb." Lia didn't know what else to say.

Lia noticed her father talking with Mr. McIntyre at the front door. "Good luck in college," Mrs. McIntyre called after them as they started down the path to the driveway.

"Did you have a good time?" It was the only question her father asked her.

"Yes, it was nice," Lia responded.

Lia was glad she had gone to the party. She did not have a particularly good time, but thought her father would be disturbed if she told him so. That night, as she lay in bed, Lia thought about the party but never thought much about it again

ξ

As she sat on the plane headed back to Levale thinking about Jordan, Lia remembered that many years ago it was a big deal to be invited to a wealthy classmate's home for a graduation party. Now, her son was going to Cape Cod for a weekend graduation celebration at the family vacation home of a white, female college friend; a wealthy one, Lia was sure. She hoped it was progress, but Lia wasn't completely sure.

ξ

"How was Jordan's graduation?"

Lia called Wanda right back in response to the message left on her machine, even though it had been a very long day and she got home late. Wanda said she had something to tell Lia, and the playful tone in her voice had aroused her curiosity too much to wait until morning.

"The graduation was great, and Jordan was super great. Rob and I took him to dinner, and he's off to Cape Cod with friends."

"Oh to be young and carefree again. How's Rob; was that okay?"

"Yeah, it was just fine. Rob is going to run for county council, and Jordan is going to work on his campaign."

"Well that's exciting; some father and son bonding, too."

"Yeah, it's about time. I'm pooped. What's up? You sounded as though something is going on."

"Ellis asked me for your telephone number."

Thank you, Lord.

"When?"

"This morning. He told me he was very taken by you, and he also said you seemed to have a lot of deep stuff going on inside."

"Oh, did he? I could say the same about him. He certainly commands attention, but in a quiet way, almost Zen."

"Oh my God, Zen? I don't know about Zen."

"You know him pretty well, though; does he realize how people respond to him?"

"I really can't say; sometimes I think he's clueless, and sometimes I think he knows exactly what he's doing, now people react to his charm. But, I like Ellis."

"I think women like Ellis." Lia was fishing for more information from Wanda.

"Not just women. I've seen men respond the same way. Oscar thinks the world of him. They've been friends for years, and now they play music together."

"Has he been married? I can't imagine that he hasn't been. Does he have a woman in his life?"

"Well, that's one of the reasons I wanted to talk with you before giving Ellis your number. Ellis was married many years ago, and he has one grown son who lives in the Seattle area. I don't think they're very close. He doesn't talk about him very often; never talks about his ex-wife that I've heard or know about. But he has been in a relationship with a woman, her name is Deborah, for a long time, about five or six years, I think. She has a son who's about seven years old, I think. The story I get from Oscar is that Ellis met her when the boy was very young, and he helped her through some very difficult times. But she moved to Mobile about a year ago, and the relationship has been up and down, off and on. I don't think it's totally over, though I don't know for sure."

"Give him my numbers, office and home."

I'm a big girl.

"Okay. I'm glad you're saying yes. I think you and Ellis would be very interesting together."

"Whoa! He just wants my number; it may not lead to anything."

"I know, but it would be interesting. Just be a little careful." Wanda was being a friend; she was trying to convey both delight and caution.

ξ PART III ξ

Summer

ξ CHAPTER 9 ξ

"Good morning."

"Hey, good morning to you," Lia responded to Wanda's cheery voice.

"You sound pretty mellow for 8:00 o'clock in the morning."

"I feel pretty good this morning. You caught me lollygagging in the sun on my deck. It's going to be really hot today. I'm having a cup of tea and thinking I should just maybe get up, maybe get dressed, and maybe go to work."

Wanda chuckled. "I'm glad you're at home; I didn't know if you were traveling or not. I just called to say happy birthday. I was going to mention it when we talked the other night, but then we got bogged down in talking about men. What can I say? I'd take you out for a birthday drink, but I have a client dinner tonight. Will you take a rain check?"

"Of course; thanks for calling. I'm hoping for a quiet, low-key day at the office. I sent myself a dozen yellow roses, my favorite, and I'm going to grill a nice t-bone for myself tonight. I don't really eat beef but once or twice a year, and I crave a nice steak. A glass of wine, a bubble bath, go to bed."

"M'mm, sounds nice."

"Have a good one."

"You, too, birthday girl."

ξ

The associates chipped in to buy a huge cake for Lia. The cake was decorated with the figure of a woman with her arms spread out as if to encircle everyone in them. "Happy Birthday Boss" was written out in big, purple lettering next to the figure. Coffee, tea and punch had been set out on the table next to the cake.

"It's a carrot cake; we know that's your favorite," Mary Carter, one of the senior associates who had organized the celebration, told Lia when they surprised her.

Many of the associates had gathered in the cafeteria after lunch. There was a lot of laughing and clapping as Lia cut and served the cake. The mood was festive and the joking was good natured. Lia was having fun.

It was short-lived. The issues with Gunther, suspiciously quiet since her staff's presentation, were placed front and center again. Sara was in the cafeteria, so the receptionist, Pam, sent one of the associates to find Lia.

"Pam has Mr. Castle holding on the phone. He wants to speak with you right away." Jeanine, the associate, had rushed upstairs to find Lia and she was out of breath.

Lia felt a sudden coldness in her chest that caused a little shiver. Dan rarely called her. Her good mood evaporated, and she struggled to maintain a cheery front.

"Maybe the big boss is calling to give us all the day off to celebrate my birthday." The associates laughed as Lia spoke to Jeanine.

"Tell Pam I'll be in my office in half a minute and she can transfer the call."

Lia headed to her office, and quickly picked up the telephone that was ringing as she entered.

"Lia, sorry to interrupt the celebration, but I need to talk with you."

"What's going on?" Lia, once again, tried to keep her voice light.

"I had a long conversation with Gunther this morning. He is very concerned about what's happening."

"What does he think is happening?"

"Gunther feels the associates and agents are out of control, that these meetings they're conducting have gone too far and the results just aren't going to be there in the long term. He's concerned because the lines of communication have changed, and he doesn't have a clear picture of what's going on. He was used to having Lucas Mayhew as his link in Levale. He questions your year-end projections. He also says the agents are disgruntled with the process and he's hearing a lot of complaints."

"Dan, that's simply not true. None of it is true. Everything we communicated in the presentation is still on course, better than we expected, in fact. I just sat in on a report from one of the process teams yesterday afternoon. They are excited about the new direction we've taken, the work they've done, and they were very specific about the results we could expect from the new process improvements they were recommending. And, they certainly understand the importance of realistic projections. We have talked about the fact that, as the process improvements continue and become more complex, they could take longer to implement and the savings and new revenue generation on service plan packages could take longer. But the payoffs are much larger and absolutely long term. They made a special point of emphasizing how important it is for all of us to be diligent and stick to it and, Dan, they also emphasized the importance of continued open communication and management support from us. I am continually impressed by their business sense."

"I'm hearing two different stories here. Can't you and Gunther get together and work this out?"

"I'm sorry that's the case. It's distressing that leaders in EPD have not embraced the fantastic work that is being done by its employees.

"You and Gunther need to talk, and soon."

"I've tried several times to have a productive conversation with Gunther, to no avail. Our initiative has empowered the agents and associates to team up and look at what we do in a whole new way. This is a big, fundamental change in the way we do things. Change can be difficult, you know."

"This has become a very difficult situation because Gunther tells me that you two have talked and that you are unwilling to listen to him."

"That is completely untrue and doesn't deserve an answer. Dan, I do not want to be put on the defensive when we're getting great results."

"Let's all try to stay calm."

Lia was determined to keep her voice level even though she was angered by this conversation.

"I'm very calm; the numbers make me calm. Jerome and I sat down earlier this morning. He factored in the last productivity gains and updated the estimates. At this point, we're projecting not only will we get the extra cost savings you requested, but a bit more, with an increase in revenue, as well. Lia thought that statement would be her trump card.

"Lia, it can't be successful without Gunther's cooperation. He can influence the agents in ways you don't understand. I know many of the technicians have been getting real involved in the initiatives, but Gunther has a lot of influence over them, and in the end, I know they will follow him."

"I don't think that's true for most of the techs. I think both you and Gunther may be misreading this situation. There are many perspectives. Maybe they need to be heard."

Dan ignored her comment and continued.

"I know your people play an important role in generating our revenues, but the agents carry out the actual service. I also need Gunther to help us make the numbers that Jud wants, now and for the long-term; he can negatively influence them if he so chooses."

"So you're saying Gunther can undermine you, me, and everybody else, and we all have to just deal with it?" Lia couldn't believe she was saying this to Dan, or having this conversation at all.

"Lia, you're going to have to placate Gunther."

"Placate him?" Lia was incredulous, and struggling to maintain a calm demeanor.

"Well, you know what I mean."

"No, Dan, I don't know what you mean. I don't intend to placate anyone. What happened to teamwork? It's never been there from Gunther. I don't think respect has been there, either. You need mutual respect to work as a team. Liking one another would be nice, but it's not necessary. But respecting one another is absolutely necessary if we're going to work together. Placating Gunther? I think it's insulting. Dan, Consumer Services is my operation, after all, not Gunther's."

Lia felt like she was preaching, but apparently Dan needed it.

"Lia, what you're saying makes sense, but I can't do what I need to do without Gunther in the loop, that's the bottom line."

"So, are you telling me to stop what I'm doing?"

"Of course not, the initiatives are great; your leadership is making a big difference, just what we needed."

"Then I don't understand what you want me to do."

"This thing has got to be done Gunther's way, or certainly with his approval. He's been in EPD for twenty-seven years, and he handles the largest service area in the country. When we complete the restructure later this year and consolidate branches, I'm probably going to give him more geography."

Lia was stunned to learn that restructure plans in the operation she was supposed to be running were obviously proceeding without her. How could she be leading process improvements and new service product initiatives if she wasn't included in the planning for how Consumer Services was going to be structured in the future? And, Gunther was actually going to be rewarded when it was all said and done despite his behavior.

What hold did he have on Castle? It must be something. What kind of shit is going on here?

"I know Gunther's not the easiest guy to deal with. He's old school and inflexible, but he has influence that you may not understand. I need him on my team."

Lia was angry now and was struggling to hold back tears.

I hate myself when I feel this way. I'll be damned if I'm going to let Dan hear tears in my voice.

"Dan, I'm having a very serious problem with this. This is not what I signed up for. I've spent months launching an initiative that has had great results, both in bringing together our employees and the savings and additional revenues we're getting. Service has true teamwork for the first time ever, employees feel empowered, and we're getting the dollars. I'd say we damn well can't beat that combination. The worst thing we can do now is give our employees the message that all their good work has been wrong or not good enough, or that Gunther's way, whatever the hell that may be, is the only way. I wouldn't know because he refuses to communicate with me. That would be a giant step backwards for everyone."

"Lia, bottom line. Call Gunther. Find out what he wants. Make it happen. This has got to be worked out. Now."

Lia was silent. She had absolutely no idea what to say. Her mind was in a fog of anger, confusion and disbelief.

Lia gritted her teeth. "Fine. I'll make another attempt at getting Gunther to understand the good work that our people are doing to take Consumer Services to the next level. Surely, he will agree that we can all benefit from joint efforts and open communications." She hung up the phone.

She knew she wasn't hanging up on him; he wanted the conversation to end just as much as she did. Lia didn't know what to do. She certainly wasn't going to call Gunther, not now anyway. She picked up the phone to call Dan back and tell him what to do with this job, but hung it up without dialing. She just sat. Sara interrupted her trance with a tap on the door, as she pushed it open and entered Lia's office.

"You never did get a piece of cake. I thought I'd bring you one."

"Thanks, Sara". That was all Lia said. Sara was observant enough to know that Lia was upset and left the office without any further conversation.

Lia stared at the piece of cake, at the thick cream cheese icing, at the bright yellow plastic plate it sat on, at the yellow plastic spoon with white "Happy Birthday" lettering on the handle. She didn't eat the cake. Her phone rang, but she ignored it. Sara would pick up the call.

"Lia?" Sara was at her office door talking to Lia's back, as she had swiveled her chair to stare out the window at the sky. "It's Jordan; I thought you'd want to take his call."

"Yes, Sara? Oh, yes." It took Lia a moment to focus on what she said and to pick up the telephone.

"Mom? Hi, happy birthday! I thought I'd call you at the office because Dad's got a fundraiser this evening, and I didn't want to miss you. You having a good day?"

Tears welled in Lia's eyes, again.

If I let these tears fall, my voice will betray me.

She swallowed hard and made an effort to put a little cheer in her voice.

"I'm having a great day. My employees presented me with a huge cake, carrot cake, of course."

"Sounds delicious; I'll bet you probably needed some fun. I know how you dive into things and barely come up for air."

"You know me too well, buddy. How's it going with your Dad?"

"Really crazy, but it's good. He's going to win; I know it. He's got these white folks wrapped up."

I'm glad somebody does.

"I'm sure this is a hell of an interesting experience for you."

"You have no idea. Next time we're together, I've got some stories to tell you. Well, I won't hold you. Have some fun!"

"I will. You take care. I love you."

"I love you too. Bye Mom."

A half hour later Lia grabbed her purse from the desk drawer, told Sara she was gone for the day, and left the building. It was a hot day, but she did not turn on the air conditioning in her car. She let the perspiration drip down her face as she drove home, and then wondered why she was doing such a strange thing. When she got home, she stripped down to her underwear, turned on her stereo, went out on her deck, and stretched out on the chaise. It was private, quiet, and hot. As the music drifted out, Lia did a rare thing. She fell asleep in the afternoon.

The strains of Sade's *Bullet Proof Soul* drifted over the heat and around Lia's relaxed body.

ξ

"I'm on a rooftop, and I've got a rifle." Without thinking about it, Lia called Laura when she woke up in near darkness.

"Hey Lia. It's going that well, huh"?

Lia had to laugh, at least for a moment.

"I hope you don't mind my calling so late at night." It was just after ten o'clock in Laura's time zone, but Lia hadn't glanced at the clock until she heard Laura's voice.

"No, not if you need to talk. Where have you been?"

"I've been traveling a lot lately, and communicating all over the place, or trying to." Lia put extra emphasis on the word "communicating."

"It's been, how should I put this, an interesting experience."

"Communicating?"

"Talking, presenting, cheerleading, challenging, cajoling, questioning, begging, you name it, with EPD people all over the country."

"What did you learn out there, anything that helps you?"

"Well, the guy who seems to be the most threatened by me probably will never change, and he's pretty much got Dan in his corner. There's a lot of historical baggage here that I don't know about and wasn't involved in, and I'm never going to know because nobody's going to tell me, but I have to live with the shit from it anyway. On the other hand, some really good people here in Levale and out in the branch offices are doing great work, and I think I have some disciples."

"Disciples? Is that what you need?"

"Yes, I do! Not in the biblical sense, of course, but we're asking these people to do so much more in an environment that is more, not less, stressful and fast moving. Dan is relentless. He's in a constant process of polishing his star with the powers that be in Fielding. And, you know, that's okay, but I don't know why these guys don't understand that you can lead people to work smarter, share power with them, and make big bucks. And, lo and behold, an African-American female can help you get there. Instead of viewing the results as a win for everybody, it seems to create nervousness and fear. It's very frustrating because it's so unnecessary. I'm not sure what I can do except keep pushing to deliver good results and look out for my employees."

"Whoa! You're preaching to the choir!"

"You know what the irony is? The overwhelming majority of people want to do their best. It has been my experience that they'll give you 150% if you just ask, and then include them in the process."

"So what are you doing about it, or going to do about it?"

"Pick off all the white boys from my rooftop bunker?"

Laura's laughter did not surprise Lia. She knew their relationship was solid enough to make that joke.

"Short of that, Lia?"

"What is there for me to do other than continue to improve EPD's Consumer Services operation and go for the goal I've been given? That's what they hired me for."

"What about the relationships?"

"If I prove I'm good at what I do, and motivate my employees to do it along with me, and continue to invite my colleagues to share in what we're doing, then I'm not sure what else I need to do, what else I can do."

"I want you to think about what you are trying to prove and why. Look, I think this is really important for you to do, to try to put things in perspective. Again, think about, specifically, what you are trying to prove to these people and exactly why. It's critical that you be precise about it because I want you to be able to clearly articulate the reasons this is so important for you."

"What is this exercise going to do for me?"

"Lia, you are no longer that young girl we've talked about who made an impression on everyone. It was great, but that was then and this is now. The stakes are different; the dynamics are different. Performing well and producing results does not give you a free pass to acceptance. We'd all like to believe it to be the case, but at some point we face reality and acknowledge that it does not. These people are going to take you, or not take you, on their own terms, Lia. That's a fact. I want you to feel fulfilled and gratified and, more importantly, happy with who you are, independent of how they react to you or feel about you. Right or wrong, and that determination is another conversation altogether, so much of who you are, or who you think you are, is tied to this, to how these people react."

"Sounds pretty depressing to me."

"Is that a question or an observation?"

"I guess it's an observation; maybe it's both."

"You've got to think about all this in a very focused way, so that you have a clear picture of the reward. What's in it for you? How does it affect your sense of well-being and accomplishment? On life's scale."

"Life's scale?"

"Yes, the yardstick you use to measure where you are, your goals, your level of happiness, if the activities in which you engage in your life are meaningful."

"Jesus," Lia mumbled.

"You haven't gotten where you are by accident. You're a brilliant businesswoman, I assume you're well paid, you've traveled the world, you raised a great son, you've got your health. What's the reward at Conallied, Lia? What is it these people can give you that you really need? Obviously, we're not talking only about a paycheck here. We're talking about what's really important to your soul. You need to decide exactly what that is."

"It's the key, isn't it?"

"Yes, Lia, it is," Laura answered, sounding tired.

"I think I've worn you out. I'm going to get off the telephone so you can go to bed."

"Don't worry about me. You owe it to yourself to go through the thought process."

"Yes, I know. I hear you. Oh, wait, I met an interesting man."

"Well, that sounds positive."

"It's nothing yet. We haven't even been out yet. In fact, he hasn't even called me yet. But it's been only a week since my girlfriend, Wanda, gave him my numbers."

I hope he calls soon. I'm not going to say this to Laura, though. I'm tired, and I don't want her jumping on my words and probing me about any anxiety I may have about Ellis. Am I feeling anxious about it? There's nothing to worry about yet. That's just what I need, more anxiety.

"Keep me posted. Have you heard from your friend, Dawson?"

I'm not even going to ask why she's asking me about Daw.

"He was down here a while back. We spent the evening together. It was nice."

"Dawson has always been good for you, Lia."

"I'll call you back soon".

"Promise?"

"Promise".

"Good, Lia. Bye."

ξ

Lia didn't know what made her walk out to her mailbox at eleven o'clock at night. Normally, if she forgot to get her mail, she simply let it sit until the next day. In the box was a large, padded envelope, and Lia smiled when she recognized the return address as Ruthie's, her aunt in California. Lia had hours ago forgotten about her birthday; it felt good that others had not. She tore open the envelope as she walked back to her front door. She pulled out a flat, heavy object protected by bubble wrap. Inside was a lovely, hand-painted ceramic tile. The scene on the tile was a twilight sky with a setting sun. The tile was inscribed with words from *My Symphony*, by William Ellery Channing. It brought Lia to tears. Inside was a short note from Ruthie wishing Lia happy birthday, telling her that she and Dalton were about to leave for a short trip to Hawaii to visit his sister, and expressing hope they would talk soon. Lia's heart dropped. She would love to talk with Ruthie tonight.

Why haven't I taken the time to call Ruthie before now? There's so many reasons to reconnect with her.

Lia washed her face and read the words on the tile again. The rest of the world was busy living life, Ruthie and Dalton were in Hawaii, Jordan was with Rob, Wanda was with Oscar. Where was she? Home alone, worried about Dan Castle and Gunther Madison.

How did I get to be this pitiful?

ξ

August 1968

Twenty one-year old Lia still felt the need from time to time to talk with and be nurtured by her favorite aunt. Ruthie was her father's youngest sister. Born late in life to Lia's paternal grandparents, she was much younger than her siblings and only ten years older than Lia. Aunt Ruthie had always understood her better than anyone else, and Lia could talk to her about anything. She encouraged Lia's love of books and reading when she was still a little girl, and Ruthie long ago suggested to Lia that she keep a journal of her thoughts.

"Writing things down always makes them clearer," she told Lia.

"Do you keep a journal, Ruthie?"

"Not anymore, sweetie. But that doesn't mean it's not a good idea for you. You have a crowded mind, but that's good. The writing will help you clear a path only for yourself. And, you'll find it very insightful to go back and read your journal later".

Lia was not at all surprised that Ruthie had kept a journal, but found it a little strange that she had stopped. It seemed to Lia that, if anyone needed to sort out all her feelings, it was Ruthie. Lia often wondered how she had endured so much pain so young. Ruthie and her boyfriend, Kermit, had been sweethearts since junior high school. She got pregnant during the spring of their senior year. Kermit was their high school's star fullback, team captain, heartthrob of all the girls, and a real jerk. As a young girl, Lia remembered that Ruthie would often bounce into their house, usually when Ruthie needed her big brother, Lia's dad, to referee a fight she was having with their parents, and she filled their house with energy. Sometimes Kermit would be with her, and Lia always felt uncomfortable around him. She thought he smiled and laughed too much, even when nothing funny was going on. Kermit had gotten athletic scholarship offers from six colleges, and his impending decision was the talk of the school and the local sports media. Ruthie's pregnancy was about to ruin Kermit's future, not to mention her own; Ruthie got the good grades, and Kermit got the points on the football field. But his mother and sisters, who spoiled him rotten, and the girls at school who had always been jealous of Ruthie, focused only on Kermit's life being ruined by that "stuck-up, smart-ass Ruthie." During their senior year-end activities, prom and graduation, Ruthie's pregnancy was starting to show, and they broke up and reconciled half a dozen times. They ended up going to the senior prom together, Ruthie wearing a dress selected to cover her pregnancy as much as possible, and they graduated two weeks later.

Two days after graduation, after Ruthie told Kermit that her family insisted that he must marry her and she didn't understand why he wasn't being the man he was on the football field, Kermit punched Ruthie twice, once in the head that spun her around and the other a direct blow in her lower back. The bleeding began immediately and, later that night, she lost the baby. Kermit never came to the hospital. No one outside the immediate family ever really knew what happened; Ruthie would not talk about it, and Kermit stayed away the entire summer. That was the end of Ruthie and Kermit. The end of Kermit came eighteen months later when failing grades, a busted knee, and rumors of drug use collaborated to send Kermit Martin back home a dropout, ex-jock failure. Ruthie had gone away to college in the Midwest, and Lia saw her only briefly during her first summer home, then once a year during the Christmas holidays. Ruthie graduated from college with a degree in nursing, and rather than returning to the West

Coast, went to work in a Chicago hospital emergency room. She met Noah Miller there. He was everything Kermit was not. Noah's large, close-knit family had helped to mold a strong, caring, hard-working doctor. Ruthie and Noah married, moved to California, and began their life together. Six years later, on an icy, mountain road above Lake Tahoe, the horror of skidding cars and screeching tires crushed Ruthie's life. Noah and their four year-old son, Noah, Jr., died instantly. Ruthie survived, and after being stabilized at a local hospital, was helicoptered to the university hospital close to home. She spent ten weeks there recovering from multiple injuries, but never really recovered from her emotional injuries. The woman who was once loving, energetic and creative lost her spirit and became an introverted loner. Ruthie never went back to nursing. She sold the home she shared with her husband and son, bought a small condo, and took an assistant librarian position at the university hospital's medical school library.

ع

When Lia called Ruthie at her condo, she was both curious and excited to be invited to a house one hundred miles south on the Monterey coast the following Saturday. Lia was not surprised something was going on in Ruthie's life; there always seemed to be something.

Lia left home very early to allow herself time to find the house and arrived forty minutes before she was expected. Ruthie answered the door in her bathrobe, and her face registered pleasant surprise. She looked as pretty as ever, fair skinned, soft features, tall but delicate. She towered over Lia. She gave Lia a long, tight hug.

"Girl, look at you; my baby niece is all the way grown up! Come on in and meet Dalton."

Ruthie had not mentioned anything about a Dalton when they talked on the telephone, just that she was spending the weekend "down the coast."

"Dalton, this is Lia, just about my favorite person in the world."

Dalton, a very tall, thin white man who Lia guessed was in his mid fifties, gave Lia a warm smile and extended his hand.

"I'm so pleased to meet you. Sorry we're still in our bathrobes; we do tend to linger at this table."

They had been having breakfast at a large, round dining table that was cluttered with dishes, newspapers and magazines. It sat just inside French doors that overlooked a garden and small wood deck and the Pacific Ocean in the distance.

"Oh, I'm early. The house was easier to find than I thought."

"You ladies have the day all to yourselves. I'm needed at the hospital today; even us old guys don't always control the schedule the way we'd like. Honey, I've got to dress and get out of here. You two stay out of trouble."

He lightly kissed Ruthie's lips, brushed his hand along her arm in one of those intimate gestures between lovers, and walked down the hall.

"Oooh! I can hear your wheels turning. I'll tell you all about Dalton later. Let me cook you some breakfast."

It was a lovely day for Lia. Ruthie prepared a breakfast of scrambled eggs, toast and fresh strawberries, and they talked almost until noontime about Lia's developing relationship with her future husband, Rob, and their growing love for one another, her career dreams and goals, and her desire to devote some time to trying her hand at writing sometime in the future.

In mid-afternoon, they were eating a late lunch of fresh crab on the balcony of a restaurant that literally hung over the ocean.

"Everything seems to be happening suddenly. Rob is finishing grad school soon. I'm trying to decide what it is I really want to do and not take a job just to be able to say that I have one. It seems like all these life decisions are floating around me, waiting for me."

"Lia, you're so young. You simply cannot imagine today the roads that will open up to you. Then, many times, you'll have to decide which direction to take.

"Jesus, it sounds so existential and a little scary."

"Just stay true to yourself."

"How do I know when I'm doing that?"

"Just follow your heart, sweetie; just follow your heart."

Later, they later strolled through the cute little shops in Carmel, and Ruthie bought Lia a sweater, and Lia purchased a small, heart pendant as a surprise for Ruthie while her aunt was down the street in another shop. She had saved money from her part-time job at J.C. Penney's, and it felt nice to spend some of it on Ruthie. They walked through a new art gallery and talked, laughed and argued about the various works of art on display. Back at the house, they rested for a while. Just as the day was winding down from late afternoon to early evening, Ruthie put salmon steaks on the grill for dinner. They again lingered at the table; the doors to the deck were slightly ajar, inviting in just enough of the outside. Lia gave Ruthie the pendant, and she seemed to really like it.

"You didn't have to buy me anything."

"I wanted to. I want you to have something from me."

"You know I'll treasure it. I'm so proud of the young women you've grown to be."

The old Ruthie was gone, and Lia knew she always would be different. The woman whose energy once filled a room, then was utterly absent, had made a passage. There was a serenity about Ruthie, and now, she glowed softly.

After the sun set in a golden glow that Lia thought must happen only on very special days, the two of them moved out to the deck and sat quietly as a bright night emerged along the coast. It had cooled down, but the temperature was still mild.

"Tell me about Dalton, Ruthie."

Ruthie turned toward Lia and smiled.

"We've talked about everything else, but we haven't managed to talk about him yet, have we? I'll keep it short and sweet."

Lia wanted every little detail, but it was Ruthie's story.

"Dalton is the chief anesthetist at the medical center. He has practiced for over twenty years. His duties are mostly administrative now; he doesn't do many surgeries anymore, unless it's a transplant or something unusual, then he'll direct the anesthesiologists. A little over a year ago, I was asked to participate on medical team that was going to make an important presentation at a conference of anesthetists; my role was research only, but I was asked to attend the conference. I wasn't particularly excited about going, but then I wasn't excited about much of anything then. Lia, I was a robot moving through life, and Dalton, for reasons I'll never quite understand, decided to make saving me his purpose in life. The attraction was mutual, slowly mutual, and so improbable. I was very afraid of it. Our relationship was slow and hesitant in the beginning, but Dalton is a wonderful man who provides me great comfort."

"He's white, Ruthie." Lia kept her voice soft to avoid sounding judgmental.

"Yes." That was all Ruthie said.

"And he's what, twenty years older than you?"

"Yes."

"Do you want me to say anything to Daddy and the others?"

"Not yet. I'll do it soon."

"Does he have a family?"

"His wife walked away four years ago and remarried the day after the divorce was final. It caught him completely by surprise. She lives in Phoenix. I'm not quite sure how much his devotion to medicine had to do with it all, but I crossed Dalton's path when he was ready for me. It was all timing for us.

"What about children?"

"He has one son, Drew, who's also a doctor. He lives in New York City.

"Is this his house?"

"Yes. But, he wants it to be mine. He says he wants to give me the damned thing."

The cliffhanger house, as Lia thought about it the moment she saw it, sat just off Highway 1 halfway between Monterey and Carmel. It was a small, charming one-story house, and it had Ruthie's touches all through it.

"Will you take it? It's got you written all over it."

"I don't know, though I love being here, and I love being with Dalton. He protects me and gives life meaning for me. I have struggled to carve out a small piece of my heart for him, and it seems to be enough. He keeps me emotionally alive. The effort makes him happy."

"God, Ruthie, if I become half the woman you are, I'll be satisfied."

"Let's go inside. Why don't you stay overnight? Have breakfast with Dalton and me in the morning. It would really please him to get to know you better. You can still make it home by midday."

"Thanks, that sounds good to me."

"Good, I'm so glad you can stay over."

"It is just too lovely here." Lia closed her eyes and let the orange light that lingered after sunset envelope her.

"Yes, it is." Ruthie replied softly. "I'm very fortunate that Dalton came into my life and brought me here."

ξ

On her drive back up to the Bay Area the following day, a warm sun competed with the fog that covered the coastline. Lia knew the sun would triumph because she was young, and hopeful, and felt good about everything after seeing Ruthie.

ξ CHAPTER 10 ξ

The morning after Lia's wonderful, horrible, disheartening birthday dawned cool and overcast in Levale, a complete turnaround from the day before and very unusual for a summer morning. Lia woke up late in her bed, but had no recollection of getting into it. She had only undressed down to her blouse and underwear. She did not want to go to the office; she wanted to snuggle further under the covers and stay there all day. But she got up, pushed all thoughts to the back of her mind as best she could, and got dressed.

I still have no idea how I'm going to deal with that ridiculous conversation with Dan.

When Lia finally walked into her office, she immediately noticed two things. A huge bouquet of brightly colored, acrylic balloons with birthday messages on them was tied to one of her conference table chairs. The big card dangling from the ribbons was signed by all of her staff. She had left the previous afternoon before they had an opportunity to present the balloons to her.

Not everyone is on my case.

She also noticed the overnight package on her desk. Lia received these packages all the time, but she was not expecting one today. She noticed the return address was the Jacksonville branch office. Lia opened the cardboard envelope and took out the one page inside. It read . . .

Dear Lia:

We are writing in support of the process improvement initiative that you launched this year. This initiative has had an overwhelmingly positive effect on the employees who have participated thus far. Their sense of empowerment and inclusion is at a high. We are pleased that the relationship between the technicians in the field and the associates in Levale has become genuinely cooperative and mutually beneficial. Most feel their work has been made easier and, most importantly, our customers are the ultimate beneficiaries.

We are not in agreement with any efforts to undermine or significantly alter the initiative as it has currently evolved. In this time of uncertainty relative to the future structure of Consumer Services, our collective long-term employment viability, and competitive market forces, we need to employ all strategies possible to strengthen EPD. We do not want to be identified as obstructionists to any progress that can be made. Hopefully, the mutual support that has been demonstrated by our employees can become a reality among management, as well. You will note that we have not copied anyone on this letter, and we would appreciate it not being passed along. This letter is for your personal knowledge.

Sincerely,

The letter was signed by Phil Barnes, Jacksonville, Glen Casey, Memphis, and Dennis DeLucca, Denver.

Half the branch managers; DeLucca's signature is a pleasant surprise, the absence of Weldon's is a surprise, too.

Lia sat and stared at the letter for several minutes. Her mind raced. She had seriously questioned her judgment and abilities during the past eighteen hours, and now she felt gratified and vindicated. She also felt bound and constrained because her first inclination was to immediately fax the letter to Castle. It seemed clear that the three guys did not want the letter out in the open. Their concern that Gunther, as much as Dan, could negatively influence the direction of their careers, was real. Gunther apparently had a lot of influence on branch manager promotions during prior administrations. In theory, Lia was the primary decision maker about career moves in Consumer Services, but that issue had not boiled up yet.

What a shit storm that could be. It shouldn't be, but I have to face the reality that everything is going to be a battle. This whole thing is a political nightmare, but there's no mistaking the fact that these branch managers felt strongly enough about the positive work being done to send me this letter.

"Knock, knock," Carl was standing at her open office door.

"Hi Carl; come on in."

"I just wanted to give you the report I promised on the customer satisfaction surveys we did two weeks ago. Overall, it looks real good. I'd like you to go over it and maybe we can sit down in a couple of days to discuss it in detail."

"That sounds good. Take a look at this." Lia handed Carl the letter.

He quickly read it, shaking his head in affirmation.

"I knew this letter was coming. I found out a little while ago".

"Really? From who?"

"I had to talk with Dennis on another matter, and he told me about it in confidence. Everybody knows Gunther is trying to shoot down the initiative; it's on the grapevine. Phil was the ringleader on the letter, but Dennis said after giving it some thought he decided it was the right thing to do. He said another interesting thing. Walter Weldon agrees with the letter, but would not sign it. He's very close to retirement, you know, and he doesn't want to risk losing his pension at the eleventh hour because of political bullshit. He's paranoid about doing anything to cross Gunther, and he has no faith that Castle will be supportive. So, Walter is in your corner, but he's not going to stand up and say so; not at this point, anyway."

"Carl, I'm not going to share this letter with anyone else. I'll just hold it for now."

"So, you're not going to give Castle a copy?"

"No. I don't want to erode their support after they've taken this risk. I will figure out another way for Dan to get the message."

At the moment, Lia had no idea how she was going to do that.

ξ

"Hello, Lia. It's Ellis. How are you?"

Here you are. I'm so glad. Save me.

"Well, hi there. I'm doing fine. How are you?"

"Actually, a bit tired. We've had a lot of gigs around the area lately, so I'm not complaining. But, along with my job at the station, it makes for some long days. Wanda tells me that you have a lot going on at work, and not all of it is pleasant."

"Oh, I might be able to give you the short version without consuming too many hours."

I haven't leaned on anyone emotionally, really leaned on someone, in so long. Someone who's emotional about me, so they'll be emotional about how I feel. I'm forgetting about Dawson. Why? Okay, focus and slow down; you haven't even had a cup of coffee with this guy.

"How about we meet for coffee tomorrow morning. I hope you'll be free since it's Saturday morning."

He read my mind.

"That sounds nice. Are you one of those early risers, up with the chickens?"

"No way! I don't see too many early mornings." Ellis laughed a deep, rich laughter that made Lia smile.

Smiling is a good tonic.

"We have a gig tonight, so I won't get home until close to 2:00 am. How about 9:30 at Katie's Tea Room?"

"Sounds good. Wanda's been telling me about Katie's because I'm a tea lover, but I haven't been there yet."

"I know."

He did some homework; brownie points.

"I'm a tea lover, too. And, I confess, a lover of sweets."

"I hear both the morning pastries and the afternoon desserts are to die for."

"So, I'll meet you there at 9:30."

"See you then. Goodbye."

"I'm looking forward to it, Lia. Goodbye."

Other than lunches and occasional dinners with Dawson, where most of our conversations have been about Conallied dramas, I have not been on a real date in years.

ξ

Lia arrived at Katie's Tea Room first, right at 9:30 in the morning. She was able to grab a small window booth for two in the corner. Perfect, as it turned out. Lia immediately liked the place. Small, only about 15 tables, the crisp white tablecloths, bright red cloth napkins, cobblestone floor and lush plants everywhere, all appealed to her. The room had a pleasant, quiet buzz of conversation; some lone patrons were reading one of the many newspapers and magazines that were laid out on an antique side table sitting against the wall just inside the entrance. She settled in the booth and adjusted her body hoping to look relaxed. She wore light slacks and a sleeveless white cotton blouse that buttoned up the front; the top buttons were left open just low enough so Lia would not be too hard on herself for wanting to appear alluring to Ellis.

I want to check my hair and lipstick again, but I don't want him to walk in and see me with my face in a mirror.

A very petite, impeccably groomed Black lady in a black uniform with a starched, white apron walked over to the booth. She set two menus on the table.

"Good morning. My name is Jean. You said they'll be two of you, correct? Can I get you something while you wait?"

"Just water, please. I'll wait for my friend before I order."

At 9:45, Lia was beginning to worry a little, but continued to sip her water with studied concentration.

He doesn't seem like the type to not show up, but you know practically nothing about this man. No, the Oscar and Wanda connection is too close for him to be a complete no-show.

"Good morning." Ellis was suddenly standing at her shoulder, and Lia jumped when she heard his voice. "I'm sorry I startled you, and I apologize for being late. I got stuck on a long- distance call."

No details.

"It's warm this morning. It'll be hot later on. I'm guessing you're still in the mood for tea?"

Lia smiled at Ellis as he settled in the booth across from her. He looked cool and casual in khaki shorts and a plain white T-shirt. He wore leather sandals that covered most of his feet.

He's probably one of those people who always look well put together with little effort.

"You guessed right. Why don't people say that to coffee drinkers; they have their coffee no matter the weather."

"So what strikes your fancy? Hmm, I think a pretty robust strong tea suits you."

"And I think some kind of herbal blend suits you. Darjeeling for me, it's full-bodied, but it's actually not too strong." Lia smiled as she responded.

"A green tea and mint blend for me," Ellis immediately shot back. They both laughed.

"So, Ellis, are you going to guess what kind of pastry I like?"

"Well, not too sweet or sticky; maybe a warm bread with some kind of fruit."

"This is getting scary. I think I'll have a slice of the cranberry nut bread. You'll have to help me eat it."

"Okay, I'm going to have a fruit tart, and we'll both go for it together."

"Are you playing tonight?" Lia asked after the waitress took their orders and went away to get the tea.

"Yes, we're playing a late show tonight at a club about thirty miles south of Levale. Kind of a strange place for a jazz club; it's in a suburban neighborhood, and it doesn't get going until late. They've booked some good musicians and built up a nice reputation. We're going to play a set at midnight. It's actually a nice gig; we play one long set and get paid more than most of the city clubs give us. The Vineyard, have you heard of it?"

"No, but I'm not very familiar with the surrounding areas, though Wanda's been great showing me around Levale and where I can get things. I've been in Levale over seven months, but I've been pretty secluded since I arrived here. My job consumes a lot of my time."

"We'll have to see what we can do about that."

Sounds like I'll see him again. I need this.

"My life is pretty full, too. My afternoons at the radio station and playing at night sometimes stretches into a lot of hours. But I must play the piano; it defines who I am in so many ways."

The waitress wheeled a white, wrought iron cart with big wheels to their booth and served from it. The tea and food were served with great care on individual flowered porcelain trays with matching china and all the requisite tea implements.

"The tea service is lovely," Lia remarked to Jean, the server.

"Katie selects beautiful things for the shop."

Lia and Ellis moved their plates to the center of the table, and they split the cranberry bread and fruit without any formality, and Lia cut off a small piece of his tart and put it on her plate. They went through the exercise of preparing their tea in silence.

This feels nice, no awful first date fanfare or tension.

"So, tell me about yourself," Ellis leaned forward when he asked the question and looked directly into Lia's eyes. "Wanda has told me a little about you, but I'm guessing there's much more."

How much do I want to tell you?

"Well, you know I'm at Conallied, transferred down here from corporate headquarters. It was a big promotion and, you were right last night on the phone, there is a lot of drama going on that I'll have to tell you about sometime. I was born and raised in San Francisco, moved east after I got married. I have one son, Jordan, who just graduated from college. He's wonderful, if I do say so myself. He's working with his Dad this summer; Rob, my ex-husband, is running for county council in the area where he lives. Big doings for him."

"Do you get back to San Francisco very often? Is your family still there?"

"Yes, they're scattered around the Bay Area. I had not been home in a while until recently when an old friend passed away, and I traveled to attend her funeral."

"I'm sorry to hear that."

"It was good to be at home, but everyone and everything there is beginning to feel a little remote to me."

Why did I tell him that, say it out loud? I've never fully acknowledged it to myself until now.

"Are you an only child; any brothers and sisters?"

"Oh no, I have a younger brother and sister. My brother is in the Air Force, but I'm the only one who flew the coop by choice, and I flew 3,000 miles away."

"Do you miss San Francisco?"

"In a general sense, yes. In a specific sense, no."

That was a weird response. Enough about me for now.

"Tell me about you."

"I'm an only child, born and raised in Seattle. My mom was white; my dad was Black. I'm a Black man with almost white skin; this is America. My mom died during my junior year in high school, and my dad died when I was thirty, so it's pretty much just me. I have a grown son, two uncles still alive, one on each side of the family; one lives in Seattle and the other lives in Houston. I have two cousins, one in Portland the one in Washington DC. I'm in touch with all of them from time to time, but I don't see them very often. My life is centered here in Levale."

"Wow, you included all the extended family. No wife anywhere along the way?"

"Not really."

What does that mean?

"Not really?"

"I got married when I was twenty years old. It lasted only two years, but we had a son, Danny. He's 29 now. We didn't have a relationship for a long time, but we're working on it now. He's a school psychologist. He visited me two months ago. We had a good long weekend together. It made me happy. I've been, was, in a long-term relationship. Deborah's son, Jason, is almost seven years old now. I've been around most of his life; he's a good kid. They live in Memphis. Deborah is a writer. We are not together now, but we do talk occasionally."

He paused before he made that last statement. I'd like to know more. This is my first date with this man, this really isn't even a formal date; I shouldn't be pressing. Lighten up.

"We had some rough times for a while, and we both agreed that going our separate ways was best."

He read my mind, or at least part of it.

"Any chance of reconciliation?"

"I'd be less than honest if I said absolutely no, but I don't think so. It's just not right anymore."

"What about her son, Jason?"

"That part makes me sad."

Enough. Not my business.

"When did you start playing the piano?"

"I started fooling around on the keyboard when I was about seven or eight years old, but I got serious about it when I was thirteen. My dad thought it was a big waste of time, so my mom paid for the after-school lessons out of the house money my dad gave her. After she died, I was devoted to it, and my dad, though he didn't encourage me, he supported it financially because he realized that he had no choice if the two of us were going to have a decent relationship."

"The piano seems so incredibly versatile musically and melodic in a hopeful, promising way."

"Promising. That's an interesting word to use. I like it."

I'm glad.

"So, is music your life's work and you do radio on the side?"

"Well, they complement one another, but I'd say that summarizes it nicely."

"You're a lucky man."

Jean rolled her cart over to their table and poured more hot water for their tea. After she rolled it away again, Ellis told Lia all about the three CD's he had recorded during his career and the gigs in the big-time clubs in New York, Chicago, Memphis and other cities, including the capitals of Europe, when he was younger, and how he settled in Levale when the radio station opportunity came to him. It provided stability. His life until then had been interesting and varied and fortunate, but nomadic. Ellis was clearly proud of his accomplishments, but he was genuinely modest about them, as well.

I like this man.

"Do you know it's almost noon," Ellis looked at his watch and smiled at Lia.

"Time flies when you're having fun. You're very easy to talk with."

"You're a good listener. I've talked about myself too much; I want to know more about you. I have a suggestion, if it works for you. I have a 12:30 meeting at the station. I should be done by 2:00. If you can hold out, how about a late lunch?" Ellis motioned for the check and took out a credit card. "My treat."

"There's an art and food festival today along North and South Main. I was planning to go down there and meander around. I'll buy you a hot dog."

"That sounds great, Lia, but I'm going to hold out for something more exotic like chicken on a stick." They both laughed. "Why don't I meet you at Main and Fifth Street in front of that big candy store at 2:30. That intersection will probably be right at the center of the action."

"I'll be there."

Lia and Ellis walked out of Katie's to the small parking lot next door to it. At her car, Ellis gave her a very quick peck on the cheek before Lia got in her car and he headed, walking, down the street.

This is a good day.

ع

Lia was right on time again, and this time Ellis was already at their meeting place looking intently at a series of oil paintings placed on a row of easels, all depicting sunsets in different locales.

I'm glad I resisted the temptation to change clothes. What I'm wearing is just fine for a street festival.

"Hi there." Lia hoped her voice sounded casual and not too expectant of a deep, long-term relationship with fun times, soulful times, sharing times, loving times, all resulting in a small, lovely wedding in a beautiful location and a long life together.

"How was your meeting?"

"Oh, I'm sure you know, another meeting to endure. What do you think?" Ellis pointed to a painting of a sunset settling over treetops along a riverbank. "I appreciate good art, but I've never invested in any good pieces. I have a few nice carved pieces from my travels and some nice posters that I've had framed; the framing is worth more than the posters."

"I've invested in a few things. I love modern art and also black and white photography. I'm not much of a landscape person, but this one is very nice."

"I'm going to think about this one. But first, we've got to find that chicken on a stick!"

Lia and Ellis whiled away the rest of the afternoon walking from one colorful booth to the next looking at paintings, sculpture, wood carvings, stained glass and all manner of truly beautiful, and incredibly tacky, artwork. To their surprise, they never found chicken on a stick, but instead feasted on teriyaki shrimp on a stick. They occasionally held hands briefly, mostly when crossing a street or moving to another display at the festival. The warm sun passed across the sky into late afternoon, and they had laughed often and shared more of themselves with one another. Little insights here and there that allowed them to know one another better, a fact that revealed what the other is, or is not.

"Damn, it's 5:45. The guys agreed to a rehearsal at 7:00. We'll probably practice 'til about 9:00. We're playing at midnight."

"You'd better get going. I think I'm intruding on your life today."

"Lia, you've provided me with a life today." Ellis' tone was so straightforward, and a little solemn, that Lia silently let his comment sink in.

He sounds so serious. I hope my comment didn't sound like I was fishing.

"Thank you."

"How about meeting me at the Vineyard around 9:30? We can have a late dinner, something light. I don't usually eat much before playing a gig, but I'd enjoy it if you could come and stay for the set. I'd love to do the gentlemanly thing and come to pick you up, but it won't work this evening."

"I'll be there."

Good, to the point, sincere, no bullshit. I want to go.

The two of them sat a little while longer on a street curb and shared a cup of strawberry ice cream, and chattered about this and that. Lia knew that Ellis would have to leave soon.

The commitment is made. We'll see one another again this evening.

Lia regretted that they had to move from the curb. The inner part of her right arm was lightly touching his left forearm and igniting dormant sensual reactions that Lia had not experienced for a long time. Lia sighed when they had to move to stand up. Ellis ran off with less than an hour to return to his condo, take a quick shower and drive to the Vineyard. Lia, at a more leisurely pace, purchased some beautifully made candles, walked back to her car, and headed home. For the first time since she came to Levale, she had not thought about EPD all day.

ξ

Lia stood in the shower for a long time and let the hot water run down her back. It was different this time, not a way to shut out the day and the relentless stress and rejection that she was refusing to fully acknowledge in the face of actions and agendas to the contrary, but a precursor to an interesting evening with a man who seemed locked into her. Their fit, the seemingly interlocking pieces of soul, thought and, maybe, heart, felt incredibly comfortable.

Whoa, girl, it's only been eleven hours, for God's sake.

ξ

Ellis was standing at the door with the Vineyard's manager, introduced as simply Skip, waiting for her when she arrived. It had taken her far too long to get dressed; it had been a long time since she worried about what to wear, except which suit and blouse would help her look strong and confident.

"You look nice."

"Thank you."

He took notice.

Skip escorted them to a table for two in a small alcove just to the left of the small stage. It was the only alcove, clearly the best and most private table in the club. They sat, Lia ordered a glass of wine, and Ellis ordered a sparkling water with lime.

"You don't drink before a set." It was more of a statement than a question.

"Never."

As they looked over the mercifully short menu, five entrees and a nightly special, Lia could feel Ellis' eyes on her; she looked up at him. He was staring intently at her. Lia stared back and smiled.

"I don't know what to make of this, Lia, of us, of what I've been feeling today."

Are we already an "us?"

Lia didn't know what to say, so she didn't say anything, and resumed studying the menu. Skip, rather than the waiter, interrupted the moment when he brought drinks and took their dinner orders. They decided to split the salmon special. Lia looked around the club for the first time. The oval-shaped space included the stage, which was already set up with the instruments of Oscar Four, although Lia did not see Oscar or the other guys in the quartet, the floor in front of it held about twenty tables for two and four, and a raised level, separated by a railing, that encircled the room, with small tables lining the railing. The tan walls were painted with over-sized vineyard scenes, and the ceiling was painted with twinkling stars in an effort to give patrons the feeling of being out of doors at night. It was an odd, but comfortable and cozy place.

After they finished the meal, Ellis again stared wordlessly at her.

"That's the second time you've done that this evening."

"What? Stare at you? I apologize. It's just that, in less than a day, I feel so connected to you. I sense, well I hope, you feel the same, but you aren't saying much."

Lia chuckled. "You don't know how unlike me that is. I'm so used to being up front and highly visible and everyone expecting me to prove that I know anything that is of value to them, that it's really nice not to have to be on."

That was the first moment EPD entered my mind today, and that was enough.

"I feel very comfortable with you. Is it okay for it to be this comfortable, this soon?"

It feels surprisingly good to not be sure, and be able to say so.

"It is completely okay."

Again, simple and to the point.

"Tell me about your job. Wanda's mentioned that you're under a lot of pressure, but we haven't talked about it at all today."

I didn't think it was possible to go this many hours without thinking about it all. Okay, I give.

She told Ellis the summary version of everything, all the gory detail, all the drama, Dan, Gunther, Conallied's culture, the other African-American executives in the company, the events on her birthday, her challenges, past and present, accomplishments, such as they were, and even the fears and tears. Ellis listened intently.

"Aren't you sorry you asked," Lia asked half joking, half serious.

"Let's pretend that this evening is your official birthday celebration."

Wow. I don't want to ruin a lovely moment by getting teary.

Lia then surprised herself by talking headlong about her longing for success and acceptance, how she thought it stemmed from being a feisty little girl who imagined another world and read books in a corner of her closet.

"Why do you do it?"

"I want to be successful. It doesn't sound so insipid when I think it. It sounds hollow when I say it out loud."

"Your demeanor, your voice, everything changes when you talk about it. Why do you care so much what these white boys think of you, whether they respect you or not? You could probably walk on water, and they won't accept you. Anyway, you're wonderful, no matter what they think."

"I'm not so wonderful all the time, just today." Lia said jokingly in an effort to lighten the mood.

"Well, I'm wonderful today, and this evening, too." Ellis laughed out loud. "But seriously, help me to understand why it's so important."

Before Lia could answer, Ellis suddenly took a deep breath, shifted his body in the chair and looked as if a thought had occurred to him.

"I'm sorry, I apologize."

"For what?"

"Instead of questioning your motives, I should be helping you to figure out a strategy to deal with the bastards, a crush-and-conquer strategy."

"I don't want to crush them; I just want to do my job well."

"I know."

Two words, but I believe he does know.

"I'd like to do something with you, wait a minute."

Ellis got up, walked to a hallway next to the club's entrance and momentarily disappeared in the midst of staff moving quietly around the room, dinner conversation, late-arriving patrons and recorded jazz music coming from somewhere. He emerged a couple of minutes later with a pen and a sheet of paper from a lined yellow pad. Without a word, he wrote a line on the sheet and turned it over.

"Have you ever done this?" He slid the sheet and pen across the table to Lia. "Write a line about what you're feeling, I'll reveal my line, and then you can reveal yours."

Out of curiosity, comfort, and basking in the glow of connecting with a new man so effortlessly, Lia wrote a line. She pushed the paper to the center of the table. Ellis smiled at Lia and read his line out loud.

"I am in wonder and gratitude for what came into my life today."

You're not breathing; breathe.

Lia very slowly read her line to Ellis.

"These hours are precious, a gift of sustenance to me."

And so it went for another twenty minutes until they eventually filled up the sheet, line by line, revelation by revelation, with their thoughts about each other, this day, this evening, life, love, fate and other thoughts, humorous and serious, random and specific. Ellis pulled his chair around to Lia's side of the table and, with their heads close together, and they read both sides again.

Lia looked up and directly into Ellis' eyes. "This means something." It was a statement, not a question.

"Yes, it does," Ellis replied as he lifted Lia's right hand up on its heel, rested it on the table, and interlaced his fingers with hers.

He let go of Lia's hand and moved back to his side of the table when dinner was served, and they ate without a lot more talking. It didn't seem necessary; the quiet between them seemed full of communication.

Later, Oscar, Johnny and Wayne walked through the club and waved at Lia as they stepped up on the stage.

"You're staying?"

"Yes."

Yes!

Lia locked on to Ellis, his body, his relationship to the keyboard, the movement of his fingers, his facial expressions, the way he shifted his weight from one side of his body to the other, the way he concentrated, and the way he seemed to draw in the audience, especially the women Lia noticed, with a glance out to the room at just the right moment in the music.

I've known the guy only one day. But, it's undeniable, I'm not the only woman in this room glued to him. But I'm the woman he invited to dinner, and spent the whole day with, and shared a lot about his life, and wrote thoughtful statements about it. You've had a wonderful day, embrace it. Vulnerable is okay; you've never allowed it for yourself. It's okay, Lia.

Since they were playing only one set, the quartet took a very short break midway. Ellis did not come over to the table, but winked at Lia before he briefly left the stage with the guys. The second half delivered the magic the first half had teased. Ellis seemed lost in the waves of his performance, just as Lia imagined he would be. When they accepted the loud and appreciative applause of the packed room, Ellis looked at Lia and winked again.

As the guys packed up their instruments and equipment and the crowd filed out of the club, Lia waited for Ellis.

I feel a little like a groupie, waiting here at the table. But, you're waiting for this man, and he wants you to wait.

Oscar came over to the table with Ellis to say hello and good night.

"You guys were wonderful," Lia remarked.

"Thanks. Good room, good crowd," Oscar replied.

They all headed out. Lia was just ahead of Ellis, and he leaned forward. "Let's make it a marathon. I'll take you home."

"I have my car."

"I'll follow you to be sure you make it safely; it'll be almost two in the morning."

"It's so much out of your way. I'm all the way up in the foothills; you'll practically pass by your condo on the way. I'll be okay."

"Can't a fellow be allowed to follow you home to be sure you're safe?"

"Yes." Lia couldn't manage to say no.

And, you can come in, we'll jump on my lavender sheets, and I'll wrap my legs around you. No, Lia, too soon.

In the middle of the night, it took only a half hour for them to pull up in front of Lia's townhouse. Lia pulled into her driveway but did not press the garage door opener. Ellis stayed on the street, stopping his car across her driveway entrance. The neighborhood was heavy with silence, and the two running car engines seemed to scream; Lia was glad to turn off her car. Before she could get out, Ellis had already gotten out of his car and bounded up her driveway. He leaned down into the open window.

"Thank you for today. You have no idea."

"No idea about what?"

"In just one day. How much you helped me to feel, how natural it is with you, how a guy with a few miles on him can actually feel life."

Jesus. I feel exactly the same way.

"I have to go to Atlanta for a couple of days. I'll call you as soon as I get back."

I'm not going to let myself think that he may really be going to Memphis.

"Thank you for tea, for the festival, for dinner, for your words, and your performance. Oh, and thank you for the winks from the stage."

"Any time, any time at all." Ellis leaned inside the window and kissed Lia softly on the lips twice.

"Good night."

Inside, she undressed quickly. She closed her mind to any thoughts; she wanted to save them for when she was under her lavender sheets.

It had been way too long since Lia felt the delicious sensation of being romantically connected and emotionally vulnerable to a man. She had no reservations, she did not hold the feelings back, she wanted to let herself sink into them.

I feel like a real person. This is real life, what it's supposed to be. I think I'll call Laura on Monday morning and tell her about Ellis. She'll enjoy this.

"I feel life, too, Ellis." Lia spoke the words out loud in the darkness. That was her last thought before she fell asleep.

ξ

The telephone rang just after 8:30 in the morning, waking Lia from a deep, dreamless sleep. It was Ellis.

"I'm at the airport about to board my flight; just wanted to say good morning."

"Hmm . . ."

"Sounds like I woke you up."

"You did, but it's nice.

"Lia . . ."

"Ellis, is everything alright?"

"Yes, it is."

That was an awfully intense "yes." What's happening?

"Lia, I want a relationship that is truly profound, not just talking about it, but living it.

I think I've always been looking for it. I feel that we, you and I, have the potential for it. I . . . more later."

My God, my God. I'm actually shaking. It feels good, though.

"Talk to you soon, Lia."

ξ CHAPTER 11 ξ

Lia spent the next few weeks at the office talking, and not talking, to various people who rightly or wrongly, were important to her well being.

Although she had no desire to do so, Lia eventually felt she had to call Gunther and try to have a productive conversation with him. She took time to collect her thoughts and made the call. It was a Thursday afternoon.

"Hi Lia." Lou's voice was cheerful as usual.

"Hi Lou. I need to speak with Gunther; can you please tell him it's urgent."

"Gunther is out of the country. He's with the group in Mexico looking at the customer service structure down there. If you like, I can try to track him down through Lucas Mayhew's office."

Lucas Mayhew!

"Lucas Mayhew?" asked Lia. The question repeated itself inside her head, and the voice was screaming in contrast to the modulated tones she used with Lou.

"Well, of course, you know he runs the new EPD manufacturing plant in Mexico now. It just started operating a couple of weeks ago."

Lia sensed that Lou suddenly realized she was delivering news. Lia had assumed Lucas was more than likely sitting at home, living off the generous severance pay he was given and conducting a job search. Running the new plant in Mexico! Lia put a hand to her forehead, her vision blurred, and she felt dizzy.

How could Lucas have been given this job without me at least knowing about it? For God's sake, how could a group travel to Mexico to look at apparently new Consumer Services issues down there without my involvement? Without me being advised of what's going on? Without me being the one to plan and lead the trip? Insulting me meant nothing. Not only is this fired bastard not sitting at home, but he's been reemployed by Conallied and given an international assignment. Keith was right; they circled the wagons around Lucas after I fired him. Has a Black woman ever had the nerve to fire a white guy, ever, in all of Conallied's history? I don't think so.

Most Conallied managers and executives alike lusted after these international assignments to advance their careers in the company, and Lucas Mayhew had obviously been rewarded with one.

Did Lucas deliberately orchestrate his own removal from my staff? Did he do it because he felt he should have gotten my job? Did he recognize that, as a result of the negative feelings he knew would be directed toward me after I fired him, he could get a really good assignment? The bastard had worked it!

Lou offered her more information. "I hear Lucas is already having some issues with the workers about salaries. They want to be paid closer to what the plant workers make here in the States. I wonder why that wasn't settled before the plant opened. I think it's pretty intense down there."

Lou was sharing critical inside information that Lia should have already been aware of, but clearly had been left out of the loop.

"I assumed you were with them, Lia, because I think they were also going to assess future Consumer Services needs. Anyway, I expect Gunther back in the office on Monday."

"I had so much going on here in Levale I couldn't get away."

I don't know why I'm bothering to lie to her.

"I'll get a report from the group when they return. Have Gunther give me a call when he gets back. Don't forget to tell him it's important."

"Will do. Hang in there, Lia."

Lia thought Lou's "hang in there" comment was deliberate and sincere. But she couldn't wait to get off the call because her heart was pounding, and she was still feeling dizzy. She sat there, yet again, feeling angry and confused. It seemed like the hundredth time. Lia swiveled from side to side in her chair, then rocked back and forth, and finally sat absolutely still staring out at the black clouds that were gathering in the hot, muggy sky. Lia knew absolutely nothing about a Mexico trip. It was clear that if a group traveled to Mexico on a mission related to Consumer Services, then she should have been the point person as the leader of Consumer Services. Why did it have to be this way? All she had done was her best, and it was pretty damned good. She was willing to bet that Donald and Virginia were part of the group. She needed to understand why this was happening. She picked up the phone and called Dan. Valerie advised her that he was in Fielding for a meeting and was then taking a long weekend on a backpacking trip. He wouldn't be back in the office until Tuesday after lunch.

ع

Lia then called both Keith and Daw, and their advice was very different. Keith was adamant that she should track down Castle and demand to know what was going on.

"If you can't find him, you should be sitting in his office when he comes back on Tuesday afternoon. This is outrageous. You're doing everything and more for those bastards. Do you think they would treat a white executive, one of their boys, like this? You know damned well they wouldn't!" Lia had never heard Keith so angry.

"You call me after you talk to Castle. I don't give a damn; we may have to do something about this."

"Oh shit, Keith." It was all Lia could think to say.

I don't want Keith sucked into my mess.

"Hey buddy, you have to pick your battles, and this damn well may be the one."

Daw, on the other hand, thought she should take a different approach.

"You'd better be careful how you play this one. I think a low-key approach may be the best."

"A low-key approach? I think I've been way too low key!"

"Carefully pick the moment to talk to Dan about this. You two definitely need to have a talk, but make sure the atmosphere is right. If you put him too much on the defensive, he may strike back."

"Oh good," snapped Lia. "I actually have to be afraid of how he's going to react? Daw, what's going on here? How do I handle this kind of shit? You know how these guys think."

"You're apparently on the outside, Lia. It appears you are too much of a threat to them with the changes you're making; it clearly doesn't matter that the changes are positive for EPD. What you've got to do is figure out what's really going on down there and exactly how to get back on the inside, be included in the conversations you're not a part of now. You stay out of that circle too long and it will become almost impossible."

"You almost make it sound like it's my fault. Why do I have to be the one to figure it out? And, I'm not sure at this point if I even want to figure it out and be in their precious circle."

"Lia, that's a decision you have to make, and you have to act accordingly."

"What does that mean, act accordingly?"

"You have to assess the entire situation and make a decision about how you want to proceed. Either way, you want to be careful and be true to yourself. Do you want me to see what I can find out?"

"No, Dawson. Has anything like this ever happened to you during all your years at Conallied?"

"No, not really." He paused. "Lia, please be careful."

Her conversation with Daw had not been helpful at all. It was as though there was some secret handshake, or code word, or established ritual that she should know about, and even Daw was hesitant to tell her.

Maybe I should have pressed him about how he, specifically, step by step, would handle this situation. Even though he cares about me, he just may not know, because as a white male, he's never had to deal with this kind of insulting dynamics.

ع

Lia's weekend was pretty much ruined because she couldn't turn off her brain. The situation at EPD, and what to do about it, played over and over in her head.

Ellis was a welcome respite from the situation, but she hadn't been able to talk to him at length, even by telephone, about the Lucas Mayhew situation because of both their conflicting schedules. Lia had met him for coffee, and again for lunch, since their magic Saturday together. His teaching and work at the radio station kept him very busy, and Oscar Four had played two consecutive weekends out of town, so he had not been around much.

Lia had been invited by Gerard to attend a weekend blues festival along with a group of his friends. She loved blues and was happy to have something to do. She went along, but did not have a very good time. The enthusiastic crowd of people sitting on blankets by the river sharing food and drink and enjoying the music did not lighten her mood. She had told Gerard the barest details of the situation, and he did not press her. Lia had to admit to herself that she was embarrassed for her staff to know she was in this situation, as though there was something she should have done, and didn't. Anyway, it was her battle to fight.

By Monday, Lia had decided to meet with Dan. She called Valerie and asked if Dan would be in the office all of Tuesday afternoon. Valerie said that he would, and Lia asked her to tell him that she would be in his office at four o'clock. Lia didn't ask if he had another appointment at that specific time, nor did she ask her to call back to confirm. Valerie was an astute executive secretary; she could tell by Lia's tone that something was up and didn't ask any probing questions. Gunther did not return Lia's call from the previous Thursday by the end of the day on Monday. She was not surprised. Keith called her on Tuesday morning.

"So what are you going to do?" He didn't say hello or ask how she was feeling, but got right to the point.

"I have a four o'clock appointment with Castle."

"What are you going to say?"

"I don't know. I've decided not to think about it too much. It'll just make me crazy. One thing I do know. I'm going to be firm and remain very calm."

"Now that I agree with. You need to show them all how well you can handle this conflict."

"You mean I can't walk into his office with my hands on my hips and cuss out the white motherfucker"?

"I'd buy a ticket to that show!"

They both took momentary refuge in laughter.

"It seems that I always, always have to show them something."

"That's right, Lia, you always do. You've always done it, so do it again, babe."

"Yeah, right."

ξ

Dan's door was open, but Lia knocked anyway.

"Lia, come on in and have a seat."

His corner office was located on the top floor of the administration building. It was huge and his office furniture was oversized and heavy. It didn't seem to suit a man as young as Dan. The desktop was neat, almost bare, but numerous stacks of papers were lined up neatly on the credenza behind his desk. He motioned Lia to a dark brown leather sofa, and he settled his large frame in the armchair opposite her. He sipped from a can of diet cola. It was a beautiful day outside, but all the window blinds were closed.

"Hello Dan. How was your weekend? I understand you were on a backpacking trip?"

Let me start out on a cordial note.

"It was great, a nice getaway." He didn't say anything else and waited for Lia to start the conversation.

"Dan, we have a problem. Or, I have a problem. I am deeply troubled and, frankly, more than a little dismayed by the events of the past couple of weeks. We are sitting here in late July, and I'm well on the way to making the third quarter goals we projected. My staff, the associates, have embraced all the goals we set for Consumer Services, and they have worked very hard. The relationships among the associates and technicians have been entirely redefined; they're well on the way to being a real team now. It didn't happen overnight, nor was it easy, but it happened more quickly than I anticipated, and they've met my challenges, more than met them."

"What's the problem, Lia?" Dan's voice betrayed an edge of impatience.

Am I wasting your time, Dan? Okay, Lia, stay calm.

"What I do and how I do it seems to be increasingly dictated by Gunther, who reports to me. And, I just learned the other day that a group traveled to Mexico on a mission related to Consumer Services. I head up Consumer Services. Why wasn't I with that group? Why didn't I even know about it? The plans to restructure EPD, and particularly Consumer Services and its branch offices, are apparently moving forward, and I have no idea what's going on. My staff asks questions that I cannot answer. Dan, I cannot and will not work this way. The strength of my career is my reputation for getting things done and doing it with integrity and, most importantly, with dignity. I think I have demonstrated thus far what I can do for EPD. I certainly want to continue, Dan. But, it isn't working for me this way."

I'm proud of myself, my choice of the words, the calm, and firm tone I think is in my voice.

"Well." Dan said, letting out a long breath. "I can see that your feelings are serious, and I'm glad that you decided to talk with me. You should have been with the group in Mexico. But, at the time it was planned, we thought it best for you to stay here in Levale with so much going on. Don and Virginia from my staff, and Gunther, also Joe Mather, went along. I figured they could report back to you."

Oh, please.

"Dan, I should have been the one to make the decision about whether I go to Mexico. Whatever issues there are down there should have been brought to my attention in advance, and then I decide if myself and any of my staff should make the trip, at least as it relates to any Consumer Services issues, especially in a new facility located in an emerging market like Mexico."

"Don and Virginia have also been working on my restructure plan. It's still in the early stages. We'll have to report to Jud Jeffries and get his approval before anything happens anyway, before we can move forward. I'm going to present the entire plan to the full staff next month so you will all know what's going on.

Nothing else about Mexico? Okay. Let's pretend it wasn't a big deal. He obviously wants to move on.

"But Dan, you've indicated that a major part of the restructure will involve Consumer Services, my operation. How can anything be analyzed and recommended without my direct involvement and input to the process? I don't think I should have to wait for the full staff meeting to find out what's going to happen in my operation."

"You have a good point."

"Yes, Dan, I think I do."

Why do I allow myself to live a professional life that results in these kinds of conversations? I could be doing some real good somewhere, making a contribution that is valued.

"I will direct Don and Virginia to keep you in the loop from now on; make sure you get all the key data, analyses, recommendations, and so forth."

"I don't think I am articulating my thoughts to you very well. What about my being in the loop during the data gathering, decision-making process, before recommendations are formulated, so I can contribute my perspectives? I am embarrassed that I have to make this request of you."

"Oh sure, I understand. But I wouldn't be too worried about that. This thing is going to change in form and substance many times before it's a done deal."

Lia still felt very uneasy. She was not at all satisfied with what Dan was saying. She had not heard any real explanation of why he made these decisions in the first place, only justifications. He did not make it right.

"About Gunther. . ." Dan continued.

"Yes, about Gunther." Lia interrupted him. "We don't communicate. Why? He refuses to do it. I have asked for his input and advice, face to face, on three different occasions. I have called him a number of times, and I never get a call back. On the other hand, he has called me a grand total of twice in seven months, and both times sent Sara looking for me because he didn't want to wait for a call back. Gunther supposedly reports to me, and I think it's time for Gunther to understand that reality."

"I know you understand how problematic this situation is. You and Gunther have to work together if Consumer Services is going to be successful."

No shit. Why is this so-called hard-charging, aggressive leader being such a wimp? He is saying words that don't communicate anything.

"Dan, my initiatives are turning around the Consumer Services operation. There is a lot of support in the branches, more than you know. I don't have to tell you that these are the best and most experienced customer service people in the world. They can distinguish good ideas from those that have no substance."

I'm dying to give Dan a copy of the letter from the three branch managers. I won't do it now, but I may have to do it soon.

"I'll call Gunther and advise him to call you. I'm going to strongly encourage him to openly discuss any problems so that you two can finally work this out. I'll call him tonight."

"Okay, Dan. I'm not sure how much good it will do. I'm learning that Gunther does exactly what he wants to do no matter what anyone else thinks or says."

Lia made the last comment in the hope that Castle would think about who was really in charge, he or Gunther. The expression on his face seemed to indicate that she had struck a nerve.

What does Gunther have on this guy?

"Dan, I'm still committed, and I want us all to be heroes, enjoy huge successes. But the work has to be gratifying as well as challenging. I don't like what's going on here. It might be best for me to consider another assignment if this situation does not work itself out soon."

She could tell he was a little shaken by the tone and resolve in her voice, but she had to say it.

"No Lia, just keep doing what you're doing and hang in there. It should get better."

If one more person tells me to "hang in there," I am going to scream.

Again, words from him that didn't have any strength or conviction behind them. He asked her a couple of questions about customer satisfaction issues, as though they were having a routine conversation, and then looked at his watch while he mumbled about having to be somewhere. The meeting was over. As Lia took the long walk back to her office on the other side of the plant grounds, her only sense of satisfaction was in knowing that she had clearly made her feelings known. She was on the record.

The next morning she again called her brain trust, Keith and Daw, not that she thought they would be any more helpful, but because she felt desperate to talk with anyone who supported her. They shared Lia's frustration, but both agreed that a wait-and-see attitude was the right approach for now. Lia relaxed just a little and went about the business of running the Consumer Services operation.

ξ

"Hey, you're still there?"

"No, I'm lying on the beach in Cancun."

Lia was working late reviewing the voluminous service reports she received each month from the branches. Wanda's call was a welcome break.

"You sound a little down; everything okay?"

"Oh, I'm all right; just tired I guess. I had a difficult meeting with Dan Castle a few days ago. You know, never-ending drama."

"Speaking of Dan Castle, I'm going to be meeting him soon."

"What the hell for?"

"About the logo project. I told you I received a written acknowledgement of my proposal package."

"Yeah, what's happening?"

"I had a meeting yesterday with a guy named Clay Simpson; he is EPD's public relations person. I thought it went pretty well. The guy is a little full of himself, but he seemed to be impressed with my proposal. He made a point of telling me how glad he was that EPD could broaden its vendor profile, especially for an important contract like this."

"Oooh! Don't you love being included in the broader vendor profile?"

"Oh honey, it gives me goose bumps!"

"Simpson and his assistant, some Barbie doll named Geanna Jones, visited my office this afternoon. At least her name wasn't Susie."

"Don't be mean, Wanda," Lia laughed.

"Ben and I gave them the complete dog and pony show. I also had a colleague, Monica Allen, at my office to participate. She's done some nice work for me. She works out of her home, but if I get this contract, I'll bring her in full-time during the project."

"Sounds good so far."

"I hope so. Simpson wants me to meet with Dan Castle. He said it would be scheduled in the next week to ten days. I'm supposed to get a call from Castle's office. I'll want to talk with you about how to approach him."

"Hah! You're asking me?"

"Yes, but let me change the subject. How's Ellis? Based on what I hear from Oscar, Ellis thinks the sun rises and sets in you."

"Well, I don't know about all that. To tell the truth, we haven't spent all that much time together. We spent that whole day and evening together, and since then we've had coffee and lunch."

"Have you told him about the stuff going on at Conallied?"

"He knows about it in a general way. We have yet to spend a long evening of quiet time together. And, I sure don't want to spend the time whining about my problems at work. It feels so needy. I feel like I might be running ahead of him in this relationship, if you can even call it that."

"Well, I don't think they have any out-of-town gigs for a while. You guys can hopefully spend some real time together."

"Good. I admit it, Wanda, I can't wait to see Ellis."

"Oooh, girl! Good night."

"Good night, Wanda." Lia giggled for the first time in days.

ξ

The week after her meeting with Castle, Lia had a number of interesting telephone conversations. She decided it was time to call Barnes, Casey and DeLucca to thank them for the letter. Enough time had passed that Lia felt they could talk without feeling too uncomfortable. The last thing she wanted to do at this point was create any more discomfort.

Not that any of this discomfort is my fault, but that doesn't mean it isn't my problem.

She needed to personally thank each of them. She called Phil first.

"Hi Lia, how are you doing?" Phil sounded like he was in a good mood about something.

"I'm doing good, Phil. I just called to say thanks for the letter. I sure do appreciate your support. I must say it came on a day when I really needed it."

"Well, we've seen the results getting better and better since the initiatives started after the beginning of the year. The employees are happy, and the customers are happy. That makes me a happy camper! This is the first time I've seen the techs and associates work this well together and, as a former tech, I certainly do know how it used to be."

"That's really good to hear," Lia responded. "Everyone has really worked hard. They're putting in lots of hours working on the process improvements, and doing their regular jobs."

"Their attitude is great. You know that we had one of their sessions here in Jacksonville, and the energy was incredible. That's why I was having a problem with what was happening. The backstabbing and misrepresentations being made to Dan were starting to get real shitty. You know, some guys want to believe all the negative crap because they can't cope with all this change. I can tell you, though, that the vast majority likes what's happening and are encouraged by it. I really hope you guys in Levale can get this worked out."

Lia knew Phil was really talking about Dan's refereeing skills between herself and Gunther.

"Well, I hope so too. I'm working on it.

Lia sensed an awkward silence on the line.

"Lia, I happen to know that Gunther told one of my senior agents that he could bury you if he wanted to do it. That's the term he used, 'bury you'. He said he didn't want to have to do it, but you have to be on the team, whatever that means to him."

That bastard has the nerve, or is it permission, spoken or unspoken, to decide what's going to happen to me.

"I'll have to speak with Gunther and learn what he means by 'team.'" Lia tried to speak evenly and muster as much strength and self-confidence in her voice as she could.

"Good."

"You'll have to come to Levale and sit in on one of the regular quarterly report sessions from the teams. They're actually a lot of fun."

"I'll do that. You hang in there."

There it is again.

Lia's conversations with Glen and Dennis had the same friendly tone, so she was not surprised by a comment Dennis made when they talked.

"Lia, you probably know that I was not real enthusiastic when you spoke to my people here in Denver. But, I've watched some of the older guys like Elmer Boone and Sam Mason get excited about the process improvement initiative. They've led the younger agents, which is a nice switch around here, and the way it should have always been. We've had some great results. We're getting positive comments from customers. But, out here, the thing I see having the most value is that the guys feel they're really part of the team as opposed to just repair robots who follow directives decreed from Levale. I signed the letter because I thought it was the right thing to do. You have my support."

"Thanks Dennis. I appreciate that. The associates love working with Elmer; he's a hero to them, a real role model."

Dennis laughed. "I'll be sure to tell Elmer. He'll get a hoot out of that."

ξ

The telephone conversations provided only a momentary boost to Lia's spirit, especially in light of Phil's revelation. She wanted to deny it in her own mind, but she had hit the wall. She finally had to consciously acknowledge that she was facing both a personal and professional crisis in her life; she had allowed disappointments in both to now become wound up into a whole life failure. Every fiber, every instinct, every hope and dream for success, wanted things to be otherwise.

Maybe I'm just not destined to have a heroic existence, professionally or personally. I want to be a hero. Is that wrong? I don't think it should be. But, maybe it is.

Lia came to Levale full of energy for the challenge. She pushed her private anxieties to the back burner, subordinated her personal needs to focus on the opportunity presented to her. She had demonstrated all the characteristics that had signaled success for her white, male counterparts. She was confident that she had been aggressive, forward-thinking, truly empowering, and had enhanced her division's bottom line. All this and her employees seemed to genuinely like her, too. She should have been the beneficiary of the kind of inclusion, and even affection, she had seen extended to others. Why was she not part of the group, included in conversations, planning sessions, off-hours gatherings? Had she done or said something inappropriate, even unforgivable? She never had much opportunity to interact with her peers or her boss. So, on what basis was she being ostracized? And, why was Dan, their so-called leader, allowing it to happen? Another question pushed at Lia's consciousness; she couldn't push this one back. Why did she care so much? Why the hell did she care? Was she fulfilled, happy? Was this real life? Was she bound and determined to have something that would forever be elusive? Laura's questions from their last long-distance telephone conversation reverberated in her head. Lia laughed out loud in response to those unanswered questions Laura had asked, and the sound of her laughter echoed around her empty office. The noise startled her.

Everything new that held hope for me seems to have been a pathetic illusion. I'm so tired.

It was late, and she was alone. After a long while, having rested under the blanket of total silence, Lia summoned her emotional energy. She continued down the road, determined, on her lonely and solitary journey.

ξ

Lia called Gunther's office the next morning. Lou advised her that he was out of town for the day and would be in the following morning.

"Louanne, I need to arrange a specific time to talk with him. Our schedules are so crazy, let's put it on our calendars. I think a half-hour will do it." Lia knew that Louanne managed Gunther's calendar and had authority to schedule, change or cancel appointments for him.

"How about four o'clock tomorrow afternoon? I'll have Gunther call you. You know how punctual he is, but he'll be in a meeting right up to four o'clock and may be a few minutes late calling. I'll call you if the delay is going to be longer."

"Thanks, Lou. It's on my calendar."

Lia knew she needed to have a no-bullshit talk with Gunther since he obviously didn't feel compelled to call her. She thought a face-to-face meeting would be more appropriate in this kind of situation, but decided to start with a telephone conversation. She was going to ask him point blank to articulate whatever issues he had, and then she would suggest they discuss them one by one. Lia had to put aside her anger at having to deal with this jerk at all, and decided to just get it done. Lia received a call from Donald Harmon later in the day.

"Hi Lia. I'm calling for Virginia and myself. We've prepared a preliminary report on the restructure for Dan. I'll fax it over to you. Review it, and if you have any questions, give me a call. You can also call Virginia, if you like." He spoke in a very clipped manner, not collegial, not rude.

"I'll look forward to getting it. As I've already discussed with Dan, I need to be in the loop and have input on any plans involving Consumer Services before anything is finalized."

"We're going to schedule a review meeting with Dan and other key people, but probably not until mid to late September. We've still got a lot of work to do to sort out our findings before we get in front of Dan. If you'd like to be there, I'll send you a copy of the agenda. The more the merrier!"

I wonder what Dan communicated to him. He doesn't seem to understand that I need to be more than just another person at the meeting, or he doesn't want to understand.

"Well, of course; that's great, thank you." Lia checked herself and held on to her professional manner. She continued.

"You can also fax or email drafts to me as you're working on them. I'll go through the document and make my comments in writing. We'll want to be sure that all the recommendations are consistent with the great process improvement work that Consumer Services employees are already doing. We don't want to do anything that interrupts or negates the improvements they have made and are continuing to make." A little preachy, but hopefully effective.

"We'll make absolutely sure that you're there".

ξ

At four o'clock the next afternoon, Lia was sitting at her desk staring at the telephone. At four-thirty, she had not heard from Gunther or Lou. By four forty-five, she was angry. She was committed; she had worked hard; she hadn't said an unfriendly word to anyone, except to Castle himself. At least demonstrate basic professional courtesy by returning her telephone call, even if he didn't want to have a real conversation with her. At five o'clock, she called Louanne to catch her before the end of the day.

"Lou, I haven't heard from Gunther." Lia was surprised and then agitated with herself because her voice trembled as she spoke.

"Lia!" At four o'clock, Gunther told me he probably wasn't going to be able to talk with you today. And, he specifically said he would give you a quick call himself to reschedule. I thought he had done it. I'm sorry."

"It's not your fault. If he's there, I'll talk to him now for a minute."

"He left for the day about fifteen minutes ago. He'll be in the office tomorrow around one o'clock."

"Thanks Louanne." Lia hung up.

Lia's hurt and confusion were dissipating fast.

Forget this bullshit. I'm done.

She was as angry as she had ever been in her life; at the rude treatment, at the arrogance, at being shut out, at the disrespect. She never dreamed she would be faced with such a lack of professionalism. She was beyond tired of reaching out to this guy.

Screw him!

ξ

Lia didn't bother to call Keith or Daw again, or anyone else, to relay what happened with Gunther. Days passed, and Gunther never called her. She had thought, for all of about ten seconds, that maybe Gunther had some kind of real emergency and good reason for not calling her. But she knew in her gut this was wishful thinking and that he was never going to call. She continued doing her job running Consumer Services. That was what she could do something about. The initiative was rolling full force on its own steam with the improvements to the operations continuing to generate impressive numbers. Lia came to the painful conclusion that the success-ful results of the process improvement activities that were now happening in varying degrees in every branch office across the country, and the new atmosphere of employee empowerment simply were not the most import-ant elements in this situation. Anything she did would have generated the same response. Clearly Gunther, not Lia's predecessor, had been in control, he had never been compelled to give up the control, and now he was in battle mode to avoid losing it. She freely gave away control and, in turn, gained more. And, even though Gunther didn't know about the letter, she presumed, he had to sense the erosion of his support base. Forget about what was best for the EPD and Conallied. As far as she was concerned, this was personal now, and Lia had to stop wishing it was otherwise.

ξ

Lia took a moment to stop talking and appreciate how easy it was to pick up the thread of past conversations with Laura. They talked as if almost no time had passed since Laura had challenged her to think about why so much of her emotional capital was invested in work and in Conallied. What Laura had done was sprinkle fertilizer on a seed that lay dormant in Lia's head, and it had begun to grow. It could not have thrived without Laura's help.

"I may have hit the wall."

"Tough work, huh."

"My forehead is bloodied and bruised from hitting the wall repeatedly. On the strictly business side, things are going really well, but I just cannot establish any kind of working relationship with the folks on Dan's staff. The employees in my operation have responded to everything I've asked of them, and instead of getting positive reinforcement, it's been nothing but sabotage and exclusion. I don't know if I'm dense or just can't face up to the truth. Every time I try to have a conversation with myself, to come to terms with it, I get too depressed to finish it."

"The answer is too tough?"

"I know they have a terribly hard time dealing with people who are different from themselves, and certainly with a Black woman who is not a subordinate. But when you are successful and add value to an organization, and I'm talking about value that is demonstrable, then what's the excuse? That I haven't tried to create a good relationship with them? I can't even get the bastards to return a simple telephone call. In the world of Conallied, and I'm sure in corporate America in general, it's the bottom-line numbers that count, the dollars. So why is that not true in my case? They may talk a good public relations game about the company's values, empowering employees, and new paradigms. Don't you hate that word 'paradigm?' I've seen it demonstrated over and over and over again that the biggest jerks continue to succeed in this company. So, whether they like me or not, or can get accustomed to my being at the table or not, why doesn't my making the numbers in response to Dan Castle's challenge and delivering on the commitments I made, hell, exceeding those commitments, not result in big success? Why does the criteria they apply to themselves not apply to me?"

Lia stopped to take a breath.

"That's a very naive question, Lia," Laura replied quietly.

"I know, I know. I'm a lot of sound and fury signifying nothing, I guess."

"You know the answer to that question."

"Yes, and it hurts. I hate the fact that the bastards can cause me to hurt."

Laura did not respond, remained silent.

"It's flashing there in the back of my head, the hurt, and the answer, like a neon sign off in the distance. I want it to remain unfocused, not come into clear view. It's so hard."

"What is it exactly that is so hard."

"The thing I need to do."

"And that is?"

"You don't let up."

Lia could not form the words. She changed the subject and started talking about Ellis.

When she originally told Laura about being introduced to him, it seemed to Lia that Laura sounded a bit conflicted about whether to cheer on or counsel Lia.

"Since we met, we've seen one another three times. It's been very intense, but we haven't been anything close to intimate yet, which feels a little weird. He hasn't even said or done anything that might lead in that direction. But, when we're together, it feels charmed. I don't think it's just me. I hope not."

"He sounds very interesting."

"He is very compelling."

"Lia, you seem to consistently follow a pattern of attraction to people and situations that have a high probability of rejection for you.

It seems to have become a theme in my life. Why don't I articulate this, express these thoughts, out loud, outside my head? I should certainly be able to articulate it to Laura. I think Laura is talking about both things now, Conallied and Ellis, too.

"Pathetic, isn't it? You always get to see, or in this case hear, the pathetic side of me. Isn't it tiring?"

"Lia, don't wallow. I want you to think about being good to yourself, giving yourself a gift."

"Can't Ellis be that gift? Put some positive energy in my life to balance my professional life?"

"Maybe, maybe not. But I'm talking about the gift of peace of mind that comes from inside you. You've trapped yourself into doing it all and being it all for people. Look, here you are once more on the telephone with me. I ask, again, about the reward for you. What's the reward to you for tap dancing for everyone?"

"I guess the reward has to come from inside me, only me."

"Bingo!"

"You're always giving me something to think about."

"But, this is the big one, my friend."

"I know."

ξ CHAPTER 12 ξ

When Lia was with Ellis, Conallied, EPD, Dan, Gunther and all the contempt and disrespect temporarily faded into the background, their importance was diminished.

I am so grateful for this reprieve from the strain.

"It was a good idea to get you out of Levale, even if it's just a day trip."

"Thank you for this. You have no idea what it means to me."

They were sitting outside on the expansive front veranda of a beautiful old house that had been converted to a restaurant on the ground floor. Harvest Restaurant sat in the middle of a beautiful vineyard situated on rolling hills in the wine country two hours outside Levale. The vines were heavy and full and ready for the upcoming harvest in a few weeks. Lia didn't even know there was a wine country in the state, and Ellis surprised her with a Saturday excursion for a winery tour and early dinner. The weather was perfect, not too hot for a late summer afternoon.

"You grew up in a state with one of the premiere wine producing areas in the whole world, so I hope this isn't a disappointment to you."

"This is such a nice getaway, I couldn't possibly be disappointed. I badly needed a day away from the salt mine." Lia responded.

The tour was interesting and entertaining, and the wine tasting was even better. Lia was beginning to feel a little woozy, and Ellis must have noticed.

"Time for lunch, Ms. Granger, before they have to roll both of us out of here. They left the cool, dark wine tasting room, and walked out into the bright sunshine. It was a short walk down a gravel path to the restaurant. They chose to sit outside.

"This is another reminder that I need to spend some time at home; hang out with my family and friends, spend a day in the Napa wine country, drive down to Carmel for a weekend with my Aunt Ruthie, spend some time up at Lake Tahoe for a few days. There are so many great things to do in Northern California."

"I've been to California several times, and I visited the wine country in Napa and Sonoma. I've never been down the coast to Carmel or been to Lake Tahoe, though I've heard both are beautiful."

"I'll have to be your tour guide one of these days."

That would be wonderful, living a healthy life doing fun things with someone I care about. I wonder how my family and friends would react to Ellis? I wonder what Ruthie would think of him. He couldn't be more different from Rob.

"I'm glad I made a reservation; this place is packed." Ellis did not comment on what Lia said.

They ordered more wine and their entrees. Everything felt enhanced, electric between them; the air, food, their conversation, when he touched her hand across the table, when they looked directly at each other, she felt an incandescence surrounding them. Lia was sure she was not the only one feeling it. Ellis kept looking at her as though he was fearful she was going to get up and leave. By the time they finished a shared fruit tart dessert, using one plate and two forks, the sexual tension between the two of them was so palpable Lia wondered if it was obvious to the people sitting around them.

"You ready to head back to Levale?" Ellis's eyes were almost pleading.

Wow. I don't know why I was worried about intimacy. We both want the same thing today. I know I want him.

"Yes."

ξ

Lia pulled the pastel green sheet up over their exposed nakedness. The linen had a clean, fresh laundered smell, just like Ellis always did.

"Thank you." Ellis had slid off her and now shifted from his stomach to his back. He was staring at the ceiling. He was silent.

Something wasn't right, and it was supposed to be so right. Their first lovemaking had been fast, somehow anxious, and it felt robotic, and then incomplete, so unlike all the time they had spent together.

What happened? He didn't like my body? It's not the most beautiful in the world, but it's not bad. Had it been too long? I want to cry. I can't cry. I won't cry.

A half moon cast an almost eerily bright light across the corner of the room where the bed sat in Ellis's bedroom. A tape of oldie, R&B ballads that Ellis had mixed himself was playing softly in the small cassette player on the nightstand. The less than symphonic sound quality was smoothed out through the glow of lust. Everything was comfortable in the room, except the two people. Lia tried to push through the creeping reality to will it all to be okay.

Well, it's our first time, and we were both probably nervous. No, I don't feel nervous, but maybe Ellis was. Why should he be nervous? I just knew this was going to be the sweetest, deepest, most passionate and spiritual lovemaking of my life. Oh God, why wasn't it?

"Are you cold?" Ellis's voice sounded distracted and the question seemed to be directed to the ceiling.

"I'm okay. I was a bit chilled for a moment without the covers, but I'm fine now." Lia responded, feeling the need to sound sexy, content, and upbeat, all at the same time.

Ellis fell quiet; not the kind of intimate quiet filled with sexual afterglow, but a brooding silence that matched Lia's mood in spite of her best effort.

Deepest lovemaking? This is sad. He has almost no penis. Even when it was erect, I could barely feel it in my wetness. I didn't even feel it filling my mouth. Maybe that's why he used his fingers so much. I need to figure out what to do about this, how to make it good. We can work on it. It's probably just a little erectile dysfunction; happens to men a lot. But it didn't feel like erectile dysfunction. I remember Rob occasionally had that kind of problem, and this is different. It felt like some kind of physical disability or impairment. Why didn't he talk to me about it, either before or even now? There's more than one way to skin a cat. I'm good at this; at least, I used to be. I wonder how many women have been through this dance with Ellis? I'll wait for him to talk.

Finally he spoke. "I was thinking that next weekend we might have dinner at Armando's. It's a new bistro owned by the husband of one my co-workers at the radio station. I'd like to support Armando on its opening weekend. He's been a good buddy. I'm very proud of my man, Mando. His parents, an Italian father and an African-American/Puerto Rican mother, owned the only genuine deli in Levale for almost twenty years, and for many years they were the one and only multi-racial family in town, believe it or not."

What?

He stopped abruptly. It was silent again. The taped music rolled on, but the mood it had set earlier was now changed to something that felt like a cruel joke.

It had been a perfect day, beyond perfect, too perfect, until we made love. Now, here we are in a moment that I can't interpret.

"Would you like a cup of tea?"

Ellis' voice in the now completely dark room startled Lia.

"Ellis, what . . ."

"Would you like a cup of tea, Lia?" His voice was low and urgent, and it frightened Lia a bit.

A cup of tea? Why aren't we wrapped in each other's arms talking softly or in the peaceful sleep of afterglow?

"Sure, that sounds fine."

He's offering me tea like it's the most important thing in the world; he wants to get out of this bed.

Ellis walked naked across the room to the closet, pulled on some sweat pants and a t-shirt, and left the room. Even then, his sensuality was overt, but it utterly belied other truths. When Lia entered the kitchen, Ellis was busying himself with the tea, and she sat at the counter and looked out the big, open window at the quiet street below. A warm rain had started to fall, and Ellis closed the window to keep out the wet.

"I don't think this rain will cool things off at all."

"You're probably right," Ellis replied as he sat one of the two cups of mint tea in front of Lia and leaned against the counter on the other side of the kitchen as he sipped his tea.

I want to get out of here. Something is happening here that I don't fully understand, and we're obviously not talking about it, and I need to go.

Lia took a couple of sips of tea and slid off the stool.

"I think I'll head home now."

"Okay." Ellis continued to hold on to his cup.

As Lia was retrieving her purse from the living room floor where she had earlier let it drop on the way to the bedroom, Ellis put his hand on her shoulder, turned her around and grabbed both her hands.

"Today, tonight was very special. You are extraordinary."

What? How? Then why am I on the way out the door, and he's not trying to stop me. This is humiliating. Get me the hell out of here.

291

In barely a whisper, because Lia was afraid if she tried to talk at this point she would cry, she responded, "really?"

She then walked out the door and out to the street. She realized for the first time that she didn't have her car; Ellis had picked her up at home.

Ellis let me leave his apartment alone, late at night, with no car.

She spotted a convenience store at the end of the block, its bright lights illuminating the wet street.

Thank God for small favors.

Lia walked to the store, straightened her clothes a bit more, ran her hands through her hair, and walked in.

"Hi, I need to call a taxi, please."

The young store clerk, and another man leaning against the counter talking to him, both stared at Lia.

"Sure, I'll call for you. Where are you going?"

"To the foothills area."

"Is that where you live?" He sounded surprised.

"Yes, in that area."

"I can drive you home." The other man, slightly older, did not leer, but Lia was not about to get in a car with a stranger."

"I'll take a taxi, thank you." He didn't look menacing, probably just wanted to make some money.

The clerk made the call. "It's going to be at least a 45-minute wait. It's Saturday night, and it's raining. Here's a chair to sit." He lifted a folding chair from behind the counter and sat it next to a stack of boxes.

"Thank you." Lia gave him a grateful smile.

No one else entered the store. Lia sat there trying not to cry and determined to look strong and confident. When the taxi finally arrived, the clerk looked out the window and remarked, "Oh, I know Pete. Let me walk out with you."

He opened the back door to the taxi, and Lia got in. He tapped on the front passenger window, and the driver lowered it. He leaned his head in the window and said, "Take good care of her, Pete, I think she's had a bad night."

How did he know? I guess he sees it all late at night in a 24-hour convenience store.

They rode in silence, and Pete let her out at home thirty minutes later. She was thankful for another small favor; a stash of cash she always kept in a small zipper compartment in her wallet. She gave him a good tip and said good night. When she entered her townhome, she stopped and stared into the wall mirror near the front door.

It was supposed to be magic. What happened to the magic? Why me, Lord, why me?

It doesn't make any sense. I can't figure anything out or understand why it has to be this way.

I want so much to figure it out, but I can't. Is this my fate? Is it supposed to be this way because this is what the universe wants for me?

ξ

Still in her pajamas and not long out of bed, Lia answered the telephone when it rang for the first time Sunday afternoon. It was Ellis.

Lia, you must not care. If you care, you'll go crazy. You'll rattle around in your solitude and go crazy.

"Hello Lia, how are you?"

"Okay, just enjoying a quiet Sunday. I eventually made it home in a taxi with the help of some sympathetic people." Ellis did not respond to her comment.

"I had to go to the station this afternoon. I may have to go in for the next couple of weekends to help with program changes that are being made."

Really? We're just going to exchange small talk and review your schedule?

"Don't work too hard, and take care of yourself," Lia unsuccessfully tried to lighten her voice.

"Lia, I can't go on. I'm sorry.

"What happened last night, Ellis? I think I deserve to know." Again, Ellis did not respond to her.

"So, the deeply profound relationship you repeatedly said you wanted is coming to an early and not-so-profound end?"

"Lia, I've thought a lot about it, and I've decided that I owe it to Deborah, and to Jason, to give our relationship another chance."

I don't believe this is happening; I don't believe I'm really having this conversation.

"Is this the excuse you use after every time you attempt to sleep with a woman that's not Deborah? You told me that you had given long and serious thought to ending your relationship with her, and you've hardly ever mentioned her son."

"I did say that, it's true. That's how I imagined it."

"So are we talking about your imagination, or about reality?" Lia was distressed by the cynicism in her voice and humiliated by the fact that she was continuing this conversation.

"You are special . . ."

"Did you meditate on that? Did you write a list on a piece of tablet paper? Did you write all your limitations on the paper? You promised to teach me how to meditate with you, but I guess meditating is just a game for you."

And, so is your tiny little penis that I might have been devoted to loving no matter the problem. What am I doing? Say goodbye and hang up the damned telephone!

"I'm sorry. I don't know what else to say. You're an extraordinary woman. You have so much to give. I can't imagine that there's not someone out there to make you happy."

Jesus, how could I have been so totally wrong?

"You have no integrity. You are a man without integrity. Goodbye Ellis." Lia hung up the telephone, walked out to the deck and sank into a chair, suspended in a silent, nightmare world of hurt, confusion and desperation, and the inability to make sense of it, or will it away, or pray it away, or demand it away.

What a cruel joke. I don't deserve this. Haven't I had enough?

Lia sat there a long time. The silence screamed, filled with her longing and fatigue. Then, she sobbed out loud.

ξ

Lia called Laura, realizing that it was very late on Sunday evening in Fielding and she likely would get her answering service. The voice on the other end of the telephone had the perfect combination of efficiency and compassion.

"Are you having an emergency?"

In other words, am I having a meltdown?

"Yes."

"Do you have any thoughts of hurting yourself, or someone else?"

Well, there's something to think about.

"No, I just need to talk with Laura as soon as possible."

"Okay, I'll page her. You should hear back soon."

I guess the service can tell when it's real.

Lia sat out on the deck again, and tried to make out the big and little dippers in a sky encrusted with stars on the August evening. It was a way to pass the time while she waited for Laura. The sky was brighter and clearer than the night before when it had been much warmer and hazy. The events of the night before seemed as though they had happened long ago, but the feelings weighed down on her with a heaviness she could physically feel. Lia tried to lose herself in the sky, lose the weight in its endless expanse, have the sky single her out, and provide the comfort that she needed, as a special favor to her.

Why can I get the gift of the sky in its majesty and not the gift of peace of mind under it?

The telephone rang, and Lia took it into the house to answer.

"Hello, Lia."

"Laura, thanks for calling me back so quickly and so late on a Sunday evening."

"What's the matter?"

"There's war in the Persian Gulf, the stock market is tanking, and my retirement fund is taking a hit." Lia's effort at humor fell flat.

"You've called me late at night. Stop avoiding. Tell me what's going on."

"I'm sinking, Laura."

Just tell her; don't leave anything out because you're humiliated.

Lia told Laura about her short, intense relationship with Ellis.

It was a nice dance, never a relationship; it never had a chance to become anything more.

"What are you feeling now, at this moment?"

"I feel like I'm sinking, emotionally and physically. I feel like I'm trying to hold on to something, anything, in the universe, but I'm disconnected, slipping. I don't mean to sound dramatic, Laura, but it's how I feel."

"Lia, I'm sorry. It's a setback, a big one, but you've got to consider a few important things."

"I'm tired of feeling disconnected." Lia was not ready to follow the path of answering probing questions from Laura. "I have nothing. No real place to call home, no family close by, and certainly no work family, to attach to. All I have is Jordan, a thousand miles away, and he deserves to live his own life. I was thinking of telling him about Ellis. I even had visions of eventually bringing Jordan down here to meet him, and Wanda and Oscar, too; now it's just humiliating. I have to laugh when I think that I ever considered that Ellis and I was a thing. I'm not making something out of nothing; well, it actually turned out to be nothing, but he was the one who characterized the two of us as profound and talked on and on about how important building a relationship was to him, and . . .

"Lia, Lia, stop. I want to ask a question."

Can't I be pathetic with my own therapist? If not her, then who?

"Lia, this man seemed to be a quality person, and he made very clear, very serious proclamations to you. He was not subtle. You did not imagine something. Do you really have to berate yourself because of a man who made a determination to do this to you? In the particular way that he did it?"

No. I don't know. Is it that simple?

"Is it that simple? I guess it is. I made a mistake; everything has been a mistake."

"For now, let's separate Ellis from whatever you mean when you use the word, 'everything.' Would you really want to be with this man now?"

"No."

"That's a start."

"But, it hurts like hell."

"I know it hurts, Lia. I'm sensing you may have looked to Ellis as a savior, particularly because the situation at Conallied has been so difficult."

"Maybe so, probably so. I seem to have no peace in my life, no peace of mind. Maybe I was thinking that Ellis would make Conallied bearable, even make it not matter any more. Add something real and valuable to my life instead of putting all my heart and soul and psychic energy into making something more valuable for others. I thought I had met a truly special man. I wanted him to think I was truly special, too. What did I do wrong?"

"Well, that question takes us back to the essential question I've asked you before. You feel humiliated and abandoned, but while you're working your way through the pain of this breakup, don't forget to keep asking yourself why pleasing others is so important to you. I want to keep you focused on that."

"I know."

I want to stop talking now. I'm so tired.

"Thank you, Laura. I appreciate your talking to me on so late Sunday night when you'd probably be in bed asleep."

"Let's talk again in a day or two."

"Good night."

Lia poured herself a glass of lemonade, took the time to find a lemon and a lime, cut slices and put them in the glass, dropped in a maraschino cherry taken from a jar that had been in her refrigerator for months, and then garnished it with a sprig of mint from a small potted plant Wanda had given to her. She took the glass out to the deck, sat down and scanned the sky again for the familiarity and dependability of the dippers.

I was so thankful for him. I thanked You, more than once. I didn't take him for granted. I thanked You for what I thought was a gift. Why is this happening? I was thankful.

Lia thought about one of her favorite songs, and in her head she could hear the voice of Richie Havens, one of the very best, singing *Follow*.

ع

Lia was late, and she ran down the short concourse to the gate where she was meeting Wanda. Thank goodness for small airports; only regular business travelers truly appreciated airports that were small enough to arrive ten minutes before departure and still make the flight. Levale's airport was one of these. Small, modern, lots of parking within walking distance of the terminal, not necessary to get on a shuttle bus to get to the rental car lot or back to the terminal. Conallied's influence in the local economy and on its politics played a major role in the airport being built, and EPD's images were everywhere. Lia arrived at the gate out of breath and was relieved to see that the boarding area was still full. The flight had not boarded yet, and it was a good thing because Wanda was nowhere to be seen. Just as the boarding announcement was made, Wanda came running down the concourse. She saw Lia, waved and laughed.

"Look at us, ain't we a pair? I saw you running ahead of me. Both of us late, staying at the office until the last minute, right? We really need this weekend".

"Yeah, this trip couldn't come too soon for me, although I had to leave a stack of work in the office and a flock of buzzards gathering to circle over my body. I stuck by our decision to take this trip, and I'm not bringing the job with me; you ought to be proud of me."

"Goodness, and you're still standing. I am proud of you! Well, as you can see, I don't have my portfolio case with me; I feel naked without that big thing hanging from my shoulder."

"And, I'm proud of you, too. We're not going to talk about business, or contracts, or dealing with white folks, or any other kind of folks, are we?"

They headed down the jetway, and after getting settled in their seats, both slept during the flight to Atlanta.

Lia and Wanda followed the game plan for a weekend of relaxation they agreed to when they decided just a few days earlier to take this trip. Play it by ear on Friday night, shopping on Saturday, splurge for dinner at an expensive restaurant on Saturday night, sleep in on Sunday morning, and have room service brunch before heading back to the airport. Lia really wanted to see a baseball game or a pre-season football game. She constantly bemoaned the lack of pro sports teams in Levale, but as luck would have it, both the Braves and Falcons were on the road the weekend they were in town.

"My heart is broken," Wanda said, suppressing a smile. She was not a sports fan.

Sitting in the restaurant late Saturday night after splurging on lobster tails and a really good Riesling, they talked about their shopping day in the boutiques and department stores of Atlanta.

"You know, it's amazing how good really expensive wine tastes. This is going down way too easy."

"I rarely drink, and look at me, on my second glass, and I'd better drink up if I'm going to keep up with you." Wanda extended her glass for Lia to refill it from the bottle sitting in the ice bucket next to her chair.

"I love the red pant suit you bought, Lia. That double-breast jacket has beautiful lines."

"I love it, too. EPD's dress code is very casual, but I had to have that pantsuit. About the only time anyone in the company is in full business dress anymore is when we're meeting with a customer, and now most of them dress casually too. I tell you, though, I don't miss the skirts and tailored blouses I used to wear daily, and I damned sure don't miss wearing pantyhose every day."

"I guess I've been lucky; I can wear just about anything to the office. When I have to meet with a client, I take a deep breath and put on a suit. It seems, though, I spend all my clothes money on lingerie; I really like it, and Oscar loves it."

"You bought some really pretty things today. You're lucky to have someone to wear them for."

"You need to find someone to wear lingerie for, Lia. Oscar told me you and Ellis don't see one another anymore, but he didn't tell me the details of what Ellis said to him about it. I doubt Ellis gave him any details. Don't let what happened with Ellis keep you from finding someone else." It was the first time Ellis's name had been mentioned all weekend, and it was enough for Lia.

"There's no one; certainly no one at EPD. My friend, Dawson, in Fielding wants something more, but that would bring a boatload of problems I don't think I'm ready to deal with. I've seen only a handful of Black men working on the line in the plant here, and none in management. I don't have a private social life, except the time I spend with you and Oscar. Anyway, I have enough problems."

"Does he have to be in management?"

"Not at all, but I've decided if I ever get involved with someone again, he will absolutely, positively have to be an honest, strong man who will take care of me emotionally; I won't have to carry the whole load. That will be a new experience for me."

"You and Rob had some good years, didn't you?"

"I guess so. The most important thing on earth to Rob is that everyone likes him and thinks he's a great guy. So, publicly, he did for Jordan and me what looked good to the outside world. Sometimes it was beneficial for us, and sometimes it wasn't. He was very successful at perpetuating that image, and still is. In our private lives, he was physically absent most of the time and emotionally all of the time. Jordan and I were a team of two. I'm a team of one now."

"Well it's time for you to give some of yourself to another person. Conallied has gotten all of you, and look at the crap you have to go through."

"You sound like my therapist."

"Good, then I'm not the only one you're hearing this from."

Lia appreciated the fact that Wanda did not comment further or probe for more about Laura and her therapy, or about Ellis.

"The reality is the man I'm emotionally closest to right now is a white man at Conallied's headquarters a thousand miles away. It's an ironic twist."

"Oh Jesus." Wanda took a long drink from her wine glass and stared at Lia.

"I know. I know. I don't really know what I'm going to do about it, but he cares a lot about me, and shows it. I always seem to be putting him to the side, but he is always there, when I turn to him. He's a real good guy. But I guess I can't help but see the shadow of the enemy in the face of Dawson, this man who wants me."

"Would it be different if he didn't work for Conallied and, wait a minute, why are you with Conallied if they are the enemy? For me, Conallied will be just one client, admittedly a big one, but your entire career is tied to these people."

"You're asking me questions right up there with 'what is the meaning of life?'"

"I am? I didn't mean to get that heavy."

"No, that's okay. I need to really think about your questions before I can answer them. I'm beginning to hear a chorus I can't ignore."

"You know I'm always around when you get the answers."

"I know; I'm so glad Clara introduced us, or I'd be completely alone down here. I admire you and your entrepreneurial spirit. It means a lot to me to have a friend in Levale. And this weekend happened right on time; you know how to just let it flow." Lia leaned back in her chair and let out a long, deep sigh. It felt as though it had been waiting to escape from Lia for months.

"After Mama died and I returned to Levale, it took a long time for me to adjust. I'd been a world traveler with my ex-husband, Kanzi, and then I was in Levale with a big house to take care of and a business to get off the ground. Early on, I often felt like I overburdened myself, but it's worked out for me. I feel like a person who is about something for the first time in my life. You're right, I do tend to let things flow, but I've had to get focused, and you've been a great role model for me to do that, Lia."

"I've come to realize that one of the casualties of corporate executive life is friendship. I think it's especially true for women, and even more so for Black women. It's still very much a man's world inside those walls, and they have numerous support systems, including wives."

"I need one of those to take care of my house and keep my schedule straight and run errands for me." Wanda chuckled and took another sip of wine.

"You find yourself geographically separated from your childhood friends, you often work in locations where there is no African-American community to speak of, and if you are lucky enough to develop friendships, then along comes a transfer. You take the transfer, of course, because it involves a promotion or an opportunity to learn another aspect of the company, or both. They say if you're not moving around, you're not moving up. But you pay a price."

"Well, you're in Levale now and you've got me, and Oscar, too."

"I'd like to think that we would have been friends anywhere at any time."

"I know we would have been, Lia."

"What actually did happen with you and Ellis? Can you talk about it?"

Oh God, here we go. I haven't offered her any details at all, except to state that it was over, and now I know she didn't hear much from Oscar.

"Oscar told me that he thought you two had mesmerized one another."

I don't want to talk about Ellis.

"We didn't know one another very long." A nothing answer.

"Well, even though he's been in some sort of relationship with Deborah forever, there's been no shortage of women buzzing around him all the time, almost all white women, by the way. I thought he was attracted to you because you didn't buzz."

Lia let out a small laugh that sounded more like a grunt.

"We couldn't believe he was developing a relationship with a Black woman, but we were happy about it; Oscar was thrilled. I don't know if he has some baggage about Black women, or he sees white women as the bigger prize; I don't think Ellis ever had any kind of a real relationship with a Black woman before you."

Hah! A relationship?

"We pretty much assumed he'd been involved with a woman during the time he spent in Europe, though we never expected he'd have a baby with one. You two talked about his daughter, Lucy, didn't you?"

Lia tried to hide her shock with an expression of knowing. She took a sip from her wine glass.

"I thought I had mentioned this to you when I told you about Deborah." Wanda must have sensed Lia's surprise in spite of her effort to hide it.

"Ellis and I talked a little bit about it," Lia lied.

Ellis never said a word to me about any child other than Jason, Deborah's son. I must be the biggest idiot on earth.

"She should be about five years old now. Oscar tells me that he doesn't think Ellis has seen her more than once or twice. I don't believe Oscar even knows the whole story about Lucy, except she lives in London with her mother who is an artist. You know men don't talk and share all the gory details about things the way we do."

"What was Deborah doing while Ellis was in London?"

"Waiting," Wanda responded, looking Lia right in the eye with an expression that women share that is part cynical judgment and part shared understanding.

Lia realized that she had been holding her breath, and she relaxed and counted her breaths for a few moments.

Don't let the scream out. Hold it together. Wanda doesn't deserve to have her weekend ruined because I lost it. I don't know why I didn't just tell her that I had no idea Ellis has a daughter. I guess I'm not ready to admit another disappointment, look like an even bigger idiot.

"For a minute there, it seemed to us that Ellis was even more meditative and spiritual than usual after he met you, even more Zen cool."

I wonder if Wanda is being cynical now. Does she know he's really a phony? I really don't want to talk about Ellis ever again.

Lia let out a short laugh of recognition. "Yeah, that's a good description."

"I was hoping it was because something good was happening between the two of you." Wanda's comment seemed to be more a statement than a question.

"Ah well, life, love and the pursuit of happiness." Another response that meant nothing; it was all Lia could muster.

"So, enough about my sad situation; how are you and Oscar doing?"

"Oscar and I are great. He wants to push right ahead, and I'm trying to take it slow and easy, but I'm falling, Lia, I'm falling hard and it feels good."

"Ooh baby, baby," Lia said in an exaggerated sexy voice.

"I have finally filed for divorce from Kanzi. The papers were mailed to Paris last week; he'll sign them. I never expected us to get back together, but I just didn't feel compelled to do anything until now. Whether Oscar and I are together long term or not, it's time."

"It will give you a sense of closure, Wanda, and then you can really move on."

"Well, Oscar and I are going to put our heads together and figure out another one of his single friends who would be a good match with you."

"Wanda, I don't want to be fixed up with anyone. My mind is too overcrowded right now."

I'm still picking myself up off the ground where Ellis left me.

"Okay, let's work on clearing your mind first, then we'll put together our Lia man- hunting strategy."

"Oh brother." Lia didn't protest any further than that. It was actually nice to have Wanda worrying about her.

"Why don't we stop at that jazz club that's connected to the hotel. There were some good sounds coming out of there when we passed by. We'll have another glass of wine, then sleep late, then have mimosas and something rich and fattening like eggs benedict in the morning, then ask for extra peanuts on the airplane. You know, one long, self-indulgent disgusting pig out."

"Girlfriend, I'm in," Lia answered.

ξ

Late August, hot, sticky, accentuated by dull, nondescript skies, came and went. Lia did not communicate directly with anyone.

Am I getting a reprieve simply because practically everyone is on vacation, or are they just avoiding any conversation with me? I haven't even thought about going on vacation. Should I go home for a week or two? It would be the normal thing to do. I think I'm afraid of leaving, because I don't know what might be done in my absence. They do what they want anyway, so my being here or not doesn't seem to matter.

The next EPD restructure planning review session had not yet been scheduled, though the latest version of the restructure document, twenty-three pages long and marked "Confidential Draft," had been sent to Lia. She sent back a three-page response outlining her thoughts on the numerous elements of the plan.

Am I wasting my time? How much of this draft is already a done deal?

A couple of weeks earlier, Donald had set up an early morning meeting with Lia and Virginia to work up getting closer to a final document for presentation at the elusive session in Fielding. Donald had also arranged for Gunther to join this meeting by teleconference, without asking Lia if it was okay to include one of her branch managers. In the end, Virginia had a crisis with one of her children and canceled at the last minute. Gunther participated for about twenty-five minutes, served up platitudes and generalities about work that had been done in the past before Lia, and begged off the call for an appointment. Lia's frustration only increased when she observed that Donald was noticeably irritated at Gunther's lack of cooperation, as if Gunther's buy-in was a deal breaker.

How the hell can I, a relatively new member of EPD's so-called leadership team, openly challenge Gunther when those who have worked with him for years won't do it?

Lia and Donald spent the balance of the morning in a polite tug of war over the scope and structure of the restructure recommendations. It was clear that neither of them was completely happy with the headway they made, so both agreed the document was still a work in progress.

At least we made an effort to work together.

A small battle won, but the undeclared war dragged on.

ξ CHAPTER 13 ξ

Lia spent some of Labor Day weekend with Wanda and Oscar, often feeling as if she was intruding on their world. On Saturday, they spent the day at Levale's annual carnival, which was held downtown in Founders Park, not far from EPD, just a few blocks from Ellis' condo. Oscar headed home around five o'clock to rest before heading to the Club Beale to play. Lia and Wanda stayed into the evening. They spread out a small blanket on the park's big lawn, and listened to an oldies band. Wanda planned to meet Oscar later. Lia didn't look forward to spending the rest of the holiday weekend alone, but she felt the loneliness would be less acute than spending it with people in love, even if they were her friends.

"Oscar told me he brought up your name again to Ellis, and Ellis refused to talk about it." Wanda was again raising the subject of Ellis. "I think men may be better than us at protecting themselves; they simply refuse to get into it. Jesus, maybe that's it, Lia. He leaves women before they can leave him."

"Wanda, I don't really want to talk about Ellis ever again. I've been struggling with this, and with things getting no better at work, I don't know what I'm going to do."

"I understand, Lia, but you may want to know that Ellis is leaving Levale."

"Where's he going?"

"He's going on tour with a group of musicians he connected with through the radio station. They got a grant from some foundation. Oscar didn't even know Ellis was doing this until a few days ago, and I think he's really hurt, though he won't admit it. Now, Oscar's group has to find a replacement keyboard player. Ellis's new group is going to travel around the world doing jazz performances and workshops and making a documentary film. They're going to some interesting places for a jazz band like Greenland, India and even parts of China, and they'll be traveling for about nine months . . ."

"Nine months?" Lia interrupted Wanda's stream of information.

"What about Deborah and her son, rebuilding that relationship?"

"Yeah, what about them?"

"Maybe he'll get to see his long-lost daughter if he gets to London during his travels." Lia tried not to sound cynical.

"Maybe he'll have a cup of that mint tea that he likes so much and meditate on the women and children he's left behind."

"So, are you going to tell me about your meeting with Dan Castle," Lia asked. "I figured you'd call me last night."

Wanda had met with Dan on Friday afternoon, and now Lia sensed she was hesitant to talk about it for some reason.

"The meeting went great, actually. I was all ready to have to tread lightly with him, based on what you've told me about the guy, but he was very charming. He asked much better questions than anyone else has. He was more knowledgeable than Clay Simpson. I'm expecting to hear something from him next week".

"Jesus, they're moving fast on this. The bureaucracy is really cranking; that's unusual."

"Well, that's what I've been told. Apparently, Castle wants to get this project moving. It's all part of the restructure that you've mentioned; they want to introduce new images along with the restructured organization."

"Who's your competition? Do you know?"

"All I know is that two other firms are being considered, but I don't know who they are."

"Good luck. I have my fingers crossed for you. Even though these white boys don't relish having to deal with a strong, Black women, hell, strong black anything, I can't imagine they'll resent a talented graphic artist like you. And, you won't have to deal with them every day, anyway. Perfect."

ξ

Lia devoted Sunday to lying on her deck in the sun, reading every newspaper and magazine article that she had put aside during the past several months. In the evening, Lia called her parents. The conversation was the usual checking in on each other's health, how Jordan was doing, and any news about her siblings or other more distant family members. Lia promised to come home for a visit sometime during the holidays.

On Labor Day, Wanda had a cookout in her backyard. She called Lia late morning and asked her to drop everything and come over. Lia hesitated, but Wanda insisted.

"It won't be a big group of people. You don't have to bring anything. Come over and enjoy the grill master Oscar's cooking."

Oscar was skillfully tending the grill when Lia arrived. About twenty people were there, friends of both Wanda and Oscar, and the wives, girlfriends and children of Oscar's quartet, minus Ellis. There was no shortage of talking, laughing and eating barbecue ribs. The mood was relaxed and fun, and everyone was friendly and sociable, but what Lia felt most keenly in the midst of a group of nice people was loneliness and a longing to be connected to someone or something.

Keep smiling, and don't get teary. It's getting tiresome.

ξ

Later, Lia lay on her back between cool sheets wide awake, staring out the open window at what seemed like a million stars. She ordinarily had no problem sleeping, and it annoyed, then depressed her when she couldn't seem to drift off. It seemed as though every person Lia ever knew, every event that ever happened in her life, was racing through her head.

I'm drowning in tension and unhappiness. I don't know what to do. I'm supposed to know what to do, but I don't.

Doing what had become a normal practice, Lia gathered the long T-shirt she slept in up around her waist and turned over on her stomach. She put her hand between her legs, spread herself open and let her fingers do the work in the wetness to quiet her mind and offer the comfort of sleep.

ξ

Lia went through the following weeks with two tracks running through her mind. Smiling, cheerleading, and counseling her staff, the associates, and the agents when they visited Levale, through the day-to-day work and challenges of servicing EPD's customers, and the continuing success of the process improvements initiatives and new service products, which had taken on a life of their own as a result of the collective enthusiasm and good ideas from the employees. At the same time, she was silently screaming to be released from her unhappiness and loneliness without being able to figure out how to do it herself. She occasionally heard from the supportive managers to follow up on a process change that had been put in place, but Gunther's communication blackout continued, and she did not talk with anyone on Dan's staff. The EPD restructure plan seemed to be in limbo with no real connection to the process improvement work the Consumer Services employees were doing.

At the end of the month, Dan Castle called Lia.

"Lia, first I want to say that you've done everything asked of you, and more." No pleasantries or preliminaries.

"But I think at this time it may be best for us to find you another assignment in Conallied."

I so needed Ellis in my life precisely for this moment. I needed him to make these white bastards irrelevant to me. I needed Ellis to have a safe place to go, safe arms to settle into and shut out the world. I would have given him my arms in return, for whatever he needed to escape from. Why in the world am I thinking about Ellis at this moment?

Lia suddenly felt light-headed, and her heart pounded.

Why are we not having this conversation face to face?

"Dan, I am stunned by the matter-of-fact sound of a statement that so seriously affects me professionally and personally." She somehow summoned the strength to keep her voice low and steely cold.

Castle ignored her remark and continued. "I know you've had an opportunity to review the initial restructure plans with Don. We'll have a lot of changes and revisions before the day is done, but I have decided to reduce the number of branch locations to three. The country will be split into three, larger regions, and Gunther will run the newly structured East region for me. It has the biggest customer base. Gunther is a long-time, valuable person in this Division. He will play a major role going forward."

That bastard must have been working overtime to undermine me and firmly position himself in Dan Castle's future at Consumer Services. It doesn't matter what Gunther has said or done, this is totally unacceptable from Dan.

"Dan, shouldn't I come over to your office so we can discuss this face to face?"

"I don't think we need to set up a big meeting. I want to keep things low-key. It'll be easier on everyone, especially you. I want you to continue keeping the people here in Levale motivated while we work with Corporate the over the next couple of months on a new assignment for you. Again, I'd like you to continue what you're doing. We'll look for an equivalent-level

assignment, or even one that represents another promotion for you, starting the first of the new year."

This bastard is a coward!

"Well, for the record, I think we should have this conversation face to
face, but I guess I won't barge into your office. Dan, let me ask you a question. What motivated this decision? What was the specific impetus for it?"

"I had a long discussion with Gunther, and this situation has to end.
This is my decision, Lia."

"Why didn't you simply put Gunther in my position at the beginning
of the year instead of bringing me down from Fielding?"

"That was then, and this is now, Lia."

"So Gunther's given you an ultimatum?"

"I don't respond to ultimatums. Gunther stated his case and the concerns he had about both of you operating in the same Division with such
different approaches to the Consumer Services operation. He's been loyal
to the Company for many, many years, and wields great influence with
the employees in the field. He's been a key player for a long time, and he's
well respected."

"I've heard all this before, Dan, and it's not accurate. Gunther, in fact,
does not have the influence you think he does. I know that I have the support of three, probably four, of the current branch managers. And, let me
say, I thought I was a key player on this team, as well, especially when you
consider the results I have gotten."

"I'm not diminishing your results, Lia. That's not what this is about.
Most of the current branch managers are going to be reassigned within the
Division. Jay Doane will run the West region, and Gunther will help us
select a new individual for the Central region".

"Is my position going to be filled with someone else?"

*What difference does it make? Why am I even asking? I can't care
any more.*

"We're still looking at that as part of the restructure."

"So, the final details of the Consumer Services restructure, the operation I was supposedly hired to run, have been decided without my final input or knowledge?"

"Ultimately, these are my decisions, Lia, and this is the new direction we're going."

He's ignoring my questions completely.

The fact that the three branch managers who sent her the letter were being reassigned stunned Lia. She felt sure Carl had not betrayed her trust. Lia had no idea if Castle knew about the existence of the letter, and she certainly did not want to mention the letter or their specific names now and possibly have a negative effect on their reassignments or their continued employment.

Why are you stunned about any of this? It should be no surprise to you. Get your thick head out of the clouds.

"Listen, Gunther clearly had his demands, and I have mine, too. Either I run my operation with the full authority I deserve, while I am still here, or I don't. I cannot continue to lead and motivate employees and not empower them forward at the same time. And, Dan, I'm not willing to be a temporary caretaker. It appears evident to me that whatever happens with my position after I'm gone, Gunther is the one who really will run this show."

Lia said what had been ringing in her brain from the start of the conversation, and Castle did not contradict any of her statements.

I'm sure that Gunther running Consumer Services is a foregone conclusion, though they'll probably wait for some agreed-upon period of time before it is announced. That's the way they do their dirt.

"Lia, I'd like to think that I can count on you to be a team player during this transition period."

I can't believe he's pulling the "team player" bullshit on me! I need to stay calm.

"Dan, I have a news flash for you. You have to be part of a team to be a team player. I need to talk with Human Resources in Fielding about this rotten situation." Lia didn't care what she said now.

"Lia, I've told you this was my decision, and EPD will take care of you. Joe Mather will call you later this morning to talk about potential opportunities. He's talking to the people in Fielding, and I've asked him to give it top priority; I'm sure he will. You'll be in demand in this company."

"So, that's it, Dan? I'm being kicked out."

"Lia, don't overreact. You've done a great job for me. This is shaping up to be a great year for Consumer Services, so much better than we anticipated. You have played a very important role in that success."

"But I can't run Consumer Services?"

"It just won't work out, Lia. However, you can count on your incentive compensation, which will reflect your contribution to the Energy Products Division this year. You'll be fine."

Dan's tone of voice signaled that the conversation was over. It was over as far as Lia was concerned, too.

ξ

Joe Mather did call Lia. She did not take the call; she had no inclination to talk with him. He never tried to call her back. Lia was angry. She didn't even feel tearful, a change from her emotional state over the past few months. She had been knocked down by situations of disrespect, minor and major, too many times during her tenure with EPD. She had gotten up every time to continued working and had not complained to anyone inside the Division. Lia felt a deep sadness; sadness because in this environment hard work wasn't enough. It was never going to be enough. It was, at last, time for her to deal with this reality. Her illusions, finally, were gone. She realized true gratification in her life was going to have to come from some-where else; within herself, a fulfilling relationship with the right person, activities in the community around her, a new direction.

Laura was right. I chose to ignore all of it thinking, if I just keep going, I could power through it. It doesn't work that way. Not for me, no matter how hard I work, no matter how much I want to belong.

Pleasing white men had consumed too much of her emotional and psychic energy for too many years. She did not feel like a failure; she felt cheated. She had to move on; not just to a new job or city, but also to a new state of mind about life and about whom she needed to please. Lia felt a physical sense of lightness in her body, and a measure of emotional relief about finally seeing the light.

Please let this feeling be real. Please don't let me slip back.

Lia sat silently at her desk for a long while. She realized, somewhat to her surprise, that she was humming the same two lines over and over from *Jesus Loves Me,* and pulled out Whitney Houston's *Bodyguard* cassette from the stack on her credenza and put it in the portable tape player. She was a little girl again singing in the youth choir in church, not quite understand-ing the rituals, but feeling they made her safe.

$$\xi$$

The next day, Lia called Jud Jeffries's office in Fielding. She knew he had bigger things to worry about than one executive in one division, but she wanted someone with authority to know what was happening. She had no expectation of getting her job back; she didn't want it back. But, someone had to know the truth.

Doesn't someone need to know? Doesn't Jud Jeffries, as leader of Conallied, want to know when someone, whether an executive or entry-level employee, has been treated so unfairly? It's hard to believe he wouldn't. But, be ready, Lia; no one in Fielding may give a damn.

Jeffries's executive assistant advised Lia that he was traveling in Asia for two weeks. She then transferred Lia to Brad Colby, the senior human resources executive who reported to Jeffries. He immediately took her call. They talked for almost an hour, and Lia told him everything. He wrapped up by saying all the right words.

"Lia, I don't know exactly what's happening down there. We were told you were looking for an assignment change, that EPD was not a good fit for you."

Who told him that? I wonder how long ago that conversation happened.

"That's a lie, Brad."

"If that's not the case, I'll certainly look into it. We have to do what's right. I don't want you to do anything you're not comfortable with. I'll talk to Dan again. Maybe your moving on to another division is the right thing to do at this point, maybe not. I'll get back to you."

Lia's kept her confidence in Brad's promises tempered with reality of how she had already been treated. Brad had been engaged during their telephone conversation, but it ultimately proved to be useless. A week passed, and he never called Lia back, never had anyone call her on his behalf, never sent her a written communication of any kind. She never heard from the man again. Nothing.

You kept your expectations low, so don't be disappointed, don't trip.

Lia placed a call to George Anderson, whose job was to focus on the Company's diversity, in Fielding. He was out of the office, but did call her back a couple of hours later. Lia had never spoken at any length with George. She had run into him at two or three Conallied events when she was in Fielding, but they never exchanged more than pleasantries. She had been told after he was hired that George was going to contact senior African-Americans around the Company to get their input on diversity issues in Conallied. He had never contacted Lia, or most of the other African-American leaders. In hindsight, Lia was not surprised given the comments about George shared during the gathering at the Farm. She told George everything, just as she had to Brad.

"I have heard that the environment at EPD is difficult. Your situation sure seems to confirm that. What do you want me to do?"

Don't ask me; you're supposed to advise me!

"George, I don't know what action you think is appropriate at this time. In fact, intervention from Fielding at this point might have a negative effect. I just wanted you to be aware of what is going on so that you can monitor it from your office. I know that part of your charge is to facilitate change in the company's environment so this kind of thing doesn't happen".

"Well, let's see what transpires in the next several days. I'll call you next week to check on what's happening."

"Good talking with you, George. Goodbye."

Lia hung up the telephone, disappointed. She really didn't want or expect George to ride in with the cavalry to rescue her, but she would have appreciated some indignation and genuine concern. He was going to call her back in a week. Well, that's certainly jumping right on the problem!"

Remember, don't expect anything. Don't slip back.

ع

"Hey Laura."

"Do you have time? I could really use your wisdom."

"For you, always. I don't like the sound of your voice today."

"Do I sound that bad?"

"Well, I usually hear a lot of things in your voice, but today is different. Your voice is flat, and that worries me".

"It looks like I'm at the end of the road, truly this time, and I'm trying to figure out how I got here. I'm desperately trying to hold on to my equilibrium and figure out my lessons learned. I've moved on intellectually, and I'm trying to do the same emotionally."

"What's happened? Something at the office? Did you hear something from Ellis?"

"No, it has nothing to do with Ellis. Well, it might in a small way, only because this has been one hell of a year."

"Maybe it's a transformational year."

"Does transformational have to be so painful?"

"Sometimes, but it can also be liberating."

"These people don't want me to succeed, or at least don't care if I succeed or not, don't even care if I make money for the company; it's unbelievable. I always thought money was the bottom line for these guys, but it's not. That surprises me, and now I feel like a naive idiot."

"If money isn't their bottom line, what is?" Lia felt Laura was trying to prompt her to talk, but she also seemed to have a real curiosity about this question.

"The bottom line is taking care of themselves, holding on to their power, staying in control."

"So how do you think you impact that?"

"I'm a leader, I always have been; people follow my lead. It's a big part of the reason I got this damn assignment in the first place. I don't think they had any idea just how significant my impact would be. That I would not only energize the associates here in Levale, but also the technicians in the field, is very threatening to the old-timers. And, on top of that, I've fundamentally changed the way things are done. I guess they just wanted me to come down here, maintain the status quo, and be quiet."

"You feel as though you should be a hero?"

"Yes", Lia answered, uncomfortable for the first time in her life, about her own aspirations. "Instead, I'm on the outside. But, Laura, I'm dealing with reality, I really am. I should have known better and I did not, but now reality has slapped me in the face. But that's not my biggest concern at the moment."

"What is, Lia?"

"Me. I feel like my spirit is in two places at the same time. I want to be this executive who is really good at her job and gets a lot of attention and approval in response. That means approval from men, white men, and some white women, too, because they're the only ones who are in the position to give approval."

"Let's be clear, Lia. They are the ones who can give approval in that particular environment."

Lia let out a long sigh. "I just want to be a real person, not necessarily big-time, well known, or anything like that, just someone that people like and look up to and feel comfortable being around. I remember feeling this way even when I was a little girl; I always wanted to do more than people expected of me. Maybe I let it get out of hand and failed to recognize when this monster called Corporate America consumed me."

"It was a path, Lia, and you took it, not failure. That was an okay thing to do. I think where it became an issue for you is when your professional life and your personal life got blurred, they became the same path, and the source of all your fulfillment.

"Well, that's obviously not healthy. I have to ask myself, if things had worked out with Ellis and me, or any of man, would we be having this conversation?"

"Were you hoping for a relationship with Ellis because of who he was as a person or because he could be a substitute for your unhappiness at Conallied?"

"If I said in my case it was because I was longing for closeness with someone, longing to belong to someone, longing to be appreciated by someone, longing to have someone real, longing for someone to provide me an escape, could that really be unhealthy?"

It could be. In your case, I think it might have been. Let me ask you, now that you have finally reached the point of disillusionment with the corporate structure, where is your comfort zone? Where is the rest of your life?"

I don't have an answer.

"When are you going to seek your own approval? Where will you find it?"

"It's hard to know what choices to make and when to make them. My divorce from Rob was the right thing to do. The timing, if anything, was late. Should I not have divorced him so that I could have someone or something, a marriage, to fall back on? Should I have worked fewer hours, even though working long hours is necessary to take on these big assignments, and spent time on my personal life, on relationships with men, and other friendships? I allowed myself to be utterly, totally vulnerable to a man like Ellis, and all I got was left. Now what? Even now, I don't want them to see me as vulnerable at Conallied, not even for a second, for fear they think I couldn't handle it. How do I know, at just the right moment, what path, what direction, to take? Hell, how does anyone know? Don't you just have to live your life as it presents itself to you?"

"That's a lot of questions, Lia. Do you now understand what I mean by blurring lines?" Laura's voice was firm, but Lia could tell she was trying to be sensitive at the same time.

"No, I admit I'm not sure I truly understand it."

"You see, Lia, when you chose. . ."

"But I don't feel like I've chosen anything, anywhere," Lia interrupted more rudely than she intended.

"Lia, you have given total time and energy to your work life, to a world that is not friendly, even hostile, to you. It became part of your heart and soul. That's a heavy dose of reality to deal with when it doesn't work out well. When it breaks you, it's devastating. Even though you energized the people who are actually closest to EPD's customers, even though you've saved them money, and even though you've generated new revenue for them, you are quite obviously being ostracized and marginalized. Have you ever genuinely asked yourself 'why do I want to be in this world?' Did you really mean it, if and when, you asked yourself the question? Did you really want to know the answer? It seems to me that's the critical question you have to ask yourself, and keep asking it until you get an answer you're comfortable with."

"I managed to raise Jordan, didn't I? Look at him; he's wonderful. I was working and traveling all the time, but I also gave him all the attention he needed, all his life. I was, in fact, doing more than just tap dancing for white guys."

Laura laughed, then apologized for doing so.

"I think that tap dancing metaphor quite aptly describes what you've been doing. You have good instincts; if you didn't, you would not be as successful as you've been. But I believe inside your head a little voice has been speaking to you, inside your gut your instinct was nudging you. Somewhere along the way those good instincts must have kicked in and caused you to pause, at least for a moment, to think about it, to question it."

"Yes, I have asked myself that question, more often than you might think. I've suppressed it, pushed it down, because I suppose I just didn't want to deal with it. I have to admit that it hurts to have to ask myself the question. I end up blaming myself; it's my fault for wanting to be in their world, rather than realizing it might be better for me to be out of it."

"This is not a blame game, Lia. That's unproductive thinking, and you need to focus now. You've been emotionally, and I would guess, also physically affected by this."

"It's all I've been thinking about lately, and it feels more like a spiritual crisis now than an emotional or physical struggle." Lia was surprised at her own statement and the quiver in her voice.

This whole thing is closer to the surface than even I realized.

"Then I don't have to tell you that a spiritual crisis requires you to make deeper, more fundamental decisions."

"Yes, I understand. I don't know anymore if I'm mad or sad. I'm both I guess, and I don't want to be either. Maybe that means I shouldn't be in Levale, maybe I shouldn't be in the corporate world at all. Laura, it seems as if we keep having the same conversation, different words, same conversation."

"It's part of the process. The process is sometimes repetitive and sometimes frustrating. You're doing fine. You do what's necessary to protect yourself professionally. But, protect your soul first. And, Lia, the two are not the same."

After Lia hung up the phone, Laura's words echoed in her head. "The two are not the same." She had spent much of her life offering words of expertise and wisdom to others. Now it was time to accept them from someone else.

ξ

By the end of the month, Lia had not talked with anyone. It was almost as though her conversations with Dan Castle and the others in Fielding had never happened. They had all closed ranks and pulled the shades down.

At some point, the Conallied grapevine would get wind of it, and everyone will hear about her "issues" quickly after that in various versions. Then, her worst nightmare. She would become the topic of discussion all over Conallied. Numerous conversations spoken in hushed tones, smirks from many of the white people, and pity from her African-American colleagues. Lia Granger would be the latest casualty to talk about, like Jake Wallace and Clark Blackburn. Lia had participated in some of those conversations in the past. She foolishly never dreamed it would happen to her, that she could have been so naïve to think she was immune from it. Now, she was in a haze, just going through the motions of a routine that was no longer normal. Her staff and employees were beginning to sense that something was wrong. Gerard tried to draw her out. A few days earlier he had stopped her in the hallway.

"I know you love Japanese food, and a new sushi bar just opened near my house. You want to try it one night this week?"

"Thanks, but this is not a good week; maybe one evening next week."

"Okay, but you've been holed up in your office so much I thought you could use a break. Come on, give your HR manager a chance to suck up."

Lia smiled. "Can I get a rain check?"

"Sure," said Gerard, and let the subject drop.

Lia had, for all intents and purposes, been discarded. Why burden her staff with her failure?

ξ

It was late when Lia arrived home from the office, and she was weary in every way. She just wanted to take a long bath and go to bed. She saw the red message light blinking on the phone on the kitchen counter.

Please let Jordan be okay; I hope everyone is okay at home.

She didn't receive many calls at home; Jordan called every Sunday afternoon when she was usually at home, and her mother called at least once a month to check in with her. Dan had called her at home on two occasions to discuss a matter that needed immediate attention the following morning. He sometimes caught up with her on the clunky car phone she rarely used, which was installed in her company car. Lia pressed the button, and a familiar voice filled the air.

"Lia, where are you? We don't want to miss you. Dalton and I are in Atlanta, on our way back from the Virgin Islands, and our flight to San Francisco has been cancelled; it's stormy here. I suggested to Dalton, and he agrees, that we should add a couple of days to our trip and detour to

Levale to see you. We can get a flight out early tomorrow morning, good Lord willing and the creek don't rise, and be in Levale at eight in the morning. We'll fly home Sunday afternoon, so I hope you are available for the weekend. Oh, I hope you get this message. I'll try to reach you later; we're going to check into a hotel right here at the airport. Call you later."

Lia didn't know if it was the fatigue or joy at hearing Ruthie's voice, or both. The universe had moved ever so slightly and made a space for Lia to receive some comfort, and the tears rolled down her cheeks.

ξ

Lia was standing in the middle of the small, second bedroom in her townhouse that she had furnished and decorated in soft tones of tan and mauve. She liked the room. It had never been used by anyone, not even Jordan, except when Dawson had used the adjourning bathroom to wash up. Lia took a small stack of thick, tan towels from the linen closet and placed them on the chest sitting at the foot of the bed. She then walked down the hall to her bedroom, moved the telephone while unraveling its cord through the doorway to her bathroom, sat it on the floor, and ran a hot tub of water.

As she soaked in the tub and waited for the phone to ring, Lia thought about how she would spend Saturday and Sunday with Ruthie and Dalton.

I will let them relax here for a while and then I'll take them to brunch at The Garden. On the way to the airport, I'll buy something to put on the grill, and good wine; we will spend the afternoon and evening here at home. It's not like Levale has great tourist attractions to show them, it doesn't. I would love for Ruthie and Wanda to meet. It's too late to call Wanda now, so I'll call her first thing in the morning and invite she and Oscar to join us in the evening. I hope they don't have plans. On Sunday morning, I'll cook breakfast, and we'll eat and be lazy out on the deck. Wow, real life, nothing to do with Conallied, real life with family and friends and no expectations or games.

The ringing telephone interrupted Lia's thoughts.

ع

Ruthie and Dalton were already standing at the arrivals curb when Lia drove up.

It's just like Ruthie and Dalton to travel thousands of miles from home with two small bags and still look great. Dalton is so tanned, and Ruthie looks beautiful and happy, as usual.

Lia jumped out of her Jeep Grand Cherokee and met the two them at the hatch door in the back. Dalton immediately gave her a big hug and a kiss on the cheek. While he put the bags in the back, Ruthie gathered Lia in her arms, and they shared a long, tight hug. Ruthie backed away and looked at Lia.

"How long has it been? Almost four years? How are you? Are you all right?"

"I'm fine, I'm great; it's so good to see you."

As they drove to Lia's house, Ruthie talked about how beautiful the Virgin Islands were and then brought Lia up to date on family and friends back home in California. Dalton spoke up from the back seat as they were nearing Lia's neighborhood in the foothills.

"We've passed some nice looking neighborhoods; they have a nice country feel to them. But I have to say there doesn't seem to be much to Levale. It doesn't feel like you, Lia; what do you do here?"

"Well, you're right, there isn't much here. Conallied is by far the largest and most visible of Levale's employers. Levale is a small city that is right on the verge of becoming a mid-size city. The town leaders want it to be a smaller version of Atlanta. It has old, southern civil war history, but there is nothing unique or particularly memorable about it. There's not much culture or entertainment, with a few exceptions; it has a handful of pretty good restaurants and, surprisingly, and a nice jazz club. I'm going to take you guys to brunch a bit later if you're up to it. The Garden is a great break-fast spot. But, it ain't sexy here!"

Lia glanced over at Ruthie who was staring intently at her. Ruthie's brows were knitted together, which gave her an inquisitive look. She smiled quickly at Lia and returned her attention to the passing landscape.

ξ

They sat on the deck outside Lia's kitchen sipping cups of tea. It was a warm, clear morning.

"It feels good out here," Ruthie murmured.

"Yeah, I actually spend a lot of time out here when I am at home."

"Are you traveling a lot?"

"No, not really. I've been on two-week long road show to our regional branch offices, and a couple of short trips up north to the Fielding area, and, of course, to Jordan's graduation, but I haven't actually done the travel to our other service facilities that I should probably have done by now. It's a long story, but I won't bore you with Conallied talk today."

"Good," Ruthie replied. "Lia, your guest room is so nice; you deco-rated it beautifully, and it's so cozy."

"You mean small," Lia laughed.

"No, I mean cozy and comfortable; it's so you."

I've forgotten the me Ruthie is talking about.

"Let's go to brunch. I'm going to feed you guys today. This evening, my friend, Wanda, and her boyfriend, Oscar, will join us. I'm so glad you will get to meet them. I'm going to put some salmon steaks on the grill; I remember that you both like salmon. Oscar is in a jazz quartet; we can catch the late show if you feel up it."

"Well, there seems to be a little taste of culture and entertainment in Levale, after all," Dalton said.

ξ

After brunch they returned to the townhouse. Dalton decided to take a nap and headed for the guest room.

"Dalton looks great," Lia commented.

"Well, he tries to stay in shape and we're careful about what we eat. He's in his late sixties, you know, and he's had health issues, but he's determined to outlive me. He always worried about leaving me behind. I always tell him I'm just going to get a new, younger model when he kicks the bucket," Ruthie laughed. Then her tone changed. "I can't imagine my life without him, so I just do my part to keep him healthy."

Lia and Ruthie settled on the deck, each with a novel. Ruthie dozed off for a short while. Lia recalled for the first time in years that Ruthie had always encouraged her love of reading and, despite their twelve-year age difference, they read some of the same books and discussed them whenever Ruthie visited. Ruthie would always ask what she was reading and showed genuine interest, in contrast to her parents' befuddled smiles and nods in response to their little girl who moped around on school holidays, loved to go to the public library alone, and read stacks of hefty books sitting on the floor of a closet with poor lighting.

After a while, Ruthie turned her body in the chaise lounger toward Lia. "You're okay, huh?" Ruthie stared at her with purpose now.

"That's the second time today that you have asked me that question."

"You seem a bit sad to me. I don't feel that old energy coming from you. When I hugged you this morning at the airport, you were trembling."

"I was?" Ruthie continued to stare at her, and Lia was certain she was not going to drop her intent gaze without a response.

Okay, here I go, talking about Conallied.

Lia relayed her experiences at the EPD Division since arriving in Levale. She offered Ruthie a narrative: a recitation of the facts and events, the challenges, responsibilities, conversations, reactions, perceptions, and the game playing. Then, she told Ruthie about her brief, ecstatic, and painful relationship with Ellis.

"Jesus, Lia, it's a wonder you're still standing. How are you feeling about all of this?"

For a moment, Lia was disappointed about Ruthie's seeming disinterest in the details of her Conallied situation or the relationship with Ellis. Lia was prepared to answer specific questions, but Ruthie didn't ask her any. Lia realized that Ruthie's concern was deeper, more focused on Lia.

"I want to know if you can muster energy for yourself rather than sapping all of it on others." She clearly was not going to let Lia get away without talking about what she was feeling.

Maybe it's time I talked about this in depth with someone other than Laura.

"I'm trying, Ruthie. For months I've been tired, emotionally tired, don't want to let them get me down, don't want to let them win. I want to be a hero, I want another success, to be successful."

"Is that all you want?"

"Isn't that a lot? I feel like it's a lot."

"It may seem like a lot Lia, but have you ever considered that it's not much?"

Lia, startled, stared back at Ruthie.

"Do you have any friends at Conallied, any real friends?"

Lia told Ruthie about Keith and how their infrequent, but supportive, conversations helped her from time to time.

"He sounds like a good guy, but do any of these people really mean anything to you, to your life? It seems like it's draining everything from you. Where is your joy? Who in the Conallied world cares about you, truly cares about you?"

Lia took a deep breath.

Ruthie is the only person in the world I can talk to about anything. Why not talk about him? If anybody would understand, she would.

Lia told Ruthie about Dawson, about their friendship, and about the connection between them that seems to defy time and geography. She talked about possibilities that neither of them, or at least she, had not stepped, or leapt into.

"So, do you really care about him? Do you want a relationship with him, a real one?"

"I don't know, Ruthie. Sometimes yes, and sometimes no. I apparently was ready to forget about him if it had worked out with Ellis. What does that say? I know I don't want to go through what I experienced with Ellis. Rob was self-centered and inattentive, but he was never cruel. I know that I trust Dawson. I . . ."

Ruthie interrupted her. "Who are your close friends that have no connection to Conallied?"

"My friends in California. I saw them all a few months ago. You heard about Gracie, didn't you? She died of cancer; I didn't even know she was sick until Dana called to tell me she had died. When I came out for the funeral, Mama told me you and Dalton were in London. I felt disconnected from my old friends, and I still think about it all the time."

"I remember Gracie well. Wow, she was a bright light that went out too early."

"I have Wanda here in Levale. We clicked and became good friends with no effort. I can't wait for you to meet her later."

"I just want you to think about this: you don't see your oldest friends at home very often, and although I'm sure Wanda is great, what happens when you are transferred to the next city for a new assignment? Dawson sounds like a good guy; maybe it's why you hold on to the kinda, sorta relationship you have with him. He's like a lighthouse for you, but does that make a genuine relationship?"

"You two seem deep in conversation," Dalton's tone was half amused and half apologetic as he stepped through the doors onto the deck.

Saved by the bell.

"Just womenfolk talking," Ruthie responded. "You look like you got your second wind."

ξ

Dalton and Oscar were sitting in a corner of the deck talking jazz. Lia, Ruthie and Wanda were in the kitchen preparing the salmon and slicing vegetables for the grill. Lia felt good; she was surrounded in her home by people she loved and liked.

"I didn't know Dalton was such a jazz aficionado."

"Oh my God, yes. You know, or maybe you don't know, that his younger brother, Bryan, is a musician. He's also a sculptor; he works with wood, and he makes the most beautiful pieces. He plays keyboards in a jazz quintet called Sound Wave. They have an interesting niche; they have regular gigs in coastal towns from Eureka down to Santa Barbara. Dalton tinkers around on keyboards and guitar, but he's not serious."

"You and Dalton always surprise me. You should see some of the work Wanda does. I'm jealous of her. Ruthie, she does wonderfully creative graphic designs for her clients. Some of her work is almost like works of art."

"Thanks, Lia. You're the one with all the balls in the air at EPD; I don't know how you handle it all." Wanda returned the compliment.

"Ladies, I'm having an Conallied-free evening."

"Good!" Ruthie and Wanda spoke in unison, and they all laughed.

It had been a long time since Lia had such a pleasant evening. The people, the food and wine, the conversation, her house, the beautiful sunset, all came together, and the pieces fit perfectly.

Oscar's quartet was playing later that evening, and he left early right after dinner. The others followed later after Ruthie and Dalton decided they had enough energy left to take in Oscar's first set. Club Beale was packed, but Oscar had reserved the same table for them that Wanda and Lia had occupied before. They all decided one more glass of wine was in order.

Thank God Ellis is wherever he is; I'm not sure I could have handled him being there on the stage, and a really nice evening would have been ruined.

When Oscar and the guys got settled on stage, Oscar spoke to the quieting crowd. "I want to dedicate our first number to friends visiting from Monterey, California, a city filled with jazz lovers. This is for Ruthie and Dalton."

Lia silently mouthed a "thank you" to Oscar for his surprise gesture. The quartet's music provided the perfect sound to end a special day.

ξ

When Lia pulled up at the departures curb at Levale Airport, Dalton squeezed Lia's shoulders from the back seat. "I'm so glad we came; thank you for a wonderful time."

After they had taken their bags out the back of the Jeep, the three of them were standing on the curb. After a silent moment filled with all their history and attachment to one another, Ruthie reached out to hug Lia, and Lia stepped into it and held on.

"I love you," Lia and Ruthie said the words at almost the same instant. Letting go of Ruthie meant aloneness, and Lia was afraid of it.

"I like Wanda. I'm glad you have her in your life. But think about moving home, starting a business, traveling the world to places you want to go, climbing a mountain. It's in you, you can do anything. It's time. Ambition is not a bad thing, but it can't be all you have, all you are."

Ruthie, you came right on time.

Lia repeated those words to herself many times in the solitude of Sunday night.

ξ PART IV ξ

Fall/Second Winter

ξ CHAPTER 14 ξ

Another quiet, tense week passed, and Lia noticed that her staff, who she had not yet gathered to explain what was going on because she could not muster the will, was now uncharacteristically tiptoeing around her and smiling sympathetically.

I owe it to my staff to let them all know what's going on, to clarify what's going on. I'm not being fair to them. God only knows what they've heard. I'll do it at our next staff meeting.

Without thinking about it, the following morning, Lia called Dawson.

"Hello Daw. You know, you guys monopolize ninety-seven percent of the top management positions in this country. Why are you all so fucking paranoid and angry?"

"Lia? Hold it. What's happened?"

"Haven't you heard anything about me?"

"No, but I've been roving around Asia with Jud. I just got back; glad to be home. What's going on?"

"I need to talk to you, to see you."

"When?"

"Tonight. I can get a flight out this afternoon and be there by early evening."

"Okay, I'll pick you up. You'll stay with me, not at a hotel." Just like Daw. No questions or comments. He was just glad she called him.

"I'll call you from the airport here to confirm my arrival time. See you later."

Once the call had been made and the arrangements set, Lia let out a deep breath. Feeling both relief and discomfort, she thought there was at least one white male who accepted her. Hell, he even wanted her!

ع

Lia left the office just after lunch, went home and packed an overnight bag, and headed for the airport. She slept during the entire flight to the East Coast. She was able to sleep on airplanes only when she was overly tired, and her body allowed it on this day. When she got off the plane, Daw was standing right there at the gate. Lia was a little startled when she saw Dawson in casual clothes. His uniform was a dark suit and white business shirt, never any pastel or patterns. He looked younger and less imposing in light khaki slacks and a dark green golf shirt. She felt no self-consciousness when he warmly embraced her and squeezed hard before letting her go. A hug was just what Lia needed, and she squeezed back in a way she had never done before. Daw took her bag, and they headed for his car.

"We're going to have three days together, so relax and we'll talk when you're ready."

"Three days?"

"You and I are going to take Monday off. I don't want you to go back until Monday evening."

"My return flight is on Sunday night, but I guess changing it to Monday won't be a problem."

She didn't want to wait. During the forty-five minute drive to Fielding, Lia told Daw everything that had happened at EPD since they last talked. She needed to talk about it, to get it outside of herself, with someone she trusted who understood Conallied. She was pretty much done when they pulled into Daw's garage.

That felt okay. I felt comfortable talking to him about it.

Lia had never been to his home before. Daw's condo sat on a rise overlooking the seventh green on the course at the Fielding Golf and Tennis Club. Although obviously expensive, it was a rather small, one-bedroom unit. He told her his former sister-in-law, an interior designer, had decorated the condo as a favor to him. It looked as though a lot of thought had been put into every room. It suited Daw well, masculine but cozy and comfortable at the same time.

This is very nice. Daw spends so much time in the office, or on the road, he obviously doesn't need much space.

"I'll put your bag in my bedroom. It's all yours. I'll sleep on the sofa; it lets out to a pretty comfortable bed, or so Meredith tells me. When she decides to come down from school, she prefers to stay here than at the house. She says Anne nags her too much."

I wonder what Daw's daughter and ex-wife would think about me being here.

"Thanks. Your place looks great. It's so neat."

"And clean, too", he grinned. "I'm very comfortable here. You lucked out; my cleaning lady comes every Friday morning. The place isn't very big, but cleaning is not my strong suit."

Lia was glad that the sleeping arrangements had been dealt with right away.

"You hungry? You want something to eat?"

"I'm not hungry, but a cup of tea would be great. I'll make it if you give me a quick tour of your kitchen."

"Okay. That will take two seconds. My kitchen can best be described as compact."

While Lia put on the tea kettle, rummaged around in the cabinets for honey, and sliced a lemon, Daw made coffee for himself. Lia noticed he had one of those mini, two-cup coffee makers. They were both going about their tasks without talking. They brushed against one another briefly in the small kitchen, and it was all right. Not electric or charged with sexual tension, but seemingly just the way it was supposed to be. It was quiet, intimate, and comfortable. It had always been that way with Daw and, for the first time, Lia realized how much she appreciated the emotional solace she felt in his presence.

I've taken this man for granted. Here I am, instead of where I thought I would be, far from where I thought I would be, and I'm lucky.

Lia took her cup of tea into the living room and sat on the sofa. Suddenly, she felt the exhaustion she had been pushing back and no longer had any more energy to talk. Daw must have sensed her mood because he didn't initiate any conversation. He started to hum along with the music on the stereo and soon Lia was humming with him; sitting there, side by side, in near darkness, humming together, sipping caffeine. It was the last thing Lia remembered before she woke with a start. Her teacup was sitting half empty on the coffee table. Daw was reading; he held a magazine in his left hand and his right arm rested lightly around Lia's shoulder. Her head rested in the hollow below his shoulder, and a blanket covered her legs. She didn't remember any of the activity that apparently had taken place. She glanced at the clock on the mantle; two hours had passed.

"Hey lady, you're sleeping on my bed." Daw was smiling down at her.

"I'm sorry." Lia sat up and yawned.

"No, no. This has been very nice for me. I like making you feel comfortable."

"I guess I'd better go to bed." Lia stood up and leaned over to kiss him on the cheek.

Dawson smiled up at her. "There are clean towels in the bathroom. "I'll see you in the morning." Lia walked down the short hallway to Daw's bedroom. She quickly undressed, bypassed the lavender satin gown that she wondered why she had packed, and slipped on a long, cotton T-shirt. She went into the bathroom to brush her teeth. It was done in rich chocolate brown and gold. As she pulled back the thick, down comforter, she noticed that all the bed linens were also coordinated in brown and gold. She got in the bed and turned out the lamp on the nightstand. The bed felt great, and Lia stared into the darkness for a while. She could see the shaft of light under the bedroom door and hear Daw moving around in the living room. When the light went out, she turned over and fell asleep.

ع

"You awake? Breakfast is on."

Daw knocked softly, opened the door a crack, and peered into the bedroom. Lia had been awake about a half hour, and had turned on the small television on the nightstand to watch the morning news. She felt cozy and safe and not ready to get out of bed.

"Breakfast? I hope you didn't do too much."

"Just my world-famous scrambled egg casserole."

"Hmm, sounds interesting. I'll be out in a few minutes."

Lia washed up, ran a comb through her hair thinking it was going to need more attention later and put on the long, lightweight robe that matched her T-shirt. She looked presentable enough. She wandered into the kitchen, and Daw handed her a glass of orange juice. The eating area in the kitchen had French doors that opened out to a small patio that looked out to the golf course, although massive oak trees provided complete privacy on the patio. Lia could hear the distant voices of golfers on the course, although she could not quite see them. The sun was bright and slashed between the trees and across one of the chairs at the table; Lia sat in that chair.

"You look nice and rested. Sleeping in agrees with you." Daw placed two plates on the table.

"I'm a real dog in the morning, no matter what I do. It's one of those sad facts of life. Daw, this looks great!"

He had prepared a casserole dish of scrambled eggs with several kinds of vegetables, ham and cheese. Warm blueberry muffins sat on a small platter, and a bowl was filled with slices of cantaloupe and honeydew melon.

"Well sir, I never." Lia used an exaggerated southern twang after she took a couple of bites.

"I know you're surprised. Actually, I'm not a half bad cook. But, I have to give credit to Nina, my cleaning lady. She shops for me and chooses some good things. And, it's nice to use some of these nice dishes once in a while."

"I guess you eat most of your meals out."

"I do, and the majority of them are business meals."

"Everything is great. I'm hungrier than I thought. You'll have to let me do the dishes."

"Okay, gladly."

They sat for a while over coffee and tea and somehow starting talking about places each had traveled around the world. It was a pleasant way to pass the time.

I'm surprised we haven't talked quite this way before. I guess most of our conversations have been centered on people and issues at Conallied.

"My good friend, Adam Grant, invited me to go out on his boat today. He called earlier to confirm, and he would love for both of us to come. He just remarried a few months ago. His wife, Kim, is good people. If you're up to it, I think it would be a lot of fun. Relaxing, quiet. They have a great boat."

"If you really want to go Daw, I'm game. I haven't been on a boat of any kind in a long time. What time are we meeting them?"

"At noon, so we had better get hopping. I'll shower while you do dishes, my dear."

Lia could hear the shower running as she cleared the table and counters and loaded the dishwasher. She could also hear the shouts, laughs and curses of the golfers beyond the patio. The sunlight spread through the entire kitchen. She felt good. Dawson came out dressed in white shorts, T-shirt, and sneakers. He looked trim and healthy and youthful, in spite of his large frame and graying hair.

"I'm going to be about a half hour or so," Lia told him.

"Okay. It will take us about twenty minutes to get to Adam's boat. I need some gas. I'll get it while you're dressing."

Lia made up the bed, showered and dressed, and fretted over her permed, neck-length hair with a hot curler.

I'm sure Daw is not used to a Black woman in his bathroom who has to do something with her hair in the morning. I can't imagine he's even really thought about it. Most of us can't just get out of bed, shower, shake our hair, and keep on going. Maybe I should simply pull it back in a headband, since we'll be out on a boat. No, I'm not going to worry about it.

She also dressed in white shorts and a T-shirt. The bathroom smelled of Daw's cologne, and she liked the feeling of familiarity. She had put Daw's tucked-away whistle charm in her bag, and she decided to wear it today. When Lia came out, Daw was sitting at the table flipping through the newspaper. They drove to the marina, chattering away about nothing in particular.

ξ

Adam and Kim were indeed good people. They seemed to bend over backwards to make Lia feel comfortable. If they had any feelings about Lia being African-American, they didn't show it.

Why do I think they might? Because those jerks in Levale do? Daw doesn't. But the reality is that I'm not threatening to them in any way.

Their boat was large and comfortable; Kim had clearly put a lot of time and effort to make it perfect, and it was filled with photos of them, their grown children from earlier marriages, and grandchildren. They brought on a cold lunch that was delicious, and Kim made strawberry margaritas all afternoon. It was a warm, lazy, wonderful day. Lia chatted, read magazines, ate, and dozed. The atmosphere was comfortable enough to do, or not do, anything you liked. Adam pulled the boat back into the dock just before six o'clock. The last red glow from the setting sun was just visible on the horizon at dusk, the beginning of Lia's favorite time of day. Adam and Kim said goodbye with hugs and kisses, and they all promised to get together again.

"Do you think you'll want to go out for dinner tonight?" Dawson asked as they were driving back to the condo.

"No. Let's do something really easy or order in. It's been a nice, lazy day; let's make it a nice, lazy evening."

They watched a movie and ordered in Chinese food, and they ate together right out of the containers. Daw poured two glasses of chardonnay and later steeped some green tea for them. By eleven o'clock Lia was fading fast, and it occurred to her that they had not talked about her troubles in Levale since the ride from the airport. But, they still had two days together, and there didn't seem to be any hurry.

"Two wine glasses, two cups, and a few forks and spoons. I'll do the dishes." Daw got up and began to clear off the coffee table.

"Don't hurt yourself," Lia chuckled. "Daw, I'm going to turn in. The sun has worn me out."

"Okay, I'm pooped too, and you're sitting on my bed again."

Daw got up from the sofa, bent over and kissed Lia four times, on the forehead, each cheek and the lips. She stood up, put her hands on each side of his waist, kissed him back with a quick peck on the lips, and went to the bedroom.

ع

Late on Sunday morning, they walked to the golf club's restaurant for brunch. The large, glass-walled restaurant, which looked out to one of the fairways, was full. Lia was the only African-American there; even the waiters and busboys were white.

"Well, it looks overdue for some color to be added to this place." Lia made the comment just after they were seated.

Daw laughed heartily. "Lia, I know you love being the one to do it. It'll be good for them; some of these monied, highly educated people are actually quite isolated and surprisingly ignorant at times about the rest of the world and the people in it."

"I'm never surprised by people anymore."

"I suppose not."

"Are you playing golf later?" Daw had mentioned a one o'clock tee time that had been arranged a week ago.

"Only if you don't want to do something else."

"Please, play golf. I'm looking forward to relaxing on the patio and reading and staring into space."

They selected from the ridiculously large and sumptuous buffet that was laid out on a series of round tables placed in the center of the room. They were both in a silly mood and told jokes and laughed a lot, about everything and nothing, while they ate. As they left, Lia saw the same glances and some outright stares that she also noticed when they were at the buffet tables. She couldn't have cared less; in fact, she took a sort of perverse pleasure in the consternation she caused some of these people.

Fuck em. Yes, girls, I'm here with Dawson Manford. Yes, boys, he's a better man, a better person, than you are.

She saw at least three familiar faces from Conallied's headquarters, but Daw didn't seem to notice or care either. He really didn't have to worry about what his colleagues thought and said about his friendship, or possibly even a relationship, with Lia. She was sure he had decades of professional good will in his pocket, and he knew the good, bad, and ugly of Conallied and where all the metaphorical bodies were buried. Daw was the soul of discretion and never discussed these things, and Lia rarely asked him about them. Whenever she did ask, he responded with vague answers like "that's been taken care of" or "we worked it out."

After Daw left for the golf course, Lia stretched out on a chaise. She put a glass of iced water and three magazines on the small table next to it.

I feel like I'm a million miles away from Levale, despite Conallied headquarters being not far up the road.

She read for a while and then began listening for Daw's foursome. She gave up on trying to distinguish his voice and went back to reading. She later curled up on the sofa in the living room and watched one of her favorite old tearjerker movies, starring Susan Hayward. She later seasoned two steaks that Daw had taken out of the freezer, got the grill going, and tossed a salad using everything green she could find in the refrigerator. She chose a bottle of rose from the two Daw had in the refrigerator and poured herself a glass. Lia put the steaks on the grill when she heard Daw's car pull into the garage.

"Hi there. How'd you do today?"

"I was great today; I was two shots over; I almost shot a par for the course! Had a drink with my buddies to celebrate; it's been so long since I've had even a decent round. It must be you."

"Oh sure. The steaks are about ready; let's eat."

After dinner, they lingered at the table; a soft, warm breeze was coming in through the open patio doors.

"I wish I always felt this relaxed." Lia leaned back in her chair

"Lia, what are you going to do?"

"Resign."

Damn. I'm surprising myself. I didn't know that was going to come out.

"Resign? Not you!"

"Yes Daw, me."

"You're too much of a fighter, way too goal-oriented, to ever quit. I can't imagine you ever running away from a challenge."

"Daw, this has nothing to do with quitting. But it has everything to do with being tired; plain, flat-out tired."

"What you do mean? Physically tired? You were really wiped out on Friday night, but you seem so much better now."

"I was physically tired, but that's temporary. A nice weekend like this can cure that. No, I'm talking about emotional fatigue, and that's long-term. I realize now it's been there a long time, and I just haven't faced up to it. I have to deal with it now because it has pretty much slapped me in the face."

"I don't really understand what you mean by emotional fatigue."

"I've always tried to please people; in fact, I've been pretty much obsessed by it. Let me be honest and just say it. I've tried to please white men all my life, and I've worn myself out doing it."

"So people like me are driving you out." Daw said this very quietly.

Oh God.

"Yes, people who look like you. But, not you, Daw, you know that. I'm removing myself first. There is no doubt I've been in a crappy situation with a bunch of jerks, some of them outright racist, and some just old school and ignorant. I know the distinction between the two, in my bones, and both are at work in my situation. I'm certainly not the first to experience this in Conallied, and I promise you I won't be the last. I've made pleasing them too important a part of my life. My definition of success, and my self-esteem, have been too much tied up in doing and pleasing, doing and pleasing. I have been like a crazed little mouse in a maze."

"It sounds like you've given this a lot of thought."

"I have. I know it's been thrashing around in my mind for a long time; I just didn't want to acknowledge it. That would be a sign of weakness, you know; at least I thought it would be. I realize now that it's just the opposite, a sign of strength, for me to face up to what I've done to myself."

"You talk as though you've injured yourself. I don't see how you have done that."

"I've been in a situation this year where I have performed beyond the call of duty, actually changed the character of how employees work together and, most important, the Holy Grail, increased revenue! My reward? My reward is to be moved aside because of some who cannot deal with what I have achieved. A Black woman comes into their territory and changes everything? Any strong woman would probably have a problem, but a Black woman? Who the hell does she think she is? I'm impacted by all of the negatives, and none of the positives, for God's sake. This is not the first time I've been faced with this kind of situation. EPD is just the worst, the most blatant. And, how do I react? How have I always reacted? I question and berate myself, try to figure out what I've done wrong! Why haven't I pleased them! Cry alone, get depressed. Well, I just don't give a shit about pleasing them any more. I can't; it has worn me down to nothing."

Daw stared at Lia. He had tears in his eyes and was struggling to maintain his composure. Lia was stunned by it. She had never seen him get overly emotional about anything; even his feelings about her had always been demonstrated in an understated way.

Oh no. Oh God. I don't want to hurt him. He's shedding tears because of me. I know what it is to be hurt. Please, I don't want to do it to someone else.

"I was hoping I would be a help to you this weekend, provide a place to escape to, be part of the solution for you. Now, I feel like I'm part of the problem".

"Not you, Daw. You and I connected the first minute we met, and we're still connected. But, let's face it, we've never really had a professional relationship. I've never had to work for you; it might be different if I had."

"I'd like to think there would have been no difference." Daw's voice shook.

"The fact of the matter is that white men, old and young, have not yet accepted African-American females as professionals and equals. We've been stereotyped in all kinds of negative ways throughout history. I mean, you all are still struggling with African-American males in your world, now here comes females, and we're a pretty aggressive group. We've had to be in order to survive."

"When you refer to white men, I feel like I'm being lumped in with all of them."

"Daw, I'm talking about the guys, and some women, too, that you've worked with, socialized with, played golf with, for years. I can tell you that many of the same guys who think so highly of you also think I don't belong in their world. Now that I'm talking about it, I wonder if they would think so much of you if they knew I was here spending the weekend with you in your home."

Daw had collected himself; his eyes were clear now.

"I wouldn't give a rat's ass what those guys think about me. I thought you knew me better than that. Have you ever thought of me as the typical Conallied clone?"

"No."

"Lia, I won't pretend to fully understand everything. But I want to support you in doing whatever you have to do. I've liked you since the moment we met. I think I have loved you for many months now. There, I've said it. It's out there, in the room, in the air. You do whatever you think is right. All I want to do is love you, right now."

Now Lia was the one with tears in her eyes, but she didn't say anything. She was dealing with too many emotions at the same time; relieved from having gotten all her feelings out in the open without going up in a poof of emotional smoke, conflicted about Daw's proclamation, and his need to make it to her at this moment.

Oh God. Again. Too many feelings.

She stood up and began clearing the dishes from the table. Together, they cleaned the kitchen in silence that was now tense rather than comforting. The clatter of dishes and silverware was jarring. Daw quickly apologized when he accidentally bumped into her. Lia noticed, for the first time, the ticking of the antique ship clock mounted on the wall. When they were done, Lia went to the bedroom, closed the door and lay across the bed. She heard the television come on in the living room. The telephone rang, and she heard Daw's muffled voice for a time.

ξ

A while later, she heard the teapot whistle, and a few minutes after that Daw tapped on the bedroom door and came in with a cup of tea for her.

"I know this is your nighttime ritual, so I thought you'd want it about now."

He's truly a sweetheart.

As Lia turned on her side to face Daw, he placed the cup on the nightstand and sat on the edge of the bed. Lia rubbed her temples, trying to press away an advancing headache. Daw put his hands over hers and moved them to her side. He then began rubbing her temples.

"Hmm, that feels good." Lia turned on her back and lowered her head into his lap, closing her eyes. "You're pretty good at this."

"Well, I know you love to be rubbed. You always used to rave about your regular massages, remember, and how you'd give up food before giving up your massage."

Something else I didn't do for myself in Levale. I've forgotten how much we used to talk when I was here in Fielding. We talked about almost everything.

"Sit up." Daw's voice was soft and soothing.

Lia looked at him as she sat up and followed his lead as he turned her back to him.

"Just relax, Lia."

Daw began massaging her shoulders. Lia was surprised how soft his touch was, but at the same time his hands were strong and sure. It was just what she needed. She relaxed and let her weight rest against his chest. Through her halter top, she could feel his skin above the v-neck shirt he had changed into, the tickle of the soft graying hair on the upper part of his chest, the creases of age, the textures of him, of this white man, which were different. Lia settled into the difference, and it enveloped her.

Do I care for this man? Genuinely care for him? I envisioned nights like this with Ellis. I never really envisioned this with Daw. Is this how it's supposed to be? He's not a substitute, is he? No, he's more. Different, but more. Less, but more.

"Let me take off your top."

Lia remained silent as Daw pulled the halter over her head. She was glad she had worn her lavender lace bra and panties; they were sexy, but not too much so. Women think of these things at moments like this, and Lia smiled to herself. As his hands massaged her bare shoulders and down to her chest, she unhooked her front-closing bra and slid her arms out of it. Daw rubbed his palms slowly down the length of her back. He played wordlessly for a moment with the chain around her neck; the gold whistle he gave her hung from it. He again put his hands on her shoulders, kneaded them softly, then more deeply, and massaged down her back again. Lia felt as if the world had slid away, and she was floating in warm, weightless space. Space that had no troubles. Space that had no rejection. She forgot about the tea.

"Lie down."

Lia turned and reclined on her back. The feel of the thick, down comforter magnified her sense of relaxation. Daw slipped off her shorts and then her panties. He looked at her for a few moments, and Lia felt both pleasure and relief because she felt completely at ease with her nudity in Daw's presence.

"I wish I had some kind of oil to rub on you."

"I have some baby oil in my travel pouch; it's in the bathroom."

Lia's voice was low and drowsy sounding, although she was hardly sleepy. Daw came back with the oil. For what seemed like more than an hour to Lia, Dawson massaged every inch of her body. He brushed her nipples with his thumbs and laid the palm of his hand between her legs with gentle pressure. He rubbed, manipulated, stroked and spread her in a way that was simultaneously gentle and strong. Somewhere along the way, he had tuned the radio to soft music and turned her over on her stomach to continue the massage. It had grown dark and the only light in the room came from the hallway. It was wonderful, and he was wonderful. Dawson then turned Lia again.

"I want to make love to you." He looked directly into her eyes, mind clear, heart open.

Lia looked directly at Dawson for the first time since he began massaging her.

"I love you, Lia. I need you, and I think you need me too."

She started to sit up again, but he bent over and kissed her on the lips. He parted his lips, and she reciprocated. She had her hands on his forearms, and she squeezed them as they kissed. He even tasted different than any man she had been with before; his kiss had a quiet passion and it was good to Lia. Lia had not been with very many men in her life, and never with a white man. But she ached for this one. He was her friend and confidant, and he always made her feel better. Now, he had demonstrated it in more ways this weekend. She struggled with her emotions.

How do I feel? How do I feel about anything?

"This is about just you and me, Lia. The rest of the world is out there, a million miles away at this moment," Daw said as if he could hear the voice in her head. "I've always felt we could be great together. Conallied will be set on its ear, but who gives a damn. That's later, not here, not now."

Daw stood up and quickly undressed. Lia threw back the comforter and he slid in bed beside her. They both turned on their sides and looked at one another without speaking. Lia drew silent comfort from Daw's presence, the warmth radiating from his naked body.

"You're beautiful," he whispered.

He moved in closer and kissed her between the breasts, then each of her nipples. He groaned as he locked on to her right breast. Just as Lia was about to reach out and reciprocate the intimate touches, Daw repositioned her, kissed Lia between her legs, and her groans drowned out his.

It's been so long. Oh God, it feels so good.

Lia sank into a warm, safe place. A place that was open to her in every way she needed it to be. As she orgasmed, Daw held her very tight. They were momentarily very still and quiet. After a time, he pulled his body up and entered her. She welcomed him, was wide open for him, and he filled her more completely than any other man she had ever been with. Lia massaged his back as he rocked inside her. When Dawson climaxed, Lia wrapped her legs around him. She wanted him to know that she had him, that he, too, was safe. He repeatedly murmured, "I love you, Lia."

This is more than sex. This is making love.

They laid there locked together for a long while. Daw rolled off Lia, and onto his back right next to her. His right arm lay lightly across her stomach, and her left hand rested on Daw's thigh. They both let the darkness and silence cocoon them in Daw's bed and in their own thoughts.

I want to long to make love to Dawson. I want to look forward to it.

Lia burst into tears, surprising even herself. Dawson looked over at her, stricken with concern.

Everything was seemingly so right; there should be no obstacles to overcome. But the barrier was there, inside Lia. She knew it, and was unable to communicate it to Daw in a way that would make everything okay. She couldn't get past the reality that if she surrendered herself to Daw, she would willingly, even eagerly, be living to please another white man. Even Dawson, ever kind, loving, strong Dawson, who wanted to rescue her, could not change this reality. She felt very angry and she did not know at whom. It couldn't be Dawson. She sat up and scooted away from him. Suddenly, she was self-conscious about her nudity and felt very vulnerable.

"I can't, Daw. Please don't expect this of me," Lia said, still crying while maneuvering to get up from the bed.

"Lia, tell me what's going on. Talk to me, please!"

She went into the bathroom, grabbed the lavender robe hanging behind the door and hurriedly put it on. She stood in the doorway of the bathroom, hugging herself.

"I would be pleasing, or trying to please, another white man, wouldn't I?" Her voice demanded an answer to a question she knew he would feel was entirely unfair.

He was still laying on the bed, but now he got up. The light from the hallway slanted across his face and settled on the far wall of the bedroom, and in the semi-darkness, Lia could see the pain in his face.

He's wide open with me. He's totally vulnerable, like I was with Ellis. God, why is Ellis even entering my mind right now? It's insulting to Dawson.

He's a quality man. A man who loves me and wants me. God, why does he have to be white. So what if he's white, so what?

"I think what we have here, Lia, is a tragedy. You see me as just another white man who needs to be made happy. But, I'm just a man. A man who cares about you deeply, who loves you. You don't have to prove anything to me, professionally or otherwise. You never have."

Dawson walked out of the room and closed the door. Lia walked over to the bed, crawled in, and pulled the covers over her head. The radio was still playing; she blocked it out. Later, she awoke from a fitful sleep. She listened for any noise from the living room but heard nothing. She turned over and fell asleep again.

ع

The next morning she found Dawson out on the patio drinking a cup of coffee and staring out toward the golf course.

"Hello," Lia said, her voice scratchy from not having slept well.

"Hi. Are you okay?"

"I will be, I guess."

"I didn't plan anything for today. I thought we would play it by ear. Do you want a cup of tea?"

"Yes, I'd like some tea, if you don't mind. Daw, I thought I would get an earlier flight out today. I'm going to take a one o'clock flight back to Levale."

"Lia, I'm sorry about you're struggling with all of this. I only wanted to make things better for you, for us."

"It's my problem, Daw, not yours."

"No Lia, that's where you're wrong. It is my problem. Damn it, it's my problem, too!"

I love you, and you're in a crisis. You're going through a tough time, and it seems to me that the line between your professional and personal well being has completely blurred.

He sounds just like Laura and Ruthie; the people who care about me.

"I happen to think I'm the perfect person to be with you, Lia. I've spent most of my professional life in Conallied, and I know the animal. I also know you and how to love you. Yes, most of these people have been colleagues and friends for a lot of years, but I don't love them. I'd like to think I could help you put everything in perspective, so you can make a good decision about what you want to do. I want you to do the right thing for everybody involved."

"Who defines the right thing? You? I think I should be the one to recite that definition, once I figure it out. I thought you cared only about me being happy. Who is this everybody that's involved?"

Lia could see that he was frustrated by her question. "I don't know exactly, Lia, but I thought I might have a place, somewhere in this scenario."

"I can't Daw; I cannot keep trying to please you white boys in the conference room and the bedroom."

"That's not fair, Lia. I don't deserve that."

"I'm sorry. Please understand, Daw. I've got to do the right thing for me. All my life, I have sought approval from everyone, especially white people and especially white men. Don't you get it? And, I'm beginning to sound like an annoying, broken record. I thought it was the key to success in the world. You know what's funny? My parents never taught that to me. It was not specifically drummed into me by anyone in my life. I simply saw it all around me from the time I was a little girl. I've just arrived, very late, at the point where I understand that I have to measure success by how I feel. Just me. Inner success, inner peace, that's what I'm talking about. I feel so dense; this is basic stuff that I should have known, figured out a long time ago, but I'm just getting it."

"I'm in a no-win situation. I don't think you can separate me from the others. You're not being fair."

"That's just it, Daw. I cannot let myself agonize over whether I'm being fair to you or whether you like it or not. Not now, anyway. I know that sounds really awful. I'm sorry."

"You don't have to be sorry, Lia."

"Daw, I know I don't. I think I finally understand that."

ξ

They drove to the airport in silence. When they arrived, Lia asked Daw to drop her off and not bother to park.

"When am I going to see you again? When will I know what you are going to do?"

"I don't know Daw; I'll call you soon. I love you for always being there for me. I mean that."

Dawson pulled to the curb in front of the terminal, and he got out of the car along with Lia. She grabbed her bag out of the back seat and turned to head into the terminal. Dawson stopped her and, without saying anything, wrapped his arms around her. Lia let her bag drop to the sidewalk, put her arms around his waist and laid her head on his chest, drawing from him a reservoir of strength and nurturing to be used later when she needed it. She let go, picked up her bag, and walked away from him.

Does Dawson have to pay for the sins of all the white boys? I'm sorry, Daw. I've got to do it this way.

As Lia settled into her seat on the airplane, *Run to You* played softly over the sound system. Whitney had come to comfort her, yet again. But, as Lia closed her eyes and quietly mouthed the lyrics, she turned her face toward the window and let the tears flow.

ξ

When Lia arrived home in Levale, she had three messages from Wanda on her answer machine. Wanda's voice sounded excited, and she wanted Lia to call her as soon as possible. The telephone rang while Lia was still listening to the messages.

"Lia, let's celebrate! I got the contract with EPD!"

"Let's not celebrate. I'm resigning from EPD."

"What?"

"Wanda, I'm sorry, but I can't talk about this right now. I'll call you soon."

"Lia, what . . .?"

Lia hung up the telephone before Wanda could say anything else. She felt the sensation of toppling over, but she didn't fall. Her body felt unbearably heavy, and she momentarily couldn't move. She became aware that she had sat in a chair, but could not remember doing so.

Jesus, what's wrong with me. Help me.

ξ CHAPTER 15 ξ

Lia sat on the side of her bed dressed in nothing but panties and a t-shirt. She had not washed her face, brushed her teeth, or combed her hair all day long.

I'm one of the sad people. Why can't I conquer feeling so down so much of the time? I'm crying way too much. There are people in this world who want me to be happy, care about me, love me. Why can't I accept genuine love? God, I'm tired. What do I have to do to stop feeling tired?

After sleep walking through the rest of the week in the office, communicating with her staff and employees only when necessary, and not at all with Wanda, Lia spent the entire Saturday wrapped in her bathrobe sitting in front of the television. Occasionally, something on the screen caught her attention, which gave her hope that she might still be interested in the world around her, but the feeling passed when she again stared into space or dozed off. When darkness inevitably enfolded the room, without any thought about it, Lia walked into her bathroom, reached up the top closet shelf for the small, carved wood box she bought to store the plastic container that held the gun and bullets. A double box to hide it from the world and any acknowledgement that it was actually there. The box was heavy, and she lifted it down slowly so she wouldn't drop it. She was still nervous about having it, about it being in her house.

I should use this wood box for something else. It's too nice for a gun.

Lia sat on the side of her bed and opened the box, then opened the container without taking it out of the wood box, and stared at the gun for what seemed a long time.

I have no one to blame but myself, no one. For God's sake, there are people in this world who deal with really terrible things every day. What's wrong with me? Some white guys have rejected me? It's a failure only because I have declared it so. I'm out of energy thinking about it. I'm on empty.

She closed the box and sat it on the nightstand.

What the hell did you think you were going to do with a damned gun? Could you actually put it to your head or in your mouth? No. It's such an act of violence. But, for people who can, I get it now.

Lia got up and changed into a long, pink flannel gown, her favorite when the weather was cold, even though the weather was unusually mild, and her house was cozy warm. She sat on the side of the bed again for a while. She got up, went to her closet, pulled out a heavy, navy blue robe, and put it on over her gown.

I can't seem to get rid of this chill. I've been wrapped up all day.

Her reverie was broken by noise out on the street. It sounded as though her next-door neighbor, who she had never gotten to know beyond a cursory greeting or wave, was greeting visitors, and there were children's voices, too. She heard someone talking in an animated voice, but she could not make out what was being said, then loud happy laughter penetrated into her bedroom.

Regular people doing regular things spending time with family or friends on a Saturday evening.

The voices subsided as they all apparently went into the house.

I need a deep sleep, just a nice escape from my screwed-up reality. I don't even want to dream. I could take pills, but I don't have any sleeping pills or anything like that. But, other things could work.

Lia went to her medicine cabinet and took out all the over-the-counter painkillers and other medicines she had accumulated. She also found one old bottle of prescription medicine for migraine headaches that had seven pills left in it. There were close to sixty pills in all. Lia went to the kitchen and filled a large drinking glass with chardonnay. In the bathroom, she started dropping pills, one by one, into the glass from the small piles she had lined up along the counter top. Some of them fizzed in the wine, and the residue settled in the bottom of the glass. The empty pill bottles lay on their sides on top of the stack of purple, mauve, and beige accent towels that sat on the bathroom counter. Soon, the light golden color of the wine had turned to a cloudy white. When she dropped the fortieth pill into the wine, the liquid had risen to the top of the glass; it dribbled down the sides when Lia dropped in the forty-first. She walked very slowly back to the bed with her eyes on the liquid, and sat the glass on the nightstand. A wet circle spread on the wood under the glass. Lia picked up the glass with both hands, and her intent to take a long, deep swallow immediately changed to just a sip.

Oh no, this tastes horrible. I'll never be able to drink all of it. I'm a complete idiot. I should have realized that it would be better to take a handful of pills with a swallow of wine until all the pills are gone. Now, I have to do it this way. No matter how horrible it is, just drink it and don't stop. So stupid; now I have to drink it if I want a real escape, a deep sleep I won't awaken from in just a few hours like I've been doing.

Lia drank the rest of the liquid in two more long swallows. She ignored the immediate rolling in her stomach and the bitterness in her mouth, got in the bed with her robe pulled around her body, and pulled the covers up to her chin. She rolled her head toward the nightstand and looked at the clock; it was 8:15 pm.

Lia stared out the window and focused on the glow coming from the streetlight, thought about Jordan, and saw shimmering multi-colored lights fading in and out behind a vision of Jordan. She began to shiver violently with cold.

Oh God, I hope I didn't swallow too many pills. I just want to sleep. I just want some peace. Help me, please.

Lia thought she heard singing in her head, and she fell asleep.

ع

It was warm, comforting; thank God it was warm. Lia lost her sense of well being when she got too cold. But it was warm here. It was very bright, white bright; not a light, but a blindingly bright day, and it was warm. She was reclined on something that felt soft and comfortable, and she was wearing a long gown made from a sort of gauzy material that gathered around her bare feet, which were tucked under the soft material. She felt somehow indulged, but she couldn't think through the sensations.

A voice spoke to Lia. "Are you okay?"

The voice seemed intimately close but echoed softly from a distance, both at the same time. It surrounded her, and added to her sense of well being. She couldn't quite make out if it was male or female. It didn't seem important who or what the voice was.

"I feel okay. Where am I? Am I okay? A bit of confusion began to intrude.

"You're where you need to be."

Lia abruptly became fully aware of her surroundings. She was in the mountains, her favorite place to be. She saw them close and far away. She began to notice the details. What seemed just beyond her reach was a meadow overflowing with flaming orange and yellow flowers that reminded her of California golden poppies. The flowers were fluttering from side to side in a gentle breeze creating the illusion of a mass movement that ebbed and flowed. In the distance beyond the meadow, purple flowers climbed up the sides of foothills that ringed snow-capped mountains rising to a majestic height, so high they were almost scary. But Lia could never be afraid of mountains. She loved them and always felt an odd combination of exhilaration and peacefulness in their majesty. It had always been one of Lia's dreams to see Mount Everest up close, to climb to base camp. She had no illusions that she could handle anything more; base camp would be challenge enough. Lia always hoped, by placing herself in the presence of something so clearly greater than her own existence, some greater under-standing would make itself known to her. She had no sense of what it was, but she had no doubt it was there.

It was looking at mountains and other wonders of nature that always confirmed for Lia the existence of a higher power. She had never been an overtly religious person, but she considered herself a spiritual being and believed that someone or something guided the universe. Lia felt sure that humankind was the weakest link in the higher power's arrangement, entangled in never-ending scrambling and reaching for something, some-thing else, perpetrating inhuman acts on each other or chiseling away at one's own personal psyche in the quest.

Oddly, Lia could not feel the breeze that seemed to meander in one direction and then another across the meadow of flowers or any chill from the snow-capped mountains. The warmth that surrounded her did not seem to be coming from the sun that she could barely make out against the background of a soft blue sky through the bright light. The warmth she felt was different and encompassed her completely. The veil of bright light held her.

"Am I alone here? Is anyone with me?"

"There is no one here with you. You came alone, but you are not alone."

"Why am I here? Is anyone else coming?"

"Lia, you are where you need to be right now; this space is for you. You found your way here yourself."

"Who are you?"

"Your friend."

"I don't know you."

"You know me. I'm always with you. I'll help you."

"Why didn't you help me before now?"

"So, Lia, you know that you need help?"

"Yes. I think I just needed to sleep deeply enough."

"I'm pleased to hear you say that. Do you know what led you here?"

"Yes . . . ," Lia hesitated. I'm not sure."

"You have good instincts, Lia. You know you're here for a purpose."

"Is anyone going to come, at any time?"

"Who do you need to come?"

"Jordan would come if he knew I needed him."

"Anyone else?"

"Well, Rob doesn't really care, but I am the mother of his son, and he adores Jordan. He'd probably send someone to take care of whatever it is I need." Lia grinned, her first outward emotion other than confusion.

"Anyone else?"

"You keep asking that. Well, my parents have never quite understood me, though I admit they were wise enough to step aside and let me go my way. They would come if they thought I was in some kind of trouble."

"You're not in trouble here. Anyone else?"

The voice seemed to be part of the air, coming from no particular direction, and it didn't seem to surround her like the warmth; it was just there, somewhere. Lia shifted her body and stared into the light and tried to fix her eyes on the sky. She didn't know where to look.

"Ruthie. She'd come without hesitation and take care of everything in a calm and elegant way."

"That's it?"

"Yes, that's it. Isn't it enough? Oh, there's Wanda, but I can't expect someone who's been a friend for less than a year to come here."

"What about your professional colleagues?"

"No. I would not want them here. It's too perfect here."

"You have friends among your professional colleagues?"

"I have a few, one a very special friend, but I don't think this is the place for colleagues."

"Why is that so?"

"This place is only for me, I think. I'm not sure the people who love me the most could find me here. I don't think the others should try. Is anything I am saying making sense?"

"You're very intuitive, Lia. That's good. You lost that skill; I'm glad you're regaining it."

"Who are you? I can't see you, but I can hear you and feel you."

"Why is it important, as long as I help you while you are here?"

"All the things I love are here. Mountains, open space, an endless sky, it's mystical, and the amazing light. The warmth is sweet icing on the cake. It's so perfect, it scares me a little."

"Interesting for a woman who has boxed herself in so much. You needed to be reminded of who and what you love most."

"I feel I've focused way too much on the what, and not the who. I let the what wipe out the who."

"Talk about the 'what'?"

"Ambition, position, validation, competition, more validation. It flattened me. I let it."

"You broke yourself against it. You ran up against it over and over, and you broke yourself."

"I want to say something wise, but I can't seem to speak from wisdom."

"You have people who love you. You are blessed, Lia. You know it. You forgot it. You know that, too."

"Yes, I do. I know I lost my way."

"You're not lost now, Lia."

"I'm blessed, I am. I sense being here is an act of grace. I know it, I know it."

"Persuasion is not needed. It is true."

"I am saved by grace."

"Yes, Lia, you are."

"I am a grateful beneficiary of grace. It has always, always been my very favorite word, grace.

"Yes, Lia, I know. . ."

Lia interrupted. "That's who you are, what you are, grace . . ."

ع

Lia awoke quietly. She opened her eyes and lay still in her bed. She was comfortable and warm. There was a very sour taste in her mouth, but she felt no other discomfort. The room glowed with the reddish light that came through the blinds and settled in nine slashes on the white wall opposite the bed. She counted them; her mind was clear. The sun was setting. The radio was on, but the volume had not wakened her.

Was the radio on last night?

Lia looked at the nightstand. The clock read 4:57.

I've been gone for almost 21 hours.

She stared at the mess on the nightstand she had left last night; the box with the gun in it, the wine glass stained with white residue down both sides, balled up tissues and, inexplicably, one of the pill bottles she remembered from the bathroom. She turned her head to the darkening sky.

Lia still didn't move her body. She was aware of coming back, of a floating sensation, and she allowed herself to return slowly back to the world.

What was that? Where did I go? A dream? A reality? What happened to me? I wanted to wake up, didn't I? Yes, I think I did. Yes, I did.

Lia focused again on the slashes of light, which were now beginning to disappear from the wall. The light disappearing from the wall and then from the sky forced her to notice the change. The light took her away, and it brought her home.

I was rescued from myself. My favorite word, grace. I remember we talked about grace. All the natural things I love joined in a chorus to sing to me, for me, to exclaim that I always had it. No recriminations, no celebrations, just amazing grace.

ξ CHAPTER 16 ξ

"Hey Laura. I have some news." Lia called her early on Monday morning after alternately reflecting on her journey and escaping back into sleep all day and evening on Sunday.

"Hey Lia. You're resigning."

"Damn you're good! Yes, it's true.

Much to the surprise of both women, Lia began to cry. She'd been doing that a lot, especially during the past few months.

"I've always been a little worried about your lack of tears. Lots of emotion, but never any tears. It's cleansing, isn't it?"

"Laura, how does that old song go? I cried a river? I've done plenty of it, but privately; you're right, letting it all hang out is very cleansing,"

Lia took a long, deep breath and blinked back more tears that were poised to spill over.

I can't tell her about what happened on Saturday night. It's my experience alone.

"I think I made the big transition."

"What transition?"

"From the intellectual truth to the actual truth."

"And that is?"

"I've finally stopped wishing and hoping and stressing and crying about why these white boys will not, actually cannot, deal with me. I wanted the same criteria that they have always applied to themselves to apply to me. I wanted all the things that bring them recognition and success to bring the same for me. I either couldn't or wouldn't cope with the reality of being viewed and measured differently by them. You have to give me an "A" for effort, though; I've been trying for years."

"Since you were a little girl." A statement, not a question.

"Yes, I have," Lia said, again fighting off more tears.

Why am I so emotional now? I've made my decision.

"I guess there's a part of me that is still the little girl who wanted to have a business. Even then, in my immature, child's mind, when I had no real concept of what it was, I wanted it."

"You regained your emotional intelligence, Lia."

"Yes, I feel like I have," Lia responded, though she had never given any thought about the year in terms of her emotional intelligence. Only her "get it done" intelligence, and it had not served her well.

"You do realize that this decision is a reward? Lia, you had to give it to yourself. It was never going to come from them. What you've done is very healthy. I imagine that you'll likely have to deal with some sound and fury as a result of your resignation. Tune it out. That's a short-term process you have to get through before you can enjoy the rewards of your decision. It will come sooner than you think. I promise."

"You do? I'll take it." Lia managed to work her face into a smile.

"Let your mind and body rest for a while. Nurture the real relationships. Spend more time with Wanda if possible; you seem to like her very much. Connect with your friend, Dawson."

"I spent a weekend with Dawson. It's a long story, but please, not today. He's a good man, but I don't know how to feel about him right now. And, I think I've totally screwed up my friendship with Wanda, the only real friend I have here. I let all my stress over these bastards contaminate my attitude about everyone. It's my own dumb fault."

Lia told Laura about Wanda's contract with Conallied.

"I should be her biggest cheerleader. She's welcomed me and shared her friends and family with me. Now that she has an opportunity to grow her business, I certainly don't need to be an issue for her."

"You can fix that Lia, so do it! Do you think you will stay in Levale or return to Fielding?"

"Neither."

"What does that mean?"

"I said that too quickly, but I'm thinking about maybe going back to the West Coast. Restart my engines there. See some good sports again."

"You're a hopeless fanatic, Lia."

"Yeah, ain't it great! For now, I'm going to relax. You know how I feel? Like a big, bright over-inflated balloon that's been floating and bouncing all over the place and, now I've stuck it with a pin, and its collapsing, and softly coming to rest on the ground. Laura, I'm going to just be still for a while."

"Have someone take a snapshot of that for me," Laura laughed heartily.

"You've helped me so much. I couldn't have made this journey without you. How many people can state that they can call their shrink long-distance at any time, and let it all hang out?"

"Well there are those in my professional community who frown upon practicing in this fashion. Us loud-mouthed Jewish babes have to lead the way for them sometimes. I'm pleased that it worked for you."

"You know, Laura, I've never once thought of you in terms of race."

"Good, I've done my job."

"And I love you for it."

They had reached an ending without saying so. It felt right.

"Stay in touch, and I mean it."

"I will, I promise."

ξ

Lia resigned later on Monday afternoon. She faxed a one-paragraph letter to Dan Castle, even though his office was in a building just on the other side of the plant, giving thirty days' notice and confirmed its receipt with Valerie. She had no intention of talking directly with Dan ever again. He'd have to trust that she would do the right thing as she wound down.

If he is concerned now, then it's too goddamned bad!

She was much more concerned about her staff and the employees of the Consumer Services. Lia dreaded the thought of having to get all the announcing done. She called in Sara first; Lia needed her to help set up the meetings and calls. Sara had been unfailingly loyal and deserved to be told one-on-one. Sara cried.

"I just want you to know you are the best boss I've ever had. You've pushed me, and I feel I've become a real administrative assistant in the time I've worked for you, because of you. I don't know how you have put up with all the crap this long, and I know you need to get out. But it will be a real loss to EPD, to the whole company."

"I appreciate that, Sara." Lia responded as she stood up and walked Sara to the door. She needed to keep moving to hold her own tears at bay.

Lia's staff was quiet during the short meeting while she spoke to them about her decision. Tears slid down Marva's cheeks, but she did not make a sound. Carl, Gordon and Jerome were uniform in holding their heads down throughout her explanation, although Carl did heave two or three loud, heavy sighs. Gerard looked stricken and stared Lia directly in the eye the entire time.

He's tried to talk with me so many times. I wonder if his obvious churning, but unspoken, feelings are directed at me or the situation.

She asked for their cooperation and assured them that Castle would be working diligently to identify her successor, though she didn't know specifically what Castle was going to do, or when. They filed out of her office, led by Marva who hurried out. Somewhat to her surprise, Gordon put a hand on her shoulder and squeezed it in a quiet gesture of something. Gerard brought up the rear.

"Can you and I talk about all of this at some point? I need to understand what has happened here, for the employees and for myself, too."

"Sure, Gerard." There would be time to have that discussion. Lia knew she was much too emotional to have it today, but she owed Gerard a one-on-one conversation. As the human resources manager, and closest confidante on her staff, it was the right thing to do.

Sara arranged a conference call with the branch managers. Lia had asked her to set it up as soon as possible, but was rattled by nerves when Sara advised that they all would be on the line in a half hour.

"Oh," Sara stopped at Lia's office door. "Gunther told Louanne that he wouldn't be available, and she should participate in the call on his behalf."

Gunther, no doubt, knew everything that was going on; he probably already knew she had resigned. Lia had always gotten good vibes from Lou, but having his secretary substitute for him, rather than one of his senior technicians in his regional office, represented the final jab of disrespect from Gunther.

So what; this will give me an opportunity to thank Lou for always being responsive and gracious.

"He's a jackass to the end." Sara's remark startled Lia because she had never heard her soft-spoken secretary use any kind of profanity.

Lia dictated a letter to the entire Consumer Services employee population. She asked Sara to walk around all the floors; she wanted her to deliver a hard copy to each of them individually. Lia knew she could not get through a series of employee meetings. She would meet with them in assembly in a few days and give them the pep talk they deserved.

No use infecting them with the same poison that has infected me.

ξ

As she sat trying to keep her mind clear, waiting for the conference call with the branch managers to materialize, Lia stared out the window toward the sky to gather in her strength. It was an oppressive Indian summer day in early November, its weight bearing down on everything. Flashes of lightning criss-crossed the sky. No thunder. No noise. Lightning lit up the sky for brief, streaking moments, but receded and left a spiritless sky behind.

"The call is ready," Sara announced and smiled at Lia as she closed the door.

Given the serious nature of the call, it seemed ridiculously brief to Lia. When she wrapped up her announcement by stating that she had enjoyed working with them, Phil Barnes interrupted.

"This is bullshit, pure bullshit. Not you, Lia, but the whole, damned situation. What can we do, what can I do?"

"Nothing, Phil. This is a done deal. For a lot of reasons, I need to do this."

"I don't know all that is going on, but I do know this just isn't right."

Glen Casey spoke up. "I think we waited too long to step up and make our feelings known."

I wonder if these guys would have been this demonstrative if Gunther had been on the line. I'd sure like to think they would be, but I'll never know.

"Your support means a lot to me, and I hope I have an opportunity to see you all before I leave." Lia's voice was wavering, and she wanted to hang up.

There was a chorus of good lucks and the last voice Lia heard was Walter's.

"I'm sorry Lia. I know you'll continue to be successful wherever you are."

Lia hung up, rose from her chair to open the door, and was startled by the booming clap of thunder that intruded on the quiet.

ξ

On the following morning, Dan Castle issued an e-mail announcement of Lia's resignation. He lauded the fact that her contributions to the Energy Products Division had made a significant and positive impact over the course of the year, expressed regret that she was leaving the "EPD family," and wished her good luck in future endeavors. Lia sat staring at the words on her computer screen and felt numb. She was old news, already, no longer part of the EPD universe.

ξ

On the same afternoon, Keith called.

"What the hell is going on? Dawson told me as much as he knows, but he said he hadn't talked with you for a couple of weeks."

Keith's voice was loud and angry, and his renowned charming demeanor was gone.

Jesus, it's already around Fielding; news travels fast.

"I quit, Keith. It's pretty simple, and I feel okay."

"Lia, this company cannot afford to lose you; this can't happen. This is outrageous!"

"Yeah, it is. But I've learned an important truth. Maybe I already knew it, but didn't want to acknowledge it, or say it out loud, because then

I would have to ask myself some painful questions about the professional decisions I have made and where I've ended up."

"As though Conallied defines the world," Keith said quietly, but he did not elaborate on his statement.

"The important truth is that white male privilege is paramount to anything else. Folks like to say that white men don't care about anything more than they care about the almighty dollar. But, you know, their precious bottom line is variable and cyclical; they understand that. White male privilege is forever, or at least they hope it is, and they will do whatever is necessary to sustain it. It's like a holy war; they're not only fighting for themselves, but the legacy they hope to hand down to their sons and grandsons. It's epic for them, and I finally get it."

"This can't happen," Keith repeated himself, but his tone sounded as if he were imploring someone else.

"It is happening Keith, and I've finally realized that it needs to happen. I feel like the weight of the world is off my shoulders. Pleasing white boys just became too important to me. I've rescued myself!"

Lia's statement seemed to stop him cold. "So what are you going to do?"

"I don't know. I'm going to give myself whatever time I need to think about everything, and then make some decisions."

"What about another assignment in Conallied, in a Division where you'll be appreciated?"

"Keith, I have absolutely no illusions about this company's support for me. I knocked heads with Dan Castle, one of their golden boys. I breached the company's etiquette. My being right is irrelevant. If I decided to make a big issue out of it, they either would have to accommodate me with a new, equivalent assignment somewhere in Conallied, which Dan said they would do, but he didn't mean it, or prepare for me to sue their asses. In whichever case, it would consume more energy than I'll ever give them again."

"Have you heard from Trisha Lyman? She'll save you. I know that Dawson is your good friend and mentor, but she was the one who originally sponsored your entry into the company".

"No."

"No? That's all?"

"Trisha has always been nice to me, but I've sometimes felt that she expected some kind of special gratitude for it. I know she likes the good press she gets in Fielding about her relationships with minority employees. All the Massas don't beat their slaves, you know."

"I do know what you're talking about, my sister."

I'm no longer into pleasing white girls, either."

"Well sweetheart, you'll be in demand on the market; you don't have to worry about that."

"You know, Keith, I have no illusions that it would be any different in any other corporate structure. I'm sure Conallied is just as bad, or as good, as any of them. It's the nature of the beast."

"I'm going to call Lance and maybe a few others. I can't just sit by." Keith had gathered a new burst of energy.

"I love you buddy, but you don't have to get crazy about this. Don't let the golden boys run the company into the ground. It could happen."

"I'll call you back." Keith hung up.

Over the next two days, Lia heard from both Doris and Cecelia. Before she called Lia, Cecelia had tried several times to contact George Anderson to talk with him about what he might be able to do.

"When I finally reached him, Lia, he was a total, fucking wimp!"

It was a week before Lia heard from anybody else. Jarvis Addison called and said he was speaking on behalf of Lance Tolliver and himself.

They wanted Lia to come to talk with them about a position in Health Industries.

Well, I'm surprised to hear from Lance, but I appreciate the support.

"Many of Conallied's leaders want to keep you in the company. And, Lance and I want to ensure that you are a success in this company, just like they ensure it for their own. I want to strategically place you, and Lance will see to it that you get all the challenges and air cover you need."

"Thanks Jarvis, but I'm giving a lot of thought to what I want to do going forward, and it doesn't include staying in Conallied."

"Don't make up your mind just yet, and don't worry about anything. Believe me, Lance has cleared it with all the right people."

All the right white people.

"We'll make this work."

Jarvis and Lance seem to be making a real effort for me. Maybe the least I should do is go and talk with them.

"Well, you know I don't mind coming to talk with you guys, but no commitments. I haven't decided what I'm going to do; I'm going to be very selective about where I commit my energy in the future. I want it to be positive energy."

"That's fine. Lance and I will coordinate schedules and my secretary will call you in the next day or two to set up a meeting."

The fact that Lance apparently needed to clear his actions with certain people sounded to Lia like he covered his backside before he dared have Jarvis call her. Even at his level, he couldn't make this particular hiring decision without first tap dancing for the right people. She decided, then and there, to listen attentively and then respectfully decline whatever offer they made to her.

Lia never heard from Jarvis or Lance again. Maybe she hadn't been appreciative enough when she talked with Jarvis. She had no idea what happened, but realized she was not at all surprised. She only needed to acknowledge it and move on.

ξ

At the end of the week, Lia left the office early and drove home. The diffused golden light of November slanted through the house and cast a glow on everything in it. Lia walked directly into her bedroom closet, shut the door, and sat on the cedar chest in the corner. The noise from her sobs startled her; letting her insides spill out staggered her. She had cried so often, but never like this. Later, left the closet, walked through the darkened house out to the deck, and sat quietly watching the sun slide behind the horizon in a red glow. Finally, a gentle breeze dried the last tears she would ever shed over Conallied.

ξ

Dan didn't call Lia once during the thirty days before her departure. A second communication went out a week before her departure announcing that Gunther would serve as the "interim" leader of Consumer Services. Lia put her townhouse up for sale. She alternately felt elated about getting out of Levale and dismayed that, for the first time in her adult life, she did not know exactly where she was headed. She had her long-delayed conversation with Gerard, and she told him as much as she was comfortable with sharing. Her last weeks in the office were filled with a variety of lunches, dinners and various send-off surprises from her employees. It was all thoughtful and sometimes emotional. It often felt as though they needed the celebratory good-byes more than Lia. Nonetheless, Lia couldn't wait to be gone. As wonderful as they were, she could not completely separate them from Conallied, the Energy Products Division, Dan, and all the others who had disrespected her.

"I know it's not fair to them for me to feel this way." Lia was talking to Keith, finally returning his calls after he left several telephone messages for her.

"Lia, you're still worrying about what's fair? Oh please, give yourself a break!"

"Don't worry my friend, I intend to do just that."

I have to admit that it is bothersome, no it's disappointing, that Keith did not have the wherewithal to exert any influence in my situation. In spite of his tenure and relationships in Fielding, he is not a power broker in the company. None of them are. Not one. Lance, with his big title, always walks on eggshells and covers his ass and, in doing so, personifies how fleeting it all is and demonstrates the fear of how easily it can disappear. So much for the emerging power of African-Americans in Conallied. There isn't any. So utterly naïve for any of us to believe otherwise.

"Lia, I know I don't need to lecture you about staying in contact, do I?"

"Of course not."

"Dawson and I were chatting about you this morning, and we're going to gang up on you about this."

"You can't gang up on me, I've escaped." Lia laughed heartily. It felt good.

ξ

One week before Lia departed Conallied, she received a telephone call from Fielding.

"Lia, hello, this is Marge Rayburn, Lawton Thorpe's secretary. He wants you to fly up to Fielding this week to meet with him."

Lawton Thorpe, Jud Jeffries's top human resources lieutenant, never had much to say to Lia in the past. Trisha had handled her recruitment into Conallied and had often dismissed Lawton as a "dinosaur." Dan never mentioned him, and she had no memory of Keith or Daw having much of anything to say about him.

What the hell is this about?

"About what?" Lia was surprised, annoyed and unyielding.

"Well, I'm sure it's probably the usual exit interview, but I think he'll probably want to seek your input on some diversity issues, as well."

Lia almost laughed out loud.

"Marge, we've talked about diversity in this company for years now, too many years. I don't have any new wisdom."

"Lia, I think he really wants you to come."

I shouldn't be, but I'm amazed at this level of arrogance. These guys condone all kinds of obnoxious, exclusionary behavior and then expect to have these polite conversations, in their ballpark, playing by their rules, reserving the prerogative to call the game complete whenever it suits their needs.

"Marge, please relay to Lawton that I don't choose to answer the summons. You have a good day. Good bye."

Lia hung up and became aware of the tension in her body. She received the reality, let it wave over her, that EPD would go on, as if she was never there, as though she never existed. She let out a long, deep breath and regained her equilibrium.

ع

In the early afternoon on Lia's final day in the office, she called Sara into her office, gave her a long hug, and literally sneaked out of the rear door of the building.

Two days later a Tiffany's traditional light blue box was delivered to her home.

Wow, Tiffany's. They must have ordered it from Atlanta.

Inside was a beautiful, crystal plate sitting on a small gold leaf easel. The plate was etched with an inscription.

To Lia Granger, With Sincere Appreciation

For Leading Us When We Needed It Most

Best Wishes

The Associates and Technicians of

Energy Products Division – Consumer Services

Lia placed the gift in the center of her mantel and stared at it for a long time.

Well, it seems I pleased the people who really count.

ξ CHAPTER 17 ξ

I need Wanda to be my friend. I want to be her friend, even though I'm leaving. She's a good, caring person. I was crazy. Her professional relationship with Conallied does not affect our friendship, not at all.

Her last telephone conversation with Wanda weeks ago rolled through her mind for the hundredth time, and she wanted to make things right in this telephone conversation.

"Lia, what the hell is going on"? Not even a hello from Wanda. "What happened, why are you resigning? All I've gotten from you about resigning is two terse statements late at night, and then a hang up. And, why are you angry about my getting the EPD contract?"

"You're wrong, I'm not angry. I wasn't angry with you that evening," replied Lia.

"You know it's the opportunity I've been waiting for to finally broaden my client base and grow my business. This is really big, Lia. This is why I started WMJ Graphic Design. It's what I've been working for."

"It's fantastic, Wanda, really great." What are you going to do to get ready for this? Are you going to need to hire someone to work with Ben?"

I'm trying to focus on the positive. She is still upset, and she's not going to let it rest.

"Lia, please, I can't let our friendship influence a business decision, and I'd really like to think that you wouldn't expect that from me."

"I don't, Wanda."

"Let's be honest here. We've only known one another a year, but I think, I hope, our friendship is strong enough that we can be honest."

Wanda's voice was angry and trembling. Suddenly Lia felt cold inside, a fearful cold. Wanda was her only real friend in Levale, a woman she related to and admired, and she needed her friendship now more than ever.

"Wanda, tell me, what is the problem"?

"I know that you do not want me to take this contract".

"That's simply not true!"

"I don't want my business to suffer because of your experience at EPD. You and I have talked many times about the shit you've gone through. I think I know how you feel and how difficult it's been for you. But, I need to separate your issues from my business and what's good for me."

"Why do you think you need to say all this to me? What do you think I might do?"

"I'd like to think you wouldn't do or say anything, Lia."

"Anything like what? What could I do at this point?"

"Well, I don't know. I've been feeling like you would think I was disloyal to you, selling out for the money, consorting with the enemy, or something like that."

Okay, I have to admit some irritation, or feelings of betrayal that I can't quite define since reading Dan's puffed up, self-serving announcement in the local newspaper about the contract award to Wanda's firm.

Lia felt the announcement read as though it came down from the mount, citing that "EPD is committed to establishing strong ties with minority-owned firms in the community and a top priority will be to build new relationships with local, 'non-traditional' business partners." Dan also stated in the announcement that the contract with WMJ was 'just the beginning of a number of aggressive initiatives of this type, and on and on, ad nauseam.

My instinct tells me that this is a move to offset the negative attention that may result from my departure; that is, if anyone gives a damn.

The Energy Products Division, the largest employer in Levale, had given quite a bit of attention to her arrival in Levale in January. Now, some positive public relations may be needed.

I could laugh at the irony of the whole scenario, if it wasn't so pathetic, and if I wasn't afraid that Wanda would take it the wrong way. Wanda should get the contract on her merit because I'm sure she will do a hell of a job for EPD.

"I, too, hope that our friendship is strong enough for complete honesty. I'm disappointed, Wanda, that you have made these assumptions about my feelings. The truth is I'm very pleased you got the contract, you deserve it, and I wish you a lot of luck in dealing with the challenges of working with Dan Castle and the others."

Oh God. I hope I don't sound cynical.

"Why do you say that? There's no reason why I wouldn't. I know these white boys are treacherous, but I'm tough enough to deal with them. I know you've had to cope with some vicious stuff, but please don't transfer your problems to me. I really can't deal with that right now".

"Wanda, there are no problems that can impact you. I've left EPD."

"Good, because I don't want them to have preconceived notions about me as an African-American woman.

"I think I'll hang up, now, before this conversation goes too far. I was only trying to help by relaying my experience so you can avoid the pitfalls."

"Lia, worry about helping yourself. Maybe you need to be with Dawson right now." Wanda paused.

"What?"

"He's a white boy. Obviously, they're okay for you sometimes."

"Good-bye Wanda."

Lia had slowly pressed down the "off" button on the telephone and held her finger there until it began to cramp. She sat quietly by the window in her kitchen. There were no stars in the sky that she could see on this night. Wanda's friendship had been a godsend to Lia; Wanda had helped her get through these awful months. Her mind simply could not absorb another failure.

Please, not now, not now.

ξ

"Oh, Lia! I didn't know you were coming by." Wanda stopped at the doorway of her office when she saw Lia sitting there. The look on her face was a combination of surprise and uneasiness.

I want Wanda to be my friend, even after I leave Levale. I think I saw a flicker of relief in her face, too.

"I'm sorry I didn't call first. I needed to talk with you, face to face."

Wanda came in, and rather than sitting behind her desk, she settled in the side chair next to Lia. A good sign. Almost a month had passed since their last, unpleasant conversation.

"Wanda, I've had one hell of a month. I've had a hell of a year, in fact. I would be lying if I said I didn't have any feelings at all about your getting the opportunity with Conallied. But the feelings are definitely not directed against you.

Wanda spoke up immediately. "I didn't know if I should call you or not. I guess I was waiting for you to call me, and suddenly weeks have gone by. I didn't know exactly what happened to you at the end; I still don't. Oscar's cousin works at the plant, has for years, and he told us that all kinds of rumors were circulating about your departure, but he didn't know what was true and what wasn't."

"Look, Wanda, I'm aware that Dan Castle created local media attention when he made a big deal out of announcing that WMJ Graphics had been awarded a contract with EPD," Lia replied. "What he was trying to accomplish is obvious. I also know the first choice was their old standby, Bastion Media Group. They have an office here just to babysit companies in Levale's corporate community; Conallied has been their biggest client. Clay Simpson convinced Dan that the selection of WMJ would prove beneficial to EPD in terms of strategic timing and community relations."

"How do you know all of this," Wanda asked quietly, warily.

"Gerard, my human resources manager, lives next door to Simpson's secretary, Alice. They talk. It all crossed her desk. But I didn't even know this until a few days ago."

"Is that so?" Wanda's voice now had an edge of cynicism, and Lia wanted to nip it in the bud.

"But, Wanda, so what? While they are busy patting themselves on the back, you can get over big time. I know you are more than qualified to do this work, and you should take full advantage of the opportunity to show them what you can do by delivering big-time on the contract. Then, leverage the hell out of the experience to market your firm's capabilities to other big companies. Maybe even make some connections at Bastion Media."

"You know, Lia, it's funny. A few weeks ago, I was on top of the world. I finally hooked a really big contract, Oscar and I are getting very serious now and it feels absolutely right, and I truly valued our friendship. Now, Oscar is warning me every day to pay attention to what happened to you and be careful dealing with these people, and there's all this tension between you and me.

"Well, Oscar and I both care about you. Don't worry about it, we'll all be okay. Just worry about them, and watch your back."

"Your advice may be too late."

"What do you mean?"

"I was on a conference call this morning with my attorney and Clay Simpson at EPD, along with their legal counsel, whose name I can't even remember now. We were trying to wrap up the final details of the contract agreement. Michael Collins is my attorney; you met him at my house on Labor Day. Anyway, we were discussing the work and reporting requirements. Simpson, as smooth and matter-of-fact as can be, informed us that Bastion would have oversight responsibility for the work I will perform, and all my reporting would go through them first."

"What the hell. . .?"

"That was my reaction. There was absolutely no indication in any of the previous discussions we had with EPD that Bastion would be involved in the project in any way. To make matters worse, my contact at Bastion would be Jim McCullagh. I know the guy from my Levale Chamber of Commerce involvement. He's a first-class jerk with a typical white bread attitude about tolerating us. I was livid, but I stayed quiet and let Michael handle it. He told Clay we would review these final details and get back to them."

"Those fuckers; it just never stops. What are you going to do?"

"Michael and I talked a little while ago, and he thinks I should take a strong position and insist on reporting directly to EPD. He's going to re-word the language in the agreement and fax it to them. It probably won't get worked out for another day or two."

"I agree with Michael."

"I called Oscar and told him about it, and that was a big mistake."

"What did he say?"

"He wants me to back out completely. He says this is just the beginning of a lot of bullshit and heartburn. We ended up arguing because I'm beginning to feel that he thinks I can't handle it."

"Oh shit. You two need to be solid on this. Wanda, I can't tell you how important that will be for you. I think my first reaction would have been the same as Oscar's, but you don't want to pass up this opportunity."

"There's more, Lia. Months ago, I submitted a bid on a contract to redesign all the national training material graphics for Cochran & Lohman. You know they have an office here, but their corporate headquarters is in Atlanta. I went through the bidder's meetings and presentations, and I never heard from them. I just assumed they selected another firm. They called me last week to come in for another meeting. Guess what?"

"You got the contract!"

"Yes, ain't it a bitch?"

"You don't mean that do you? This is great!"

"When it rains, it pours, but this takes care of my drought. It's not quite as big as the Conallied job, but it is a substantial contract with a national firm. There's also a lot less bureaucratic crap in dealing with them."

"Well, girlfriend, you are really going to have to expand your operation. You'll be able to hire two people. Jesus, you may need larger office space."

"Hold it, hold it. I'm seriously thinking about telling Conallied to keep their damned contract. If it's going to keep me stressed out, I don't need it. Look what it did to you. I don't know exactly what happened at the end, but I can tell that you've really been through something. Lia, you fearlessly took up space in a universe that has not made space for Black women before."

"Well, in the end, I sincerely hope I created some space for other Black women, minority women in general. They'll have to be stronger and more resilient than me. I think what happened to me was I didn't have enough emotional insight; hell, maybe none at all. Ambition and smarts, and knowing how to run a business are not enough. I needed to recognize my own emotions, and those of others, maybe think more about all the different feelings, and do a better job of managing all the emotional information, adjusting to it, so I could achieve my goals.

"You may be overthinking it too much. Don't let them off the hook by apologizing for what you think you didn't do. I hope I'm as strong as you."

"Oh, you're plenty strong. This is your decision. You've got to determine what is best for the well being of your business and yourself. But whatever you do, please don't, I repeat, please don't factor me into your decision making. As far as I am concerned, you and I are fine regardless of what work you do."

"I'll tell you what. I refuse to let all this shit stress me out for too long. I'm going to make some final decisions by the end of the week, and then move on with doing what I do."

"Good for you. Be selfish about your stress level and what you will tolerate. Believe me, I know what I'm talking about; I've been there big time."

"Lia, just let me say that I am sorry for the comment I made on the telephone about you and your friend, Dawson. I don't know the guy. I really don't have any appreciation for your relationship. You know, we didn't meet him when he was in town last spring. I've sometimes wondered why."

"To be honest, I didn't think about it until after he left. He was in town for only one day and practically had to sneak away from meetings so that we could spend a few hours together. I spent a weekend with him not long ago. He's a very special person, but for a lot of reasons, I don't think it can work out."

"I'm sorry, I really am. Are you okay?"

"I will be. I'm flying up to New York City early Thanksgiving morning to meet Jordan there. A quick trip; I'm flying back on Friday afternoon. After that, I'm going to advise on some loose ends at EPD's Consumer Services; they keep calling me now for information and advice. I'm going to spend most of December packing up my townhouse. I think I may have a buyer already. Then, I'm going to hibernate for a while, so if I don't call, don't worry."

"Where do you think you will end up?"

"I'm still undecided, but wherever I am I hope you and Oscar will come to visit."

"You do know that I'm here anytime you need me?"

"I know."

"I won't worry as long as you don't take too long to call."

"You've got a deal, girlfriend." The tired lines in Lia's face smoothed out in a smile.

"Hey, the Berlin Wall came down, we can't let a little thing like EPD come between us."

"So true." Lia's gaze at Wanda reflected her respect and affection.

They reached across the gulf, much narrower now, and closed it with a hug.

ξ CHAPTER 18 ξ

Lia continued to take occasional telephone calls at home from Consumer Services until things quieted down for the Christmas holidays. They called for help on strategies to continue the process improvement initiatives, clarification of longer-term issues, problem-solving advice, and pep talks. It was all teleconferences, which Lia felt she could handle. She helped when she could, but was relieved as the calls slowed to a trickle.

I've cut the cord, and they need to do the same.

ξ

Other than weekly telephone conversations with Jordan, Lia had no desire to talk with anyone else. She faced the hard reality that her reticence came from accepting the fact that many of Conallied's African-American executives had not called her, in the office before she departed, or at home. Keith would wait for her to call him as she promised to do. Both Cecelia and Doris, her African-American female colleagues in Conallied, had both left commiserating messages on her answer machine at home, but no one else did. Lia decided that she did not have hard feelings about it; she did not condemn them. She was sure they were sympathetic, but they had to disconnect from her failure to avoid being infected by it. They were all, in varying degrees, vulnerable. What happened to Lia could happen to any of them; it had in the past and would again in the future. They all knew it and, worse, the white boys, from their position of power, knew it, too.

Ɛ

Lia negotiated a generous separation package with Conallied's legal counsel at corporate headquarters in Fielding, taking full advantage of their fear that she was going to create a big stink and sue the hell out of them.

One day, Lia's mail included an envelope from Trisha Lyman. The thick, ivory stationery, embossed with her initials, was impressive. The brief note expressed her satisfaction that Lia had reached an amicable settlement with the company and offered to provide any recommendation Lia might need in the future. No mention of regret, no curiosity about the facts, no telephone call at any time prior to sending the note. Lia tore it in half and dropped it in the trash can.

Ɛ

Lia fell off the post-Conallied wagon, one time only, for a few hours. The universe shifted just slightly in the inexplicable way that it does sometimes and caused her copy of Conallied's annual report to land in her mailbox in Levale almost nine months after it was apparently mailed in error to her old address in Fielding. After she scanned the financials, Lia stared at the photographs of featured senior executives, many of whom she had worked with, almost all of them white males, along with two white females. Lance was the only Black face among the chosen ones, standing in the back of a group photo. A couple of the smiling, younger white faces had been managed and counseled by Lia during her time with Conallied. Hurt and anger fought for control of her emotions and then joined in an attack on her calm.

Was I not clever enough, or hardworking enough, or white enough, or what enough?

Lia knew the answer to these self-flogging questions, acknowledged the true answers, and found her strength again. It was the final time she would backslide.

ξ

It was time to call Dawson. He deserved to have whatever loose ends he felt existed between them tied up. But Lia had a loose end, too. She had to say it to him. Emotionally, it had been on her mind since she resigned. Daw had fought for Lia on a personal level, but had not done the same for her professionally in Conallied. If he had tried to do anything, it was not apparent to Lia.

Lia came to grips with the fact that, deep down, she did want Daw to charge, outraged, into Jud Jeffries's office and demand a stop to the way she was being treated by the Energy Products Division. Go beyond Castle right to the top to Jud, where Daw had a years-long professional and personal relationship, where reason and fairness were supposed to prevail.

Lia called Daw, and they exchanged pleasantries as though nothing had happened at Conallied or between the two of them. She then shared with Daw what had been on her mind.

"Lia, I'm not surprised that you wondered why I didn't intervene on your behalf with Jud. He doesn't get involved in the operations of the Divisions; he leaves it to the Division leaders. He's only concerned with their bottom lines. He has stuck to that practice, except in the case of an extraordinary situation with the Division leader himself. Yes, I could have talked to Jud, but I'm pretty confident it wouldn't have done any good. But, Lia, I want you to understand the more important reason why I didn't talk to Jud about you."

"Why, Daw?"

"Because you need to leave Conallied. You need to be where you fit. You're a no-bullshit lady trying to operate in an environment that thrives on bullshit. I know I'm a cynical bastard who's a lifer here, but I also know it's true."

"Daw, there's bullshit everywhere, every day. I'm not a china doll, I can handle it."

"That's just my point, my love. These guys are not ready for you; they're afraid and angry!"

"Is that good or bad?"

"Good or bad for whom, Lia?"

"You know, I have struggled mightily, both intellectually and emotionally, with this whole white male anger thing. When you look at the real statistics, that ninety-seven percent of all corporate executives are white male, you have to wonder what is all the resentment and anger about? Or ninety percent, or even eighty percent for that matter! Now, Daw, I get it; I finally get it. You all don't view ninety-seven percent as having the enormous lion's share. No, you focus on the three percent. It's viewed as a loss and, worse, as the beginning of a threatening trend. It's like you all must draw a line in the sand right now or it will get out of your control. I've always thought that the fear was totally illogical, but now I understand there is an absolute, clear logic to it. I feel like an idiot for taking so long to figure this out. I don't have the power to do anything about it at Conallied, except not allow myself to be a victim of it."

"I hated hearing you question yourself, and I'm so glad you seem to have figured it out. This is Conallied's loss; they have no idea. Now you need to get on and live your life."

Daw sounded just enough like he was lecturing her, and it set Lia on edge.

Not even you can do it, Daw, not even you.

She snapped back more sharply than she intended. "You know, you're right. But what I do is up to me, not you."

"Lia, please, of course it is. But, when you say 'you' sound as though you somehow blame me for something."

"No, Daw, I don't. I've liberated myself from Conallied. I really don't need to talk about it any more. One day, a fantastic Black woman, who is much stronger and smarter than I am, will end up with her photograph featured among Conallied's executive elite in the annual report, and she won't have sacrificed herself to be there. When it happens, I'll raise a toast to her."

"No, Lia, she'll raise a toast to you."

"Thank you, Dawson."

"Am I ever going to see you again? Lia, that's all I really care about."

"I know you care, and I've always been grateful that you do. Your friendship has saved me in ways you'll never understand. I wear your whistle all the time. It signifies for me what was good about being in the Conallied galaxy, and that is knowing you. Daw, I won't ever forget you, and you will be the first to know where I am and what I'm doing."

"This doesn't feel right, Lia."

I'm hanging up now. I can't talk with him about this any more.

Lia laughed softly. "You're right, Daw; but, it will. I love you. Goodbye, my friend."

She hung up feeling a comfortable sense of closure.

I do feel love for Dawson. But, I'm not compelled to make him happy. I can't be.

She had taken control of what she had to do, and at the same time, what she could no longer do.

ع

Lia spent the week leading to the Christmas holidays resting and keeping a journal. She had created a monster, though a friendly one, with the journal.

She recorded all her thoughts and feelings and consumed many pages as she wrote in it several times a day. It was both cathartic and relaxing. She spent time thinking about what she would eventually do with herself, but not nearly as much as she anticipated she would. There was no angst, no worry. Lia considered it a personal victory.

She was truly surprised at how physically tired she really was. When Lia stopped, she stopped cold. For the first two weeks after she left Conallied, she was generally in bed by ten in the evening and slept soundly through the night. She stayed in bed until mid-morning each day, not lingering, but sleeping. Her constant bad dreams were mostly gone. The jarring, lingering disturbance of them was matched only by how silently they slipped away, releasing their grip on Lia. She walked three miles every day, and the exercise energized her. She sometimes wondered if she actually had been depressed for a long, long time. Clearly her body was doing what it needed to do, and Lia followed its lead.

ع

Lia diverged from her journal one morning. Peculiarly, without any conscious forethought whatsoever, she sat in front of her computer and composed a letter. She walked the two blocks to the mailbox, and without hesitation, mailed the letter to Jud Jeffries, Conallied's CEO.

Dear Jud:

With a great deal of regret, I recently resigned my service with Conallied (the "Company"). As you know, I was recruited during an initiative to diversify the executive ranks of the Company with experienced, proven leaders. My final assignment with the Company was Senior Vice President of Consumer Services for the Energy Products Division.

I am writing for a specific reason: to communicate directly to you the sense of disillusionment and dismay that developed from what began

with great excitement and strong commitment. The disappoint-
ment comes from the awful reality that, notwithstanding consistent
demonstration of the characteristics that have historically defined
success in the Company -- strong leadership, proven organizational
skills, empowerment philosophy (long before it was in vogue), abil-
ity to bridge a variety of cultural barriers, build cooperative rela-
tionships, and most importantly, deliver on financial commitments
-- African-American females in the Company are overwhelmingly
trapped within narrowly drawn borders that largely restrict us to
selected support roles rather than business leadership positions. I was
an exception and, regrettably, the Energy Products Division was not
ready. While many in the Company now feel that cultural diversity
at the most senior levels has largely failed, it is acknowledged that
primarily white females and, to a lesser degree, African-American
males, have begun to make some progress in scaling the walls that
are erected throughout the Company. However, the Company has
not addressed the cultural stereotypes and professional perceptions
that stubbornly remain intact relative to African-American females.

In spite of an attractive salary, incentive compensation, stock
options, training at the Farm, etc., and entreaties by my employees
to reconsider resignation, the reality of the resentments and limita-
tions imposed by the Company necessitated a serious reassessment of
my future course. Consequently, with a twenty-year career of accom-
plishment minimized, the sense of belonging extinguished, long-held
core values sorely tested, and a dream denied, I was compelled to
move toward new challenges that demand the best I have to offer,
require total commitment and, above all, reject any attitudes and
barriers to maximizing business leadership potential.

Jud, I hope you might come to appreciate that my reflections are
enlightening and helpful to you as Conallied's leader and will posi-
tively impact those African-American females in the Company who
come behind me.

Sincerely,

Lia Granger

"There, it's out of my system," Lia said aloud to herself as she dropped the envelope in the mailbox and walked away from it. She didn't want or expect a reply. Lia preferred to hold onto a kernel of hope that her letter would spur Jeffries to some action, as opposed to sending her a pro forma letter signed by himself or one of his lieutenants, which would signal to her nothing was going to change.

She let out a long, deep breath. It had become a nice habit.

ξ

Lia awoke with a start from a dream about Dawson. He was on a huge motorcycle, and he pulled up close to her. She was standing on gravel and could feel the heat from the bike's engine. Daw leaned over and touched her bare arm. His touch raised the hair on her arm, and she felt soothing, sensual warmth. She was standing in front of a small cabin that sat alone in the middle of what seemed to be a large plateau overgrown with tall, dry grass. Mountains in the distance seemed to rise out of a horizon that was blazing bright red tinged with gold. Daw was not wearing a helmet, and his hair, normally well groomed, was longer and blowing in the breeze. Lia asked him about a helmet, and as he started to speak, the insistence of the telephone ringing dissolved the scene. Lia glanced at the illuminated clock on her night table; it was after midnight.

Jordan is okay. Is Jordan okay?

"Lia, I'm so sorry to wake you in the middle of the night; I'm just so upset."

"What's wrong, Wanda?"

"Someone broke into my office tonight, and the place is a mess."

"Oh my God! Where are you?"

"I'm back at home now. I got a call around 8:30 from my security company telling me the alarm had been triggered in the office and the police had been called to investigate. I called Ben, and he met me at the office."

"Is Oscar still traveling?" Lia remembered that Oscar Four was playing dates in Nashville and Memphis. "Was anything stolen?"

"I haven't reached him yet. Two computers and a very expensive color printer were stolen. I had a small, inexpensive tape player they took. But what upsets me the most, beside the fact that this is supposed to be the fucking season of goodwill to all men, is they vandalized the place. All of our tools, supplies, design boards, photographs, files, you name it, were thrown all over the office. The low-life bastards took the time trash my office. One of the police officers told me it's 50-50 if they are ever caught. The more I think about it, the angrier I get. You understand more than anyone what my office means to me."

"Are you okay? I can hear you are angry, but you also sound pretty shaky."

"I'm okay; I felt a little shaky driving home. Thank goodness we don't have any deliverables until after the holidays. It's going to take us a couple of days just to clean up and take stock of where we are. They got in through the glass door on the lake side of the building, and it has to be replaced. Ben made me leave and go home."

"Do you want me to come over?"

"No, I'm okay." Wanda didn't sound okay.

"I'm getting dressed and coming over right now."

"No, stay in bed. I just took a sleeping pill, and I'm sipping a glass of wine. I'll be out like a light soon."

"I'll come to the office first thing in the morning and help you clean up. I'll bring some bagels and juice."

"Can you bring coffee, too? The coffee maker is in pieces on the floor."

"I can do that. Get some rest. I'll see you in the morning. You and I will get you up and going again."

"Thanks, girlfriend."

ξ

Lia refilled the vase with fresh water. The yellow roses, her favorite, that Jordan sent her had opened perfectly.

After Lia resigned, she had to convince Jordan repeatedly that she was not dying or seriously ill. After a few weeks, he began to relax about it.

"In all my life, I've never known you to be so laid back, really relaxing. You've always worked so hard; sometimes you seemed absolutely driven. Even Dad is worried. I'm going to ask one last time and then let it go. Are you really okay?"

"Better than I have ever been. I can't believe I waited so long to give myself a break."

"Mom, you're a superwoman. But even you need a break sometime. I think this is good."

"Well, listen to my son, all grown up and making wise statements." They both laughed, a knowing laughter, shared in a moment of casual affection that delicately arrives between parents and adult children.

"Mom, think about what you want us to do for Christmas. Dad is all revved up now that he is Mr. County Councilman; you know he thrives on that stuff. My new job at the Institute doesn't start until mid January."

Jordan was fortunate enough to land a research assistant position at the prestigious Institute for New Urban Renewal Policy in Washington, DC. The Institute had received a large grant from a consortium of major corporations, Conallied among them. The irony of Conallied's indirect influence on creating a job for her son was not lost on Lia. He would be working on a newly formed team to study the efficacy of creating new models for urban communities. It sounded very interesting to Lia, and she was going to enjoy discussing Jordan's work with him.

"I like the path you are taking, Jordan."

Lia was very frankly pleased that Jordan had not been seduced by corporate America; a number of companies had tried during his senior year in college. He had expressed disdain about the entire corporate world many times as he grew into a young man, and Lia's experiences over the years only reinforced his feelings. If the day ever came that corporate America presented a great opportunity to Jordan, an offer he could not refuse, if he asked for her advice, Lia was not at all sure what she would say to him.

"I think you had a monster mid-life crisis, Mom."

"No, I had an awakening."

"Mom, you're better than they are, always have been."

"Thank you, sweetie. I just wanted to do good, do right. I think I'm better at being self aware."

"You were always self aware, Mom, or it sure seemed like you were."

"I'm better now at understanding restraint and the impact of actions, mine and others."

"We could spend a couple of weeks together, forget about all the work stuff, and maybe go somewhere fun, if you're able to finance your poverty-stricken son."

"I can do that. Christmas sneaked up on me this year. I'd like us to spend part of the holiday with my Aunt Ruthie. She's always been a special person to me, and I'd like you to know her better. We can spend a few days with the family and then go down to Monterey to spend some time with Ruthie and Dalton. We've had too many quick visits and phone calls for too many years. I want to reconnect with her and connect you with her. Then, maybe just the two of us can spend a couple of days driving up the northern California coast. It's spectacularly beautiful. You were just a little boy when your Dad and I did that drive; you were with us, but I'm sure you don't remember it."

"Whatever you want to do, Mom, is okay with me. It'll be fun. I'll see you soon."

Lia was glad Jordan was going to spend the holidays with her. She knew that she would get all the unconditional love she could handle between Jordan, her parents, and Ruthie.

It's time to get in the Christmas mood. Lia dug out her Christmas cassettes. Luther Vandross and The Whispers never failed her.

ξ EPILOGUE ξ

As she filled the final pages of the second volume of her journal, Lia's place in time and mind came together. She was acutely aware and deeply grateful for the endowment of grace; she had been given the gift of enlightenment. In the quiet after the holiday celebrations and reunions with loved ones start to recede into the space of pleasant memories, a new beginning was taking shape for her. It was punctuated by an inescapable theme that emerged in her writings, like a neon sign whose repeated flashing demanded her attention. Lia, the little girl, and Lia, the woman, had exhausted her internal fortitude by relentlessly seeking approval. Whatever spiritual and intellectual energy, which was gifted to her and powered the will to push forward, had been sapped by this life-long exercise. Lia asked herself if she would regret no longer being part of a driven and seductive world that included beautiful, manicured surroundings, conferences at posh resorts, trips abroad, meetings with industry leaders, and substantial salaries, all infused with a sense of exceptionalism and privilege. A world that is, oddly enough, highly visible and discreetly cloistered at the same time.

She tried to delve into the origins of her compulsions and could not discern any tangible connections. She had spent many hours in therapy. Her sessions with Laura in Fielding and the telephone conversations from Levale had surely saved her, allowed Lia to maintain her balance while walking along the tightrope. Lia needed to call Laura soon. She would be happy to hear that her efforts had not been in vain. Why had the approval of white folks, and white men in particular, been so important to her? What voice, or which signal, implanted itself, took root, and became part of her psyche? Why had her definition of success been so inextricably connected to approval by these people? Certainly her parents had never sent her any signals; they never dreamed their daughter would operate in this world that they never quite understood. It is an environment that defines success by arbitrary standards. Relationships, professional and personal, suffer from relentless pressure, lack of time, and loss of focus on the need to connect with others on a more fundamental, human level. The longing was still palpable, the searing heat of a primal wound, which might always be there. Lia was growing to understand, finally, that trying to figure it out, consuming the time and energy to try to get to the core of it, would only continue the unhealthy cycle. Even if she did figure it out, so what? It was done, water under the bridge. The important thing was to not let it happen again. It was painful for Lia to decide, in spite of every instinct tugging at her, to declare failure for not being able to answer all these questions. She instinctively knew it would be the passage of time that ultimately would allow her to declare a true victory. Her professional and personal crises, sometimes she couldn't separate them from one another, brought disillusionment and self-examination. It also created the opportunity to start over again. Lia had not yet focused on what she wanted to do for a living; that, too, would come with time. But, most joyfully, she had come to know what she wanted to do about living.

ξ

The will of the gods, some higher power looking out for her by sending a wake-up call? Is that what brought her to this point? Lia pondered this final question over many pages as she reached the end of the journal, the need to continue keeping it, the need to lose herself in it. As if ordained, she had been directed down the very long path to find herself. She felt a new way to be human, which is to live with content in a world in which one's destiny is never entirely of one's own choosing. Lia closed the journal, her hands folded over the flowered cloth cover. She closed her eyes and let the new peace of mind embrace her. It felt so good. At that moment, a stream of sunshine, just a sliver really, slipped through the gray sky and searched out the blinds at her kitchen window near where she sat. Some things, thankfully, did not change. It settled around her shoulders.

END